ST/ESA/SER.A/129/Add. 1

Department for Economic and Social Information and Policy Analysis

Abortion Policies: A Global Review

Volume II
Gabon to Norway

 United Nations   New York, 1993

NOTE

The designations employed and the presentation of the material in this publication do not imply the expression of any opinion whatsoever on the part of the Secretariat of the United Nations concerning the legal status of any country, territory, city or area or of its authorities, or concerning the delimitation of its frontiers or boundaries.

The designations "developed" and "developing" economies are intended for statistical convenience and do not necessarily express á judgement about the stage reached by a particular country or area in the development process.

The term "country" as used in the text of this publication also refers, as appropriate, to territories or areas.

The report has been edited and consolidated in accordance with United Nations practice.

ST/ESA/SER.A/129/Add.1

UNITED NATIONS PUBLICATION

Sales No. E.94.XIII.2

ISBN 92-1-151258-1

PREFACE

Abortion Policies: A Global Review presents, in three volumes, a country-by-country examination of national policies concerning induced abortion and the context within which abortion takes place. Comparable information is presented for all Member States and non-Member States of the United Nations. The countries are arranged in alphabetical order: volume I covers from Afghanistan to France; volume II from Gabon to Norway; and volume III from Oman to Zimbabwe. In volume I, the country names are those in use as of 31 December 1992.

Information on the abortion policies of four countries that gained independence following the publication of volume I (Armenia, Azerbaijan, Bosnia and Herzegovina, and Croatia) are included in the present volume, as are the abortion policies of the Democratic People's Republic of Korea. In addition, the sections on the policies of Belarus and China, which were presented in volume I, have been revised and are included in this volume.

Responsibility for this report rests with the United Nations Secretariat. The assessment was facilitated to a great extent, however, by the close cooperation among the United Nations bodies. In particular, the contribution of the United Nations Population Fund (UNFPA) in support of this publication is gratefully acknowledged. The assistance of national experts who reviewed early drafts of country profiles and provided additional information and comments is greatly appreciated.

Although for many countries current information on the status of abortion policy is relatively easy to obtain, for some countries that is not the case. Information on some countries is incomplete; in others it is noticeably lacking. Readers are therefore invited to send any information, comments or corrections they deem useful to the Director, Population Division, Department for Economic and Social Information and Policy Analysis, United Nations Secretariat, New York, NY 10017, United States of America.

CONTENTS

ANNEX

Explanatory notes

Symbols of United Nations documents are composed of capital letters combined with figures.

Reference to "dollars" ($) indicates United States dollars, unless otherwise stated.

Reference to "tons" indicates metric tons, unless otherwise stated.

The term "billion" signifies a thousand million.

A hyphen between years (e.g., 1984-1985) indicates the full period involved, including the beginning and end years; a slash (e.g., 1984/85) indicates a financial year, school or crop year.

A point (.) is used to indicate decimals.

The following symbols have been used in the tables:

Two dots (..) indicate that data are not available or are not separately reported.

A dash (—) indicates that the amount is nil or negligible.

A hyphen (-) indicates that the item is not applicable.

A minus sign (-) before a number indicates a deficit or decrease, except as indicated.

Details and percentages in tables do not necessarily add to totals because of rounding.

The following abbreviations are used in this volume:

ASFR	age-specific fertility rate
HIV	human immunodeficiency virus
HR	hospital admission records
IPPF	International Planned Parenthood Federation
IUD	intra-uterine device
MCH	maternal and child health
PAHO	Pan American Health Organization
PR	provider registration
SP	surveys of providers
SW	surveys of women
TFR	total fertility rate
UNICEF	United Nations Children's Fund
UNFPA	United Nations Population Fund
WHO	World Health Organization

INTRODUCTION

Induced abortion has attained high public visibility in many countries, both developed and developing. In some contexts, public concern has been voiced primarily because of the alarmingly high levels of maternal mortality and morbidity that have resulted from unsafe illegal abortion. In others, the visibility has resulted more from public debate concerning the legal status of abortion and the role the State should play in permitting or denying access to induced abortion. More often than not, both the concern with health consequences and the political controversy play an important part in the saliency of induced abortion in the public eye.

Induced abortion is one of the oldest methods of fertility control and one of the most widely used. Induced abortion is practised both in remote rural societies and in large modern urban centres. It is practised in all regions of the world, although with differing consequences. In countries where abortion is legal and widely available, abortions pose a minimum threat to women's health. Where abortion is illegal, however, abortions are usually performed in substandard and unsanitary conditions, leading to a high incidence of complications and resulting chronic morbidity and often death.

Regional variations concerning the consequences of induced abortion are not due solely to differences in national abortion laws. Differences in interpretation by the local legal authorities and the extent to which the laws are enforced also affect the conditions under which abortions are performed. Although laws and policies are a product of the social, cultural, political and religious context in which they were developed, the same context also mediates the outcome of those policies. Thus, the consequences of induced abortion are the result of a complex interplay of factors.

As the topic of induced abortion has gained increased attention, the number of studies on the subject has multiplied. Some studies have focused on specific regions and/or legal traditions,[1] while others have taken a global approach.[2] Most studies document the current status of abortion laws and policies in various countries and analyse trends in legal reform. The legal aspects of abortion are, in general, the easiest to record because they are codified. More difficult to document are instances where policy deviates from legal precepts, and fewer studies address this aspect. Great strides have also been made in documenting the incidence of abortion and its consequences for women's health. Earlier studies focused on legal abortion because the data were more readily available, but more recent studies are attempting to document and to estimate the extent of illegal abortion in different contexts.

This study examines the major dimensions of induced abortion on a country-by-country basis, with the objective of providing information not only on the legal and policy status of abortion but on the ways in which abortion laws have evolved over time, the manner in which they have been interpreted and enforced and the context within which abortion usually takes place. Where possible, data on the incidence of induced abortion are included. Although information on the incidence of abortion and the setting within which abortion takes place are not the focus of the study, these data are provided to enrich the policy picture.

Several publications provide detailed analyses of the abortion situation in a variety of countries, but they focus on a limited number of countries, usually on those for which ample information is available. This publication is intended to serve as a reference book on abortion policy, providing pertinent information on induced abortion for every country in the world, even those for which data are scarce.

NOTES

[1]For example, Cairns, 1984; Cook and Dickens, 1979, 1986; Glendon, 1987; Knoppers and Brault, 1989; and Sachdev, 1988.
[2]For example, Moore-Čavar, 1974; Cook, 1989; David, 1983; Henshaw and Morrow, 1990; Lee and Larson, 1971; Liskin, 1980; Tietze and Henshaw, 1986; Royston and Armstrong, 1989; and UNFPA, 1979.

I. MAJOR DIMENSIONS OF ABORTION POLICY

Broadly speaking, the abortion policy of a country is the product of the social, political, economic and religious context in which it is embedded. More specifically, the nature of abortion laws and policies depends upon their legal heritage, that is, the legal system to which the country adheres, upon the interactions of that legal system with concurrent or prior legal systems and upon the ways in which laws are interpreted and enforced. Because a detailed analysis of the social, political, economic and religious factors affecting abortion policy is beyond the scope of this study, these dimensions of the policy context are mentioned to illustrate certain important points.

The majority of contemporary legal systems throughout the world have been shaped to some extent by one or more of the three main legal families: common law; civil law; or socialist law. For instance, Japan, whose Government formally embraces Buddhism and Shintoism, adopted a civil-law system based primarily on French civil law during the Meiji era in the late 1890s. Turkey, once the capital of the Islamic world, adopted a version of the Swiss Civil Code in 1926. Although other systems of law do exist, such as religious and customary laws, their importance has declined as aspects of the major legal systems have replaced or been incorporated into existent systems. Religious and customary law have, however, had an important effect on the content of contemporary legal systems, particularly in the area of private law.[1]

Customary law and law linked to religion, such as Islamic, Hindu, Jewish and canon law, can have a significant influence on human behaviour and on the content of secular law even in countries where they are not enforced by the courts. For instance, the French Civil Code borrowed statutes on marriage and filiation from canon law (David and Brierley, 1978). The Islamic and Hindu systems, although not influential in many realms of public law,[2] have had considerable influence in the area of family law and law regulating interpersonal relations. The laws contained in the "personal statutes"[3] of the Koran and the Hindu Sastras regulate individual social behaviour; and in some Islamic countries, such statutes have even been codified.

The type of legal system to which a country adheres affects the content of its abortion laws, the flexibility with which they may be interpreted and the ease with which legislation may be introduced and modified. Law is developed in one of three ways: by statute law, passed by legislatures or parliaments; by case law, based on court precedents; or by administrative decree (Moore-Čavar, 1974). In the common-law system, law is defined primarily by judicial precedent, and judicial interpretation plays an important role in court decisions. Common law emerged originally as a means for judges to resolve individual disputes. Thus, its objective was to provide solutions to disputes rather than to define rules of conduct. Common law places greater emphasis on individual rights and self-reliance than does civil law. Private rights, such as the right to privacy, private property and freedom of contract, take precedence over social rights designed to protect social welfare (David and Brierley, 1978; Glendon, 1987).

In civil law, or Romano-Germanic law, as it is often called, law is conceptualized as a guide of conduct seeking to protect justice and morality. In general, civil law views individual rights within a social context, placing great emphasis on social responsibility (David and Brierley, 1978; Glendon, 1987). Law is defined primarily by statutes, and interpretation of enacted law usually plays a minor role.

Socialist law,[4] although included here as a distinct system, is not always considered a separate system of law because it formerly belonged to the Romano-Germanic group. In fact, it has retained the terminology and structure of that group (David and Brierley, 1978). As in the civil-law systems, legislation is the main source of socialist law, but the role of legislation differs. Because the primary goal of socialist Governments was to bring about radical change, the function of law was not to serve as a guide of conduct, as is the case in civil law, but rather actively to transform the economic forces of the country and the behaviour and attitudes of its people. The role of legislation was to create a new social order based on Marxist principles. The role of jurists and

2

judges was to ensure that the law should be interpreted in the manner intended by the authors. Because existing laws were few, judges were required to look to Marxist doctrine to determine the solution to a dispute. As the socialist legal system developed, the number and detail of laws increased, limiting the role of the judges to the application of the laws. Thus, interpretation of enacted law has played a limited role in socialist systems. To the extent that law has been interpreted, it has been interpreted to protect Marxist principles.

Islamic law has had an important influence in abortion laws in many Islamic countries. Islamic law, known as the shariah (the way to follow), is also a codified system that specifies rules of conduct. Law is defined both by statutes (the "personal statutes" contained in the Koran and in the Sunna, the collection of acts and statements made by the Prophet), and by scholarly interpretation and analogical reasoning. As the Koran and the Sunna do not cover all aspects of behaviour, Islamic scholars are called upon to rule on situations not covered by these works, through a process of interpretation employing deductive or analogical reasoning and leading to consensus. The interpretation adopted depends upon the school of Sunni or Shiah law followed (El-Kammash, 1971).

Lastly, a word must be added about cases where legal heritage has had limited effect on the content of abortion law and policy. Such is the case among a handful of countries where abortion policy has been introduced for primarily demographic considerations. Albania and Romania are examples of countries that had introduced highly restrictive abortion laws with pronatalist intentions. Recently, both countries liberalized their abortion laws. China is an example of the opposite policy, that is, a Government that permits abortion in an effort to achieve a drastic reduction in fertility.

In general, a codified system is more static than one based on judicial precedent. Common-law systems, in which the limits of the law are constantly being tested and extended through court precedents and changes in the interpretation of the law are routinely incorporated through court rulings, are more fluid than civil-law systems, in which legal codes take precedence. In legislation-based systems, such as civil-law and socialist-law systems, the degree to which interpretation of the law is permitted determines its openness to change. For instance, among the countries with a civil-law system, the Nordic countries have demonstrated greater flexibility to change than have the Iberian countries. In Islamic law systems, the school of Sunni or Shiah law to which the country adheres is also an important factor affecting the extent to which flexibility of interpretation is permitted.

The common-law, civil-law and socialist-law systems described above are the principal families of law in existence today. Most existing contemporary legal systems have drawn some or many elements from one or more of these families. Although these legal systems have been described in their pure form, in reality legal systems are hybrids of various systems. The trend has been for common-law and civil-law systems to merge. Countries with common-law legacies have adopted legal codes, and case law has been gaining importance in some civil-law systems.

The three systems, along with some religious legal systems, such as Islamic and canon law, have influenced the content of most abortion laws today. Civil law, as it is known today, originated in continental Europe and, in many cases, was spread to other countries through colonization. Thus, the countries colonized by Belgium, France, Germany, Italy, the Netherlands, Portugal and Spain inherited a version of the civil-law system of the mother country and its statutes concerning abortion. As a result, the legal codes of numerous countries in Africa, Asia, Latin America and Oceania are based on civil law. Common law, the legal system that developed in England, forms the basis of the legal codes of most Commonwealth countries and the United States of America. Common-law systems are found in anglophone Africa, Northern America, the Caribbean, Asia and Oceania. Despite recent events, socialist law still forms the basis of the legal systems in most countries of Eastern Europe. It is also the basis of the legal system in Cuba. Several countries that are considered socialist States do not adhere to the socialist legal system described above. Their legal systems are so varied that it is difficult to classify them under a single generic group. Likewise, the legal systems of some countries, such as Israel, the Philippines and South Africa, are hard to classify because they contain important elements from both civil-law and common-law systems, as well as religious law. Islamic law has shaped family law in many Islamic countries in Africa and Asia. Canon law, which had an early influence on both common law and civil law, continues to exert its influence, particularly in predominantly Catholic countries.

Although many countries adopted the abortion laws of the colonial authority almost verbatim, others introduced important modifications. The version adopted by a country depended upon its indigenous legal systems and how those systems fit in with the law of the colonial authority. A common outcome is that different branches or sub-branches of law may be moulded by different legal systems. For instance, in many Muslim countries, numerous branches of law have been secularized. The main exceptions are laws concerning the family and interpersonal relations, which are influenced by Islamic and customary law. Thus, although most laws in Bangladesh have been patterned after English common law, those relating to the family and, in this case, abortion are influenced by religious and customary law.

Laws concerning abortion frequently appear to be inconsistent because they are addressed in multiple simultaneous codes. When abortion is considered a crime, it is addressed in a penal code. However, States that address abortion in their penal code may permit abortion in some or all circumstances, that is, they define situations where abortion is considered lawful in separate laws or decrees, or in statutes in health codes, social welfare codes and the section of civil codes covering personal statutes or those on relations between persons. Thus, while the penal code may express the punishments for the crime of abortion, the health code or instruction may specify the conditions under which abortion could be lawfully performed, and the social welfare code may stipulate under what conditions the State might pay for abortions.

Laws may also appear to be inconsistent within the same code because laws affecting the legality of abortion may not specifically address abortion. For instance, in many countries where abortion is strictly forbidden in any circumstance under the criminal code, other sections within the same code, that is, sections concerning the state of necessity, will permit abortion when the life of the pregnant woman is in immediate danger, because it can be justified as a defense of necessity (Glendon, 1987). In Egypt, for instance, sections 260-262 of the Penal Code forbid abortion in any circumstance. Section 61 of the Penal Code, however, provides that "a person who commits a crime in case of necessity to prevent a grave and imminent danger which threatens him or another person shall not be punished, on condition that he has not caused it on his own volition or prevented it by other means" (quoted in El-Moiz Nigm, 1986).

NOTES

[1]Private law includes spheres of law governing relations between private persons, such as laws on property, inheritance, marriage and filiation, and commercial law.

[2]Public law includes branches of law covering the sphere of relations between those governing and those governed, such as criminal law, labour law, public international law, law of procedure, administrative law and constitutional law. In some Islamic countries, including Pakistan and Saudi Arabia, Islamic law has shaped criminal law.

[3]The "personal statutes" include the law of persons, family relations and inheritance.

[4]As of the preparation of this volume, it is unclear what changes will be introduced in the legal systems of the newly independent former Soviet republics or what course the former USSR will take. A discussion of socialist law is included because it was the basis for abortion laws in Eastern Europe and in the USSR.

II. THE ORIGINS OF ABORTION LEGISLATION

The view that abortion is a reprehensible criminal act was first expressed explicitly in religious law. For example, the first collection of canon law, compiled in the twelfth century, considered abortion a homicide if it was performed after quickening. Quickening was assumed to take place 40 days after conception for the male foetus and 80 days after conception for the female foetus. In practice, however, movement of the foetus was taken as the sign that formation of the foetus had taken place; thus, abortion was sometimes performed as late as the fifth month of gestation. Except for a brief period in the mid-sixteenth century, when abortion could be punished by excommunication, the view that abortion was not a punishable act if it occurred in early pregnancy was held by the Christian Church until 1869, when the Pope decreed that quickening takes place at conception and that, for Roman Catholics, excommunication was once more the punishment for abortion (Paiewonsky, 1988).

The first instance of a secular law concerning abortion occurred in England in 1803 (Cook and Dickens, 1979; Francome, 1988). Before 1803, abortion was considered a common-law misdemeanor and was punishable only if performed after quickening. Although canon laws were influential in shaping the English abortion laws, other social and economic factors were equally influential. The early nineteenth century was a period of great economic and geographical expansion. It witnessed the rise of modern medicine and the introduction of sweeping public-health measures leading to dramatic improvements in public health. The growth of industrial capitalism led to the rise of the middle class, to its establishment as a political force and to the establishment of its moralistic values as the values of the time. This period was also one of colonial expansion, leading many States to adopt pronatalist policies in order to have the labour necessary to administer and to populate the new colonies (Paiewonsky, 1988). Repressive attitudes towards sexuality, combined with pronatalist policies, and mounting evidence that abortion was the cause of much maternal mortality and morbidity, resulted in the passage of the Irish Chalking Act in 1803. This Act, in an early amendment of its section 58, punished a woman obtaining an abortion, whether self-induced or not, by life imprisonment (Francome, 1988).

The Act of 1803 and its amendments paved the way for the Offences Against the Person Act of 1861 (sections 58 and 59). This Act stipulates that it is a felony punishable by life imprisonment for any woman "with child" unlawfully to procure or attempt to procure her own miscarriage and for any other person to do any similar act with similar intent "whether she be with child or not" (Cook and Dickens, 1982). The word "unlawfully" is not defined. A person supplying any instrument or poison to be used to induce an abortion is guilty of a misdemeanor and liable to three years in prison (Francome, 1988).

An important judicial precedent, the case of *Rex* v. *Bourne* in 1938, clarified the Act of 1861 by specifying instances when abortion would be "lawful". In the *Bourne* case, a physician was accused of performing an abortion on a 14-year old girl who had been raped. Dr. Bourne was acquitted of the offence on the grounds that continuation of the pregnancy would have caused the girl to become a "mental wreck". The judge explained that the word "unlawfully" in the Act of 1861 implied that abortion performed with the intent of preserving the woman's life or health was not a criminal act and that health included both mental and physical health (Cook and Dickens, 1982; Kloss and Raisbeck, 1973).

The Offences Against the Person Act of 1861 formed the basis of abortion law throughout the Commonwealth. In some countries, the Act was retained in its original form. In others, it was adopted including the *Bourne* decision of 1938 or was modified on the basis of local court precedents. The wording of these laws is, in general, very similar to the Act of 1861, but there is ample variation in punishments for unlawful abortion (Cook and Dickens, 1979).

In civil law, the first widely adopted statute concerning induced abortion appeared in the Napoleonic Code of 1810.[1] It was enacted during the same period as the first abortion legislation in common law and was similarly influenced by canon law. The French Penal Code (section 317) prescribed harsh sentences for women procuring an abortion and for any person performing an abortion. Subsequent reforms in 1920 and 1923 changed abortion from a crime to a misdemeanor, with reduced although still harsh sentences.

The Napoleonic Code forms the basis of abortion legislation in many countries with a civil-law system. Wide variation exists among the existing civil-law systems, with those of the Iberian Peninsula and Italy being more influenced by canon law and the Nordic systems being the most secular.

Reflecting its civil-law origins, socialist law prior to 1920 considered abortion a crime. Concerned with women's status, health and welfare, the Government of the former Union of Soviet Socialist Republics legalized abortion in 1920. Abortion became available in the former Soviet republics if performed during the first trimester (Law of 8 November 1920). In 1936, the abortion legislation was reversed for demographic considerations (Law of 27 June 1936), permitting abortion only for serious therapeutic reasons. In 1955, the abortion law was liberalized once more in recognition of the increased maternal mortality and morbidity resulting from illegal induced abortion (Decree of 23 November 1955). The Supreme Soviet made abortion available on demand in all the former Soviet republics during the first 12 weeks of pregnancy (Hecht, 1987). Several countries of Eastern Europe had similar legislation. However, in the wake of recent political changes, several Eastern European countries either revised or enacted new legislation dealing with abortion.

In Islamic law, abortion is addressed in the "personal statutes" of the Koran. Although the different schools of Islamic law differ somewhat in their interpretation, there are some commonalities. Islam forbids the killing of the soul, but the various schools of Islamic law disagree as to when a foetus acquires a soul. Some schools of Islam identify that time as 40 days after conception and others as 120 days. Most schools adhere to the 120-day definition. Some schools permit abortion prior to quickening only with justifiable grounds, and others forbid abortion even before quickening (that is, before the foetus acquires a soul). Islam permits abortion, however, when the pregnancy endangers the mother's life, regardless of the duration of gestation (El-Kammash, 1971).

NOTE

[1]The Napoleonic Code was not the first codification of civil law but was the first to be widely adopted (David and Brierley, 1978; Glendon, 1987). The Napoleonic Code, also known as the Code civil des Français, includes five codes promulgated in the first decade of the nineteenth century. The Napoleonic Code dealing with civil matters was promulgated in 1804. The Penal Code, containing punishments for the crime of abortion, was promulgated in 1810.

6

III. COUNTRY PROFILES: DESCRIPTION AND DISCUSSION OF VARIABLES

This chapter contains a detailed description of the variables included in the first page of each country profile. An attempt has been made to provide comparable information for each country. Because abortion laws can be complex and diverse, considerable space is dedicated to the description of how the legal grounds for abortion are coded. The section on abortion policy addresses the grounds on which abortion is permitted; it is followed by a short section describing any additional conditions required by the law. The causes and consequences of induced abortion differ from one country to another. In order to capture some of these differences, a number of fertility and mortality indicators are given in the following section. In the background section of each country profile, the national context is described in further detail. The last section provides statistics on induced abortion, when such data are available.

A. ABORTION POLICY

1. *Grounds on which abortion is permitted*

The most commonly cited grounds on which abortion is permitted include: *(a)* to save the life of the mother (life grounds); *(b)* to preserve her physical (narrow health grounds) and/or mental health (broad health grounds); *(c)* in cases of rape or incest (juridical grounds); *(d)* when foetal impairment is suspected (eugenic grounds); and *(e)* social or economic reasons (social grounds). These are the grounds coded in the first section. Although some countries include additional grounds, for example, when there is contraceptive failure, when the pregnant woman has tested positive for the human immunodeficiency virus (HIV), when the pregnant woman is a minor or when the pregnancy is the result of an illegitimate relationship, they are not coded in this variable because of their limited applicability. When they are applicable, however, these grounds are described in the section under "additional requirements" and are described in detail in the background section of the country profile. Because the wording of the laws differs substantially, the variation in language and interpretation of each of the grounds is also discussed in detail on the second page. When it is evident that policy deviates from law, an asterisk is placed next to the pertinent ground indicating that although unlawful, the legal or official interpretation usually allows the abortion to be performed on the particular ground. For example, in countries where abortion is considered unlawful in any circumstance but performing an abortion to save the life of the pregnant woman is permitted in "defense of necessity", the ground to "save the life of the woman" is coded as not permitted but is followed by an asterisk.

Because some countries have both national and subnational abortion laws, and it is not always clear which takes precedence, the most liberal of the national or subnational laws was coded. A detailed description of the local laws is contained in the text.

To save the life of the woman

Permitting abortion to save the life of the pregnant woman is the most clearly interpreted ground. Although some countries attempt to provide detailed lists of what they consider life-threatening conditions, there is, in general, a tacit agreement on the conditions that permit this ground to be invoked. It is true that there is some room for interpretation as to what can be considered life-threatening, which allows some courts to show greater leniency, but it is less ambiguous than the other grounds usually considered. This ground is also the most universally permitted. A notable exception is Malta, which has one of the most restrictive abortion laws among the European countries and prohibits abortion on any grounds. Another exception is the Holy See, whose opposition is based on the premise that life is a divine property and as such is sacred from its beginning.

To preserve the physical health of the woman

Performing an abortion on the ground that it is necessary to preserve the physical health of the pregnant woman or more precisely, in cases where the continuation of the pregnancy would involve a risk of injury to the physical health of the woman, is also permitted in a majority of countries. The term "physical health", however, has been variously defined. In some countries, the definition is narrow, often including a list of conditions that are considered to fall under this category; in other countries, the term "physical health" is broadly defined and allows much room for interpretation. Where possible, the range of interpretation allowed is discussed in the text. In general, Commonwealth countries permit a broader definition of health than do African or Latin American countries adhering to civil law.

In many cases, the law does not specify the aspects of health that are concerned but merely states that abortion is permitted when it averts a risk of injury to the pregnant woman's health. As a rule, the interpretation of health tends to be narrow, referring only to physical health. In some cases, however, it is not possible to determine if mental health is also implied. Nevertheless, laws permitting abortion on the ground of preserving the woman's mental health generally specify that ground.

To preserve the mental health of the woman

Many abortion laws specifically state that abortion is legally permitted when the continuance of the pregnancy would involve greater risk of injury to the physical and mental health of the pregnant woman than if the pregnancy were terminated. The definition of "mental health" grounds varies significantly. Mental health is sometimes interpreted to include some or all of the other grounds to be discussed. It can refer to anything from psychological distress caused by the fact that the pregnancy was the result of rape or by the scientific opinion that there is a risk that the foetus may be mentally or physically impaired, to situations where the pregnancy is interpreted as causing mental distress because of the socio-economic context in which it occurred. This phrasing of the law is employed primarily in Commonwealth countries. Most other countries specify the grounds directly, that is, juridical, eugenic and/or social or economic grounds, rather than making reference to a catch-all term like "mental health". Some Commonwealth countries do, however, specify additional grounds, as is the case in Ghana, Guyana, India, Malaysia and New Zealand.

A word should be added about *Rex* v. *Bourne* (1938) at this point. As previously mentioned, this was a landmark case in Commonwealth law. It set a judicial precedent that resulted in a broader definition of lawful abortion, extending it to include cases where abortion could be performed to safeguard the physical health of the pregnant woman and in order to "prevent her from becoming a mental wreck". The manner in which the *Bourne* decision was adopted by the colonial possessions of the United Kingdom of Great Britain and Northern Ireland often differs. Because the *Bourne* case is invoked only after a physician has been accused of performing an abortion (and perhaps arrested), many physicians do not want to risk arrest. Thus, in countries where arrest is a possibility, the *Bourne* case tends to be interpreted more narrowly, to include only physical health. Kenya is a case in point. In these instances, the law is coded as excluding the mental health ground.[1]

Pregnancy as a result of rape or incest

When a pregnancy is caused by rape or incest, abortion is often permitted even in countries with restrictive legislation, as is the case in most Latin American countries. It may be worded as "when necessary to defend the pregnant woman's honour", or simply, when the pregnancy is the result of sexual violence. Some specifically mention both rape and incest; others make reference to rape only. Because many countries require that the case be brought to court or be reported to the authorities before permission for abortion can be granted, many women are discouraged from opting for an abortion on this ground. Several countries that do not permit abortion on juridical grounds, for example, Jordan and Lebanon, do apply reduced sentences when the abortion was performed to defend the woman's honour. In many Commonwealth countries, no specific reference is made to juridical grounds because such cases are interpreted as falling within the mental health grounds.

Possibility of foetal impairment

As is the case with juridical grounds for abortion, eugenic grounds are often permitted in countries with restrictive abortion laws. In many Commonwealth countries, no specific reference is made to eugenic grounds because they are interpreted as causing the mother mental stress and are therefore considered to fall within the mental health grounds. Several countries specify the type and level of impairment necessary to justify this ground.

Economic or social reasons

The phrasing of laws permitting abortion on socio-medical, social or economic grounds varies widely. Some specifically mention social or economic conditions while others merely imply them. For instance, in Luxembourg, the law mentions the living conditions that may result from the birth of a child and considers them as a ground for abortion when they are likely to endanger the physical or mental health of the pregnant woman. Similarly, in Italy, the law specifies that the economic, social and family situation must be taken into account in determining if continuation of the pregnancy or childbirth would seriously endanger the physical or mental health of the pregnant woman. In other cases, as in Iceland, the law expressly lists in detail the social and economic conditions for permitting an abortion. The list of social reasons includes high parity and short interval between births, youth or lack of maturity of the future mother which may prejudice the child and difficult family circumstances, such as ill health of a member of the household. There are also instances, as in India, when abortion is not explicitly permitted on social and economic grounds but the law specifies that in the determination of whether the continuation of the pregnancy would involve a risk of injury to the health of the pregnant woman, the physician may take into account the woman's actual or reasonably foreseeable socio-economic environment.

Although it may be difficult to detect major policy differences between countries that permit abortion when necessary to preserve the physical and mental health of the pregnant woman and interpret those grounds very liberally and those in which abortion is available for social or economic reasons, they are coded differently because they imply different legal approaches and philosophies. The ambiguity of the "mental health" ground leaves much room for interpretation, leading some countries to interpret the grounds very narrowly and others very liberally. With regard to social and economic grounds, however, liberal interpretation is the rule.

Available upon request: permitted on all grounds

The major difference between laws permitting abortion on social and economic grounds and those permitting abortion on demand is that a woman may simply request an abortion. She need not justify it in the eyes of the law. It must be noted that in many cases the difference may be purely in terms of the philosophical orientation of the law as women may have the same access to abortion in both situations. Thus, such countries as Norway and Greece have abortion on demand, whereas in Hungary, a woman seeking an abortion must be in a crisis situation and must have a compulsory consultation with a nurse. In Italy, she must attest to her physician that continuation of the pregnancy or childbirth would seriously endanger her physical or mental health, based on broad considerations which include economic, social and family conditions.

2. Additional requirements

This section concerns the additional legal requirements that must be observed to qualify for a lawful abortion. It may encompass consent clauses, personnel permitted to perform abortions and where they may be performed, and any gestation limits that need to be observed. For instance, abortion on demand can generally be performed without the approval of authorities if performed within a given gestation duration, usually 12 weeks.

B. FERTILITY AND MORTALITY CONTEXT

1. *Government's view of fertility level*

This variable identifies the Government's perception of the overall acceptability of aggregate national fertility; it is divided into three categories: "not satisfactory because too low"; "satisfactory"; and "not satisfactory because too high".

2. *Government's intervention concerning fertility level*

Governmental intervention concerning the level of fertility is classified as four types: (*a*) to raise the fertility level; (*b*) to maintain the fertility level; (*c*) to lower the fertility level; and (*d*) no intervention or no policy formulated.

3. *Government's policies concerning effective use of modern methods of contraception*

Four categories of governmental policy concerning individual fertility behaviour were adopted to categorize countries according to their level of support for modern methods of contraception:

(*a*) The Government limits access to information, guidance and materials in respect of modern methods of contraception that would enable persons to regulate their fertility more effectively and would help them achieve the desired timing of births and completed family size;

(*b*) The Government does not limit access to information, guidance and materials but provides no support—direct or indirect—for their dissemination;

(*c*) The Government provides indirect support for the dissemination of information, guidance and materials by subsidizing the operating costs of organizations supporting such activities outside the Government's own services. The indirect support may take various forms, such as direct grants, tax reductions or rebates, or assignment of special status;

(*d*) The Government provides direct support for the dissemination of information, guidance and materials within government facilities.

4. *Use of contraception*

The percentage of currently married women aged 15-49 years that use modern contraception provides an indication of the actual availability of contraceptives. Use of contraception is inversely associated with abortion at the aggregate level. A low availability of modern contraceptives tends to be correlated with high abortion rates. Conversely, when modern contraceptive methods are widely available and are used effectively, abortion rates tend to be relatively lower. At the individual level, the use of contraception is positively associated with the practice of abortion. That is, women that have ever used a contraceptive method are, on average, more likely to resort to abortion than never-users. On the other hand, women that have had an abortion are more likely to use contraception than women that have never done so. It has been suggested that contraceptive use increases after an abortion because of the provision of contraceptives and counselling in abortion clinics.

Information on contraceptive use was obtained primarily from representative national sample surveys of women of reproductive age conducted by various governmental and non-governmental agencies. The data pertain to women currently married or in a consensual union (United Nations, 1992).

5. Total fertility rate

The total fertility rate (TFR) measures the number of children a woman would have over her lifetime if she were to follow current age-specific fertility rates. For most countries, the rates presented here are medium-variant estimates for the period 1990-1995 unless otherwise specified and are based on available data that have been adjusted to reflect rates for the same five-year period. Estimated rather than actual TFRs were used to permit comparisons across countries. For countries for which data for the period 1990-1995 were not available, data for the period 1985-1990 are provided.

6. Age-specific fertility rate for women aged 15-19

The age-specific fertility rate (ASFR) for women aged 15-19 is an indicator of current rates of adolescent fertility. Specifically, the rate is the number of births to women aged 15-19 per 1,000 women in that age group. In general, adolescent fertility has been increasing in a number of countries in recent years. Because many of these young mothers are unmarried, have no means of economic support and may face social disgrace as a result of the pregnancy, many resort to abortion.

Adolescent abortion rates are high in developed countries, such as the United States of America, and in less developed regions, particularly in sub-Saharan Africa and the Caribbean. In developed countries, between 5 (in Japan) and 26 (in the United Kingdom and in the United States of America) per cent of all legal abortions during the period from around 1985 to 1987 were to women aged 15-19 (Henshaw and Morrow, 1990). Estimates of abortion rates in many developing countries are unreliable because abortion is generally illegal and most abortions are not reported. However, estimates indicate very high rates of abortion. Studies of the hospital records of women hospitalized with complications arising from induced abortion have found that in 1977 the average age of abortion patients in the Congo was 22 years, and in Benin the average was 19 years.

ASFRs pertain to the years in which the data were gathered in each country. Comparable estimates of ASFR for women aged 15-19 years are not available. Because people tend to round their age to digits ending in zero or five and because adolescent women giving birth tend to overstate their age, it is likely that many births occurring to women under age 20 are recorded as occurring at age 20, thus underestimating actual adolescent fertility (United Nations, 1989a).

7. Government's concern about morbidity and mortality resulting from induced abortion

This variable indicates whether the Government views existing health complications due to induced abortion with special concern. The information was obtained from the Government's reply to the Sixth United Nations Population Inquiry among Governments in 1987 and the Seventh Inquiry in 1992, conducted by the Population Division of the then Department for Economic and Social Development of the United Nations Secretariat. If a Government did not respond to the Inquiry, statements made in official government documents and publications were reviewed in order to determine that Government's concern about morbidity and mortality resulting from induced abortion.

8. Government's concern about complications of child-bearing and childbirth

This variable indicates whether the Government views existing health complications due to child-bearing and childbirth with special concern. The information was obtained from the Government's reply to the Sixth and Seventh United Nations Population Inquiries among Governments, conducted by the Population Division. If a

Government did not respond to the Inquiry, statements made in official government documents and publications were reviewed in order to determine that Government's concern about complications of child-bearing and childbirth.

9. Maternal mortality rate[2]

Induced abortion accounts for a large percentage share of maternal mortality in developing countries, particularly in those with very restrictive abortion laws. As many as 54 per cent of all maternal deaths in Ethiopia and in Trinidad and Tobago have been attributed to abortion. In Mauritius, 50 per cent of maternal deaths were abortion-related; in Matlab, Bangladesh, 31 per cent. The corresponding figures are 37 per cent for Argentina, 23 per cent for Venezuela and 18 per cent for the United States[3] (PAHO, 1990; WHO, 1991a; Royston and Armstrong, 1989).

According to the World Health Organization (WHO), a maternal death is defined as "the death of a woman while pregnant or within 42 days of termination of pregnancy regardless of the duration and site of the pregnancy, from any cause related to or aggravated by the pregnancy or its management, but not from accidental or incidental causes" (WHO, 1974, p. 764, cited in PAHO, 1990). Thus, the maternal mortality rate measures the number of maternal deaths occurring in a given year per 100,000 live births during that year. Ideally, both that rate and the proportion of deaths attributable to abortion should be included. Because induced abortion is frequently performed illegally, however, only deaths occurring in hospitals are reported and even then the cause of death is often omitted. This practice greatly underestimates the number of deaths caused by abortion. Given these additional reasons for unreliability of data, the proportion of deaths attributable to abortion was not included.

Caution should be exercised when examining maternal mortality rates and making comparisons across countries. Underregistration of maternal deaths varies by country, as does underregistration of cause of death. Even in developed countries, such as the United States, maternal mortality has been found to be underregistered by as much as 27 per cent (PAHO, 1990). Underregistration of births is also significant, and when the degree of underreporting of births and deaths differs, the direction of the bias will also differ. Limiting the puerperal period to 42 days also introduces a downward bias. Studies conducted in the United States have shown that 16 per cent of the "deaths associated with pregnancy, delivery, and the puerperium occur between 42 days and one year afterwards" (PAHO, 1990, p. 119). Given that data on maternal mortality are often unreliable and that many countries lack information, rates for both the country and the region were included. Where both figures are available and it is thought that the country in question might have very deficient vital statistics, the regional figure provides an idea as to the extent of possible bias of the national figures.

10. Female life expectancy at birth

Female life expectancy at birth is included as a measure of women's overall health. The figure represents the number of years that a newborn female child would live, on average, if she were subjected during her lifetime to the risk of dying observed for each age group in the current year. For most countries, all the measures are medium-variant estimates for the period 1990-1995 unless otherwise specified (taken from United Nations, 1993) and therefore permit cross-country comparisons. For countries for which data for the period 1990-1995 were not available, data for the period 1985-1990 are provided.

C. STATISTICS ON INDUCED ABORTION

The most commonly employed sources of abortion statistics include official statistics provided by Governments on legal abortions performed, surveys of abortion service providers, hospital admission records on women admitted for abortion complications and household surveys containing information on women's pregnancy history. The last-named source may provide both period and lifetime abortion experience.

12

In general, countries with liberal abortion laws require that all abortions performed be reported to the Government. These statistics are usually published by national health statistics agencies. In countries where abortion is available on demand, where abortion services are sufficient and adequate and where there is compliance with reporting requirements, one may expect government figures to provide the most unbiased estimate of abortions performed. The same may be said of countries where abortion is de facto available for socio-economic reasons. If abortion is not readily available, even when legal, abortions may be sought in other countries or in illegal facilities, in which case official figures would underestimate the actual number of women obtaining abortions. Insufficient access to legal abortion may be the result of burdensome procedures required to obtain an abortion (as was the case in the former USSR) or of insufficient service availability, including both clinics and physicians (as in Zambia), or simply due to the refusal by available staff to perform the abortion on moral grounds (as in Austria).

Not all countries, however, require providers to register abortions performed in their facilities. In these cases, statistics are often available from other health agencies and associations or from individual surveys of abortion service providers. Surveys of providers are the next least biased source of abortion data. These surveys have been conducted in countries with liberal abortion laws which have no official reporting requirements. They have also been conducted where abortion is illegal in order to estimate abortion rates. Where abortion is legal, surveys of providers generally give good estimates of abortion rates. Where abortion is illegal, however, providers may not be willing to give the information in order to protect the women's confidentiality and to avoid prosecution. Moreover, non-medical providers may be difficult to identify. Women successfully inducing their own abortion are also missed.

Surveys of women, either as part of a general household survey or in a more specialized demographic or health survey, can also be a source of information on abortion. This category includes abortion statistics based on personal interviews with women in households or hospitals, or as participants in specific programmes, concerning their reproductive history, or more specifically, their abortion experience. This source is useful regardless of the legal status of abortion because it provides measures both of prevalence and of incidence. However, survey data have their drawbacks. Underreporting of induced abortion in surveys has been found to be considerable even when abortion is legal because of fear of social disapproval and poor recall. In addition, the statistics obtained from pregnancy histories are retrospective and are usually presented as lifetime measures rather than annual measures. These statistics were employed only when they were calculated as annual rates and when they were based on representative samples of the population.

Where abortion is illegal, the most commonly used source of information on abortion statistics is hospital admission records. Hospital admission records include all women admitted for treatment of complications of abortion, whether spontaneous or induced. In these cases, the underestimation of true induced abortion rates can be substantial, as only those cases in which an abortion resulted in complications are hospitalized. Furthermore, only hospital-based treatments are included. Deaths occurring before a hospital has been contacted also go unreported. Despite problems with underestimation of induced abortion, hospital admission records are useful because they give an indication as to the minimum incidence of abortion in a given region.

In addition to the potential biases mentioned above, all measures miss self-induced abortion employing prostaglandins during very early pregnancy. They may also miss abortions performed by menstrual regulation because in some places it is considered a family planning method, not an abortifacient. The use of RU486, the Roussel-UCLAF "abortion pill", might also go undetected.

NOTES

[1]Most of the comparative studies on abortion law in Commonwealth countries were conducted by Cook and Dickens. They surveyed all Commonwealth countries to inquire whether the *Bourne* case was applicable in each country in question. When a country responded in the affirmative, they considered that country to permit abortion on both physical and mental health grounds, regardless of whether a court precedent had been set in that country. That is, in some cases, mental health grounds are assumed to be permitted, when in fact no case has

tested those grounds. In this publication, only those countries where local court precedents have tested the legality of mental health grounds are coded as permitting this ground.

[2]Major sources of information on maternal mortality were WHO, 1991a and 1991b.

[3]Figures for Argentina, Mauritius, Trinidad and Tobago, and the United States of America are for the late 1980s; for Matlab, Bangladesh, 1982; for Ethiopia, 1987; and for Venezuela, 1985.

IV. COUNTRY PROFILES:
GABON TO NORWAY

ABORTION POLICY

Grounds on which abortion is permitted:

To save the life of the woman	Yes
To preserve physical health	No
To preserve mental health	No
Rape or incest	No
Foetal impairment	No
Economic or social reasons	No
Available on request	No

Additional requirements:

The physician performing the abortion must obtain the advice of two consulting physicians, one of whom must be taken from a list of experts provided by the court. The physician must attest to the fact that the life of the woman cannot be saved by any means other than the intervention contemplated.

FERTILITY AND MORTALITY CONTEXT

Government's view on fertility level:	Too low
Government's intervention concerning fertility level:	To raise
Government's policy on contraceptive use:	No support provided
Percentage of currently married women using modern contraception (aged 15-49):	..
Total fertility rate (1990-1995):	5.3
Age-specific fertility rate (per 1,000 women aged 15-19, 1990-1995):	163
Government has expressed particular concern about:	
Morbidity and mortality resulting from induced abortion	Yes
Complications of child-bearing and childbirth	Yes
Maternal mortality rate (per 100,000 live births):	
National (1983)	190
Middle Africa (around 1988)	710
Female life expectancy at birth (1990-1995):	55.2

Gabon

In Gabon, as in many other former French colonies, the Penal Code (Law No. 21-63 of 31 May 1963) derives from the French penal codes elaborated in the early nineteenth century. Article 244 of the Penal Code forbids abortion except to save the life of the woman. The Penal Code provides that anyone performing or attempting to perform an abortion is subject to imprisonment for from one to five years and a fine of from 24,000 to 500,000 CFA francs (CFAF). These penalties are increased to 5-10 years and a fine of CFAF 50,000-1,000,000 if the person habitually performs abortions. Members of the medical or paramedical profession that perform an abortion can be suspended for a minimum of five years or be forbidden to practice. The woman is subject to from six months to two years of imprisonment and/or a fine of CFAF 24,000-240,000.

According to Ordinance No. 64/69 of 4 October 1969, contraceptives can be obtained only by prescription for therapeutic purposes. The law provides that in exceptional cases contraceptive products may be prescribed where the woman's health could be endangered by a further pregnancy or where the well-being of the family so requires. The decision may be made only by a commission of three physicians.

The fact that abortion is generally illegal in Gabon under the Penal Code and access to contraceptive information and services is limited is partially explained by the fact that the Government is concerned by the perceived low fertility and high level of infertility. For this reason, up to the beginning of 1990s, the Government did not provide any support for family planning activities and was opposed to family planning.

The rate of maternal mortality in Gabon has been increasing, largely as a result of the consequences of illegal abortion. The problem of infertility is also related to complications arising from abortion (70 per cent of infertility in Gabon is related to secondary sterility caused by sexually transmitted diseases and abortion). To reduce maternal mortality and morbidity and to address the problems posed by sterility, the Government is receiving international assistance to expand the Safe Motherhood Initiative to more of the provinces of Gabon, as part of the public health system.

INCIDENCE OF ABORTION

Place	Year	Measurement	Coverage

Information not readily available.

Source: The Population Policy Data Bank maintained by the Population Division of the Department for Economic and Social Information and Policy Analysis of the United Nations Secretariat. For additional sources, see list of references.

ABORTION POLICY

Grounds on which abortion is permitted:

To save the life of the woman	Yes
To preserve physical health	Yes
To preserve mental health	Yes
Rape or incest	No
Foetal impairment	No
Economic or social reasons	No
Available on request	No

Additional requirements:

Information is not readily available.

FERTILITY AND MORTALITY CONTEXT

Government's view on fertility level:	Too high
Government's intervention concerning fertility level:	To lower
Government's policy on contraceptive use:	Direct support provided
Percentage of currently married women using modern contraception (aged 15-49, 1991)	7
Total fertility rate (1990-1995)	6.1
Age-specific fertility rate (per 1,000 women aged 15-19, 1990-1995):	204
Government has expressed particular concern about:	
Morbidity and mortality resulting from induced abortion	Yes
Complications of child-bearing and childbirth	Yes
Maternal mortality rate (per 100,000 live births):	
National (1984)	1,500
Western Africa (around 1988)	760
Female life expectancy at birth (1990-1995):	46.6

Gambia

BACKGROUND

BACKGROUND

The Gambia Criminal Code of 1 October 1934 (cap. 37, sections 15, 140-142) prohibits abortion except when necessary to save the life of the pregnant woman or to preserve her health. In addition, the British case *Rex* v. *Bourne* (1938), in which the concept of health is broadly interpreted to include mental health, is applied. Any person that assists in performing or induces an illegal abortion, including the pregnant woman, is subject to imprisonment. The person performing an illegal abortion is subject to imprisonment for 14 years. A woman that induces her own abortion is subject to imprisonment for seven years, and any person that supplies instruments with the knowledge that they are intended to be used for an abortion is liable to imprisonment for three years.

Although no official statistics on abortion are available in the Gambia, a study conducted in the greater Banjul region in 1988 suggests a high incidence of abortion. The study, conducted among women aged 14-24 years, showed that 11 per cent of women that had ever been pregnant terminated their first pregnancy through induced abortion. The maternal mortality rate is quite high and is much higher than the rate for Western Africa as a whole. A 1987 study estimated a maternal mortality rate of 1,005 per 100,000 live births.

Family planning services have been provided in the Gambia since the late 1960s, even though the Government did not adopt an explicit population policy until 1979. The overall objectives of the family planning programme are to reduce the number of abortions and maternal deaths and to improve maternal and child nutrition, education and the family economy in general. Contraceptives are available in the private sector through pharmacies and community-based distribution systems initiated by the Gambia Family Planning Association, as well as in Government clinics and in the five major health-care centres. The contraceptive prevalence rate is very low in the Gambia; only 7 per cent of women of reproductive age use modern methods of family planning. Low contraceptive use rates can be attributed to several factors. One of the most important is that contraceptive services are not provided to women under age 21, even though 45 per cent of the Gambian population are under age 15 and the median age is 18.8 years. Unmarried mothers must obtain parental consent in order to receive family planning services. Other factors contributing to low rates include illiteracy, traditional practices, the low status of women, inadequate and undertrained medical personnel, low morale among family planning workers, poor communication and insufficient funding.

INCIDENCE OF ABORTION

Place	Year	Measurement	Coverage

Information not readily available.

Source: The Population Policy Data Bank maintained by the Population Division of the Department for Economic and Social Information and Policy Analysis of the United Nations Secretariat. For additional sources, see list of references.

ABORTION POLICY

Grounds on which abortion is permitted:

To save the life of the woman	Yes
To preserve physical health	Yes
To preserve mental health	Yes
Rape or incest	Yes
Foetal impairment	Yes
Economic or social reasons	Yes
Available on request	Yes

Additional requirements:

An abortion requires the consent of the pregnant woman; it is authorized if performed by a licensed physician in a hospital or other recognized medical institution. Abortion is available on request during the first 12 weeks of gestation. Thereafter, induced abortion is available within 28 weeks from conception on judicial, genetic, vital, broad medical and social grounds, as well as for personal reasons if authorized by a commission of local physicians.

FERTILITY AND MORTALITY CONTEXT

Government's view on fertility level:	Satisfactory
Government's intervention concerning fertility level:	To maintain
Government's policy on contraceptive use:	Direct support provided
Percentage of currently married women using modern contraception (aged 15-49, 1990):	8
Total fertility rate (1985-1990):	2.3
Age-specific fertility rate (per 1,000 women aged 15-19, 1985-1990):	55

Government has expressed particular concern about:
Morbidity and mortality resulting from induced abortion	Yes
Complications of child-bearing and childbirth	Yes

Maternal mortality rate (per 100,000 live births):
National (1990)	20.5
Developed countries (around 1988)	26

Female life expectancy at birth (1985-1990):	75.6

Georgia

As was the case with all of the former Soviet republics, Georgia, known prior to 1992 as the Georgian Soviet Socialist Republic, was subject to the abortion legislation and regulations of the former Union of Soviet Socialist Republics. As a result, abortion practices in Georgia were similar to those throughout the former USSR.

The description given below pertains to the situation in Georgia prior to independence.

The Soviet law of 27 June 1936 prohibited induced abortion in most circumstances, permitting it only for eugenic reasons. Physicians and non-medical personnel that performed abortions in hospitals or as part of an out-patient service were subject to a maximum of three years in prison. A husband, relative or physician who pressured a woman into having an abortion could be sentenced to a maximum of two years in prison. The pregnant woman could be prosecuted by public trial and/or be required to pay a large fine.

In a decree of 23 November 1955, the Soviet Government repealed the prohibition of abortion. Regulations issued in 1956 and subsequently in 1982 specified that abortions could be performed during the first 12 weeks of gestation, although not less than six months after a woman's previous abortion. An abortion was considered illegal if not performed in a hospital or if the person performing the abortion did not have an advanced medical education. The maximum penalty for an illegal abortion was set at eight years in a labour camp.

In 1974, the Ministry of Public Health of the USSR published a document entitled "On the side-effects and complications of oral contraceptives", in which the mass use of oral contraception was de facto prohibited. On 5 June 1987, in Order No. 757, the Ministry of Public Health legalized and officially permitted the provision of early vacuum aspirations in any clinic regardless of the place of residence of the woman. Vacuum aspiration had been the method of induced abortion provided during the first 20 days of pregnancy with the obligatory diagnosis of pregnancy.

During the 1980s, the Ministry of Public Health continued its efforts to decrease the number of illegal abortions by formally broadening the grounds on which abortions were legal and increasing their availability. Most of the later changes were not followed by a simultaneous increase in actual de facto accessibility of abortion services. On 31 December 1987, the Ministry of Public Health published Order No. 1342, which permits induced abortion during the first 28 weeks of gestation on judicial, genetic, broad medical and social grounds (for example, more than five children in the family), as well as on demand with the special authorization of a commission of local physicians.

The high incidence of abortion has been attributed to a number of factors, including shortages of high-quality modern contraceptives and reliance upon less reliable traditional methods, a lack of knowledge among couples of contraception and of the detrimental health consequences of frequent abortions and the absence of adequate training for physicians, nurses, teachers and other specialists. In 1989, the availability of condoms in the entire former Soviet Union amounted to only 11 per cent of demand; intra-uterine devices (IUDs), 30 per cent; and pills, 2 per cent. Data from the All-Union sample survey of contraceptive use conducted in 1990 indicate that in Georgia, 8 per cent of all women aged 15-49 years regularly used contraception, 9 per cent sometimes used contraception, 60 per cent did not use any contraceptive method and 20 per cent knew nothing about contraception. Sample survey data for 1988 show that at Tbilisi, the capital of Georgia, the proportion of contraceptive users was 12-16 per cent and that of every 100 contraceptive users, 40 per cent used the vaginal douche method and 21 per cent practised coitus interruptus; the proportion using IUD or the pill was very low.

In 1989, a total of 68,833 induced abortions were registered in Georgia, giving an abortion rate of 51.1 per 1,000 women aged 15-49 years. The actual figure is much higher, because this total does not include most abortions performed in departmental health services and commercial clinics, early vacuum aspirations and self-induced abortions. At Tbilisi, over 70 per cent of all induced abortions were performed on women aged 20-35 years and were intended to prevent subsequent births. In 1988, 2 per cent of all induced abortions were performed on primigravidae and 3.5 per cent of all induced abortions were vacuum aspirations. In 1989, illegal abortions, calculated on the basis of their registered complications, accounted for 12 per cent of all abortions and 46 per cent of all abortions among primigravidae. Among women under age 17, they accounted for 18 per cent of all induced abortions.

Maternal mortality rates in Georgia were 25.7 and 22.8 per 100,000 births in 1980 and 1988, respectively, one of the lowest rates in the former Soviet Union; in 1988, 76 per cent of all maternal deaths were due to unknown or "other" causes.

INCIDENCE OF ABORTION

Place	Year	Measurement	Coverage
National	1970	40.6 abortions/1,000 women aged 15-49	PR
National	1975	74.0 abortions/1,000 women aged 15-49	PR
National	1980	67.7 abortions/1,000 women aged 15-49	PR
National	1985	52.4 abortions/1,000 women aged 15-49	PR
National	1988	58.8 abortions/1,000 women aged 15-49	PR
National	1989	51.1 abortions/1,000 women aged 15-49	PR
National	1990	45.7 abortions/1,000 women aged 15-49	PR

Note: PR = provider registration; SP = survey provider; SW = survey of women; HR = hospital admission records. For a detailed description of these abbreviations and information on sources of the data, see technical notes in the annex.

Source: The Population Policy Data Bank maintained by the Population Division of the Department for Economic and Social Information and Policy Analysis of the United Nations Secretariat. For additional sources, see list of references.

Germany

ABORTION POLICY

Grounds on which abortion is permitted:

To save the life of the woman	Yes
To preserve physical health	Yes
To preserve mental health	Yes
Rape or incest	Yes
Foetal impairment	Yes
Economic or social reasons	No[*]
Available on request	No[*]

Additional requirements:

Except for abortion on medical grounds, the woman must attend a pre-abortion social counselling session with a physician. The intervention must be performed in a hospital or other authorized facility.

---

[*] Abortion on this ground may be considered in exceptional circumstances, based on the Federal Constitutional Court decision of 28 May 1993.

FERTILITY AND MORTALITY CONTEXT

Government's view on fertility level:	Too low
Government's intervention concerning fertility level:	No intervention
Government's policy on contraceptive use:	Indirect support provided
Percentage of currently married women using modern contraception (aged 15-44, 1985):	68[*]
Total fertility rate (1990-1995):	1.5
Age-specific fertility rate (per 1,000 women aged 15-19, 1990-1995):	17
Government has expressed particular concern about:	
Morbidity and mortality resulting from induced abortion	No
Complications of child-bearing and childbirth	No
Maternal mortality rate (per 100,000 live births):	
National (1990)	7.3[*]
Developed countries (around 1988)	26
Female life expectancy at birth (1990-1995):	79.0

---

[*] Data refer to the former Federal Republic of Germany.

Until the end of 1992, the legal status of abortion in Germany was provisionally based on a compromise (covenant) according to which the respective laws of the two former States (the Federal Republic of Germany and the German Democratic Republic) would continue to be applied within the previous geographical borders of their respective jurisdictions. Abortion law has been one of the more complex questions to resolve among those resulting from the unification of the two German States in October 1990. Abortion law was a focal point of discussions surrounding the treaty of unification, with the former German Democratic Republic having difficulties if the more restrictive abortion law of the Federal Republic of Germany was applied to the eastern Länder (federal states). Long negotiations eventually resulted in a compromise: that the decision was to be postponed for two years (i.e., until the end of 1992), during which time the two laws would continue to apply within the former geographical borders. According to the agreement, counselling centres were to be established, with federal financial help, in the eastern Länder.

The sensitivity of the issue led to a long debate among the political parties in Germany, and it was only on 26 June 1992 that the Parliament adopted the new law. The new law retained the medical, eugenic and ethical reasons, and it also allowed abortion during the first trimester of pregnancy, if the woman received counselling of physicians, psychologists or social workers whom she had to convince that given her present and future situation there was no remedy other than abortion. The woman then had the entire responsibility for the decision. At the request of its opponents, this law was submitted to the Federal Constitutional Court in order to explore its compatibility with the Basic Law of the State (Constitution) and, in particular, to decide if the counselling offered adequate protection for the foetus, in line with its decision of February 1975. In August 1992, the Court suspended application of the new law, pending its decision, which was announced on 28 May 1993. In its decision, the Constitutional Court ruled that the proposed new abortion law was unconstitutional because it did not protect the life of the unborn. According to the Court, an abortion may be performed only in exceptional circumstances and the compulsory counselling must be an active effort to dissuade the pregnant woman from having an abortion; however, the pregnant woman and the physician performing an abortion will not be prosecuted, even though the abortion is illegal. One of the implications of this ruling is that an abortion performed for other than medical, eugenic or ethical reasons will not be subsidized under compulsory health insurance. This will not apply to women living on social aid. In addition, the court made it clear that the right of the unborn child is to take precedence over the right of the woman to self-determination. This will have an impact on family planning counsellors, who will now be required by law to offer only counselling geared to the protection of unborn life. The counselling given in many centres, in which all alternatives are considered, is now illegal. The Court ruling was to take effect on 16 June 1993. As a consequence of this ruling, the German Parliament will have to formulate a new abortion law in harmony with the guidelines set by the Constitutional Court.

In the former German Democratic Republic, the law of 9 March 1972 stated that during the first 12 weeks of gestation, the woman could decide whether she would give birth, thereby allowing abortion on request during the first trimester of pregnancy (*Fristenregelung*). The abortion was denied, however, if a period of less than six months had elapsed since the woman's most recent previous pregnancy termination. After the first trimester, the pregnancy termination was permitted only by a decision of a commission of medical specialists taken in order to safeguard the woman's life or to respond to "circumstances of a serious nature".

A similar procedure, although one requiring counselling by a physician or by an approved organization, existed in the Federal Republic of Germany for a short period, from June 1974 to February 1975. Subsequently, a decision of the Federal Constitutional Court found this procedure to be in conflict with the constitutionally protected right to life and the duty of the State to secure human dignity. With the reform of February 1976, the Penal Code of the Federal Republic was modified along the lines of the Constitutional Court decision. The new law considered abortion to be illegal unless specific conditions were applicable

Germany

(*Indikationsregelung*). Abortion was not punishable if it was performed with the consent of the woman by a physician who considered that her situation posed a threat to her life or physical or mental health (medical reason). A physician could also allow an abortion if there were risks of permanent damage to the health of the child (eugenic reason), if the pregnancy resulted from rape or incest (ethical reason) or if other situations were causing serious distress for the mother (social reason). Only the physician could decide on the reason. Also, the woman was required to go through social counselling and then she could obtain an abortion from an approved physician different from the one deciding on the reason. There were wide differences in the availability of abortion among the different Länder, with states with large Catholic populations urging that counselling conform to Catholic teachings and stressing the sanctity of life. Consequently, a number of women sought abortion in neighbouring states with more liberal abortion practices or in other countries. All abortions (except those abroad) were subsidized by compulsory health insurance which covers 90 per cent of the population.

Prior to unification, the level of induced abortion was viewed as a matter of concern by the Government of the Federal Republic of Germany, as many pregnancies were terminated for social reasons (i.e., situation of serious distress for the mother). In 1984, the Government initiated a major counselling and assistance programme—Mutter und Kind, Schutz des ungeborenen Lebens (Mother and Child, Protection of Unborn Life). A counselling law was introduced in order to ensure comprehensive counselling before a pregnancy was terminated. Although the official number of abortions performed in the western Länder is lower than that in the eastern Länder, a significant number of abortions took place in neighbouring countries with more liberal abortion laws.

The reaching of a compromise between the liberal abortion law of the eastern Länder and the law of the more conservative western Länder was made even more difficult by major differences in the enforcement of the law in the western states that have a large Catholic population. In addition, the establishment of counselling centres in the eastern states was controversial, as their essential purpose was protecting unborn life and encouraging the pregnant woman to continue her pregnancy. On the other hand, the abortion law of the eastern states was viewed by some groups in the western states as being too permissive and as treating abortion as a family planning method.

In 1989, it was reported that in the former German Democratic Republic about one pregnancy in four was terminated; in the Federal Republic of Germany, the rate was estimated at one abortion in five or six pregnancies. In 1991, there were 49,806 abortions in the eastern states, a rate of 465 abortions per 1,000 live births, while there were 74,570 abortions in the western states, a rate of 103 per 1,000 live births. The data for the eastern Länder may have been biased by the widespread uncertainties related to the unification process. Apparently, large numbers of women had their pregnancies terminated in the period 1989-1991 because of fears about the impending socio-economic changes. These concerns included the fear of losing a job because of pregnancy when unemployment might rise and the possibility of loss of maternity benefits, such as the child care that had been provided by the former German Democratic Republic. It is estimated that in the former German Democratic Republic the number of abortions performed in 1990 increased by 30 per cent. The higher abortion rate in the eastern Länder may also be explained by the fact that abortion was more easily obtained there and alternatives were rarely discussed. However, given that the information for the former Federal Republic of Germany includes only official data, which omit underreporting and abortions performed abroad, it is felt that the abortion rate may be substantially higher.

INCIDENCE OF ABORTION

Place	Year	Measurement	Coverage
A. Federal Republic of Germany (former)			
National	1975	1.5 abortions/1,000 women aged 15-44	PR
National	1978	5.6 abortions/1,000 women aged 15-44	PR
National	1980	6.6 abortions/1,000 women aged 15-44	PR
National	1982	6.6 abortions/1,000 women aged 15-44	PR
National	1985	6.1 abortions/1,000 women aged 15-44	PR
National	1986	6.3 abortions/1,000 women aged 15-44	PR
National	1987	6.6 abortions/1,000 women aged 15-44	PR
National	1988	6.3 abortions/1,000 women aged 15-44	PR
National	1989	5.6 abortions/1,000 women aged 15-44	PR
National	1990	5.8 abortions/1,000 women aged 15-44	PR
B. German Democratic Republic (former)			
National	1975	25.2 abortions/1,000 women aged 15-44	PR
National	1978	22.2 abortions/1,000 women aged 15-44	PR
National	1980	24.4 abortions/1,000 women aged 15-44	PR
National	1982	26.5 abortions/1,000 women aged 15-44	PR
National	1985	25.5 abortions/1,000 women aged 15-44	PR
National	1986	24.4 abortions/1,000 women aged 15-44	PR
National	1987	23.5 abortions/1,000 women aged 15-44	PR
National	1988	23.3 abortions/1,000 women aged 15-44	PR
National	1989	22.0 abortions/1,000 women aged 15-44	PR
National	1990	20.1 abortions/1,000 women aged 15-44	PR
C. Germany			
National	1975	6.6 abortions/1,000 women aged 15-44	PR
National	1980	10.4 abortions/1,000 women aged 15-44	PR
National	1985	10.3 abortions/1,000 women aged 15-44	PR
National	1989	8.9 abortions/1,000 women aged 15-44	PR
National	1990	8.7 abortions/1,000 women aged 15-44	PR

Note: PR = provider registration; SP = survey provider; SW = survey of women; HR = hospital admission records. For a detailed description of these abbreviations and information on sources of the data, see technical notes in the annex.

Source: The Population Policy Data Bank maintained by the Population Division of the Department for Economic and Social Information and Policy Analysis of the United Nations Secretariat. For additional sources, see list of references.

Ghana

Grounds on which abortion is permitted:

To save the life of the woman	Yes
To preserve physical health	Yes
To preserve mental health	Yes
Rape or incest	Yes
Foetal impairment	Yes
Economic or social reasons	No
Available on request	No

Additional requirements:

An abortion must be performed by a registered physician with the consent of the pregnant woman. The consent of kin or a guardian is required if the woman is not capable of giving consent. The abortion must be performed in a government hospital or a private hospital or clinic registered under the Private Hospitals or Maternity Homes Act of 1958 (No. 9) or in a place approved for the purpose.

FERTILITY AND MORTALITY CONTEXT

Government's view on fertility level:	Too high
Government's intervention concerning fertility level:	To lower
Government's policy on contraceptive use:	Direct support provided
Percentage of currently married women using modern contraception (aged 15-49, 1988):	5
Total fertility rate (1990-1995):	6.0
Age-specific fertility rate (per 1,000 women aged 15-19, 1990-1995):	127

Government has expressed particular concern about:
Morbidity and mortality resulting from induced abortion	Yes
Complications of child-bearing and childbirth	Yes

Maternal mortality rate (per 100,000 live births):
National (1984)	500-1,500
Western Africa (around 1988)	760

Female life expectancy at birth (1990-1995):	57.8

BACKGROUND

Until 1985, abortion was illegal in Ghana unless performed in good faith and without negligence for medical or surgical treatment of the pregnant woman. The Criminal Code of 1960 (Act 29, sections 58-59 and 76) stated that anyone causing or attempting to cause an abortion, regardless of whether the woman was pregnant, could be imprisoned for up to 10 years and/or fined. A woman inducing her own abortion or undergoing an illegal abortion was subject to the same punishment.

The law of 1960 was not sufficiently clear on several issues. It did not, for example, clarify who was qualified to perform an abortion, whether the consent of the woman (or guardian) was required, the gestation limits and where a legal abortion could be performed. Two studies conducted among physicians and lawyers in the early 1970s confirmed that the law was so vague that different persons had varying interpretations of it. The studies also found that the overwhelming majority of physicians supported the drafting of a clearer and more liberal abortion law in Ghana.

Ghana liberalized its abortion law in 1985 (Law No. 102 of 22 February). Abortion is currently legal if the continuation of the pregnancy would involve risk to the life or to the physical or mental health of the pregnant woman, or if there is substantial risk that the child might suffer from or later develop a serious physical abnormality or disease. Abortion is also legal if the pregnancy resulted from rape, incest or defilement of a mentally handicapped woman.

A legal abortion must be performed by a registered physician and with the consent of the pregnant woman. If the woman lacks the capacity to give her own consent, the consent of her next of kin or guardian is required. The abortion must be performed in a government hospital or a private hospital or clinic registered under the Private Hospitals and Maternity Homes Act of 1958 (No. 9) or in a place approved for that purpose by the law.

Any person administering any poison or other noxious substance to a woman or using any instruments or other means to cause an abortion is guilty of an offence and is liable to imprisonment for a term not exceeding five years, regardless of whether the woman is pregnant or has given her consent. Any person encouraging a woman to cause or consent to an abortion, assisting a woman to cause an abortion or attempting to cause an abortion may also be imprisoned for a term not exceeding five years. A person who provides any poison, drug or instrument or any other thing knowing that it will be used to perform an abortion is also subject to the same punishment.

Although there are no official statistics on abortion in Ghana, recent studies suggest that it is a common practice. For example, a 1987 study conducted at Accra and Tamale suggested that abortion was commonly used as a method of birth control. In 1984, a survey carried out at Accra among obstetric patients also found that 20 per cent of the women who had at least one previous hospital delivery had had at least one induced abortion. Despite the relaxation of abortion restrictions in Ghana, limitations on resources restrict the number of legal abortions performed. Therefore, women sometimes attempt illegal abortions and then go to a hospital for treatment of abortion complications. The complications associated with illegal abortion have had serious public health implications in Ghana because they raise maternal mortality and morbidity and divert limited health resources. A study conducted at Korle-Bu Teaching Hospital in 1968-1969 found that 41 per cent of the hospital blood supply was used to treat abortion complications. There is a higher incidence of abortion among young educated women that want to delay their first birth or to space births.

Following the conclusions of an in-depth analysis of the Ghana National Family Planning Programme conducted in 1991, the population policy adopted in 1969 will probably be revised. In addition, it is expected that a National Population Council will be created to monitor and coordinate the activities of governmental and non-governmental bodies involved in population and family planning. The likely revision in policy is in part a response to the results of the Ghana Demographic and Health Survey of 1988, which indicated a

Ghana

total fertility rate of 6.4 children per woman. The survey also found that 13 per cent of currently married women were using some method of family planning and 5 per cent were using modern methods.

INCIDENCE OF ABORTION			
Place	Year	Measurement	Coverage

Information not readily available.

Source: The Population Policy Data Bank maintained by the Population Division of the Department for Economic and Social Information and Policy Analysis of the United Nations Secretariat. For additional sources, see list of references.

ABORTION POLICY

Grounds on which abortion is permitted:

To save the life of the woman	Yes
To preserve physical health	Yes
To preserve mental health	Yes
Rape or incest	Yes
Foetal impairment	Yes
Economic or social reasons	Yes
Available on request	Yes

Additional requirements:

The abortion must be performed by a practising physician in a private clinic or hospital. A physician other than the one performing the abortion must confirm the existence of valid grounds for the abortion. A minor must obtain the written consent of her parents or guardian.

FERTILITY AND MORTALITY CONTEXT

Government's view on fertility level:	Too low
Government's intervention concerning fertility level:	To raise
Government's policy on contraceptive use:	Direct support provided
Percentage of currently married women using modern contraception (aged 15-49):	..
Total fertility rate (1990-1995):	1.5
Age-specific fertility rate (per 1,000 women aged 15-19, 1990-1995):	27
Government has expressed particular concern about:	
Morbidity and mortality resulting from induced abortion	No
Complications of child-bearing and childbirth	No
Maternal mortality rate (per 100,000 live births):	
National (1989)	4
Developed countries (around 1988)	26
Female life expectancy at birth (1990-1995):	80.2

Greece

Until the Second World War, the Government of Greece was strictly opposed to induced abortion, except on medical grounds. The Greek Orthodox Church considers abortion to be a crime and has therefore prohibited and condemned the act. Religious tenets have inevitably influenced legislation and attitudes in Greece concerning abortion. Under the Greek Penal Code of 1950, heavy penalties were imposed on both the woman and the person performing the abortion. Abortion was permitted only in the following exceptional circumstances: if the pregnancy presented a threat to the life or serious or permanent damage to the health of the pregnant woman; if the pregnancy was the result of rape or incest; or if the woman was under age 15.

Due to the efforts of various organizations, such as the Family Planning Association of Greece, the law on abortion in Greece was liberalized in 1978 (Law No. 821 of 14 October). The new law expanded the reasons for permitting therapeutic abortion. Abortion was thereafter permitted for eugenic reasons during the first 20 weeks of gestation. It was also allowed in cases of risk to the mental health of the mother, as determined by a psychiatrist on the staff of a public hospital, but only in the first 12 weeks of gestation.

Until 1980, family planning was illegal in Greece. According to the Fertility Survey conducted in 1983, the general pattern in Greece was for children to be born early in the marriage and for family size to be carefully controlled by the use of withdrawal and condoms, backed up by abortion. Abortion in Greece was used mainly as a form of birth control, and despite being illegal, it was widespread.

Abortion was further liberalized by Law No. 1609 of 28 June 1986. Thereafter, abortion on request could legally be obtained in Greece during the first 12 weeks of pregnancy. Also, if the pregnancy was a result of rape, incest or seduction of a minor, abortion was permitted during the first 19 weeks of gestation. Lastly, in the case of foetal abnormalities, the legal limit was extended to 24 weeks.

It is widely believed that the liberalization of the abortion law in Greece has made little difference in the abortion rate because, prior to its liberalization, a person performing an abortion or a woman undergoing an illegal abortion was rarely prosecuted. Indeed, it is believed that one of the main motives for the liberalization of abortion law was to preserve the integrity of the legal system, which was threatened by the increasing incidence of illegally performed abortions that were not prosecuted.

Although many women having abortions in Greece use the National Health Care System, the majority resort to private gynaecologists, primarily because private abortions are performed immediately. In contrast, the Government-run system is characterized by bureaucratic procedures and resultant delays. A large number of illegal abortions are still performed in Greece, because the public is not yet fully aware of the new abortion law. Despite liberalization of the law on abortion, advertising of abortion services (excluding information supplied in family planning centres) remains a criminal offence.

INCIDENCE OF ABORTION

Place	Year	Measurement	Coverage
National	1989	3.6 abortions/1,000 women aged 15-44	PR
National	1989	7.2 abortions/100 live births	PR

Note: PR = provider registration; SP = survey provider; SW = survey of women; HR = hospital admission records. For a detailed description of these abbreviations and information on sources of the data, see technical notes in the annex.

Source: The Population Policy Data Bank maintained by the Population Division of the Department for Economic and Social Information and Policy Analysis of the United Nations Secretariat. For additional sources, see list of references.

Grenada

ABORTION POLICY

Grounds on which abortion is permitted:

To save the life of the woman	Yes
To preserve physical health	Yes
To preserve mental health	Yes
Rape or incest	No
Foetal impairment	No
Economic or social reasons	No
Available on request	No

Additional requirements:

Information is not readily available.

FERTILITY AND MORTALITY CONTEXT

Government's view on fertility level:	Too high
Government's intervention concerning fertility level:	To lower
Government's policy on contraceptive use:	Direct support provided
Percentage of currently married women using modern contraception (aged 15-44, 1985):	27
Total fertility rate (1990-1995):	..
Age-specific fertility rate (per 1,000 women aged 15-19, 1990-1995):	..
Government has expressed particular concern about:	
Morbidity and mortality resulting from induced abortion	..
Complications of child-bearing and childbirth	..
Maternal mortality rate (per 100,000 live births):	
National (1985-1987)	64
Caribbean (around 1988)	260
Female life expectancy at birth (1990-1995):	..

BACKGROUND

In Grenada, the Criminal Code of 1958 (chap. 76, sects. 238, 250-251, 254 and 263) provides that abortion is illegal on all grounds. However, the British case of *Rex* v. *Bourne* (1938), which established the legality of abortion to preserve not only the woman's life but also her health and, in particular, her mental health, applies. Both a person performing an illegal abortion and a woman inducing her own miscarriage are subject to imprisonment for up to 10 years.

Contraceptive awareness is widespread in Grenada. According to a survey in 1987, 90 per cent of women knew of at least one contraceptive method and 73 per cent knew of three or more methods. However, only 37 per cent of the currently married women reported that they practised contraception. The main reasons given for not using contraception were the desire for more children and fear of the side-effects of contraceptives.

Although the Government basically holds the position that family planning is an individual matter, it recognizes that family planning plays an important role in socio-economic development and is receiving international assistance to support its population programmes. One such project, which was begun in 1985, is directed to increasing contraceptive use and reducing the incidence of teenage pregnancy in Grenada. The percentage of births delivered to teenage mothers is, in fact, relatively high, representing 26 per cent of total births in 1987. In 1974, the Government began integrating family planning services into the National Health Programme. As of 1990, family planning services were available in all health-care clinics throughout the country. The Grenada Planned Parenthood Association provides family planning services through government health centres and a community-based distribution programme, with support from the Ministry of Health.

INCIDENCE OF ABORTION

Place	Year	Measurement	Coverage

Information not readily available.

Source: The Population Policy Data Bank maintained by the Population Division of the Department for Economic and Social Information and Policy Analysis of the United Nations Secretariat. For additional sources, see list of references.

Guatemala

ABORTION POLICY

Grounds on which abortion is permitted:

To save the life of the woman	Yes
To preserve physical health	No
To preserve mental health	No
Rape or incest	No
Foetal impairment	No
Economic or social reasons	No
Available on request	No

Additional requirements:

Consent of the woman is necessary and third-party authorization is required. The physician performing the abortion must consult with another licensed general practitioner prior to the procedure.

FERTILITY AND MORTALITY CONTEXT

Government's view on fertility level:	Too high
Government's intervention concerning fertility level:	To lower
Government's policy on contraceptive use:	Direct support provided
Percentage of currently married women using modern contraception (aged 15-44, 1987):	19
Total fertility rate (1990-1995):	5.4
Age-specific fertility rate (per 1,000 women aged 15-19, 1990-1995):	123

Government has expressed particular concern about:

Morbidity and mortality resulting from induced abortion	Yes
Complications of child-bearing and childbirth	Yes

Maternal mortality rate (per 100,000 live births):

National (1984)	300
Central America (around 1988)	160

Female life expectancy at birth (1990-1995):	67.3

BACKGROUND

In September 1973, sections 133-140 of the Penal Code of Guatemala were amended by Congressional Decree 17-73. This legislation provided that a therapeutic abortion performed by a physician to save a woman's life was not punishable. Abortion remained illegal, however, in instances where the woman was raped, foetal deformity was suspected or there were socio-economic constraints.

Since the amendment to the Penal Code in 1973, the Government has expressed concern about the occurrence of induced abortion, given that article 3 of the Constitution declares the right to life from the moment of conception (even if a portion of article 47 emphasizes individuals' right to decide the number and spacing of their children).

The woman's consent and third-party authorization (approval by one other physician) are prerequisites of any legal abortion in Guatemala. Furthermore, abortion is permissible only if all other options have been considered. The abortion must be conducted without the specific aim of terminating the life of the foetus and with the single purpose of preventing what is deemed to be inevitable harm to the health of the mother.

The prison term for performing an illegal abortion is from one to three years. Medical personnel performing an unauthorized abortion are subject to harsher penalties.

One of the objectives of the family planning programme is to lower maternal and infant mortality. Although the Government has advocated the utilization of contraceptives as a preventive measure, the level of contraceptive use was only 25 per cent for married Guatemalan women of child-bearing age as of 1983. Among native American Indian women, the contraceptive prevalence rate was less than 5 per cent. Sterilization was by far the most prevalent method, accounting for 45 per cent of all contraceptive use. The results of the maternal and child health survey in 1987, however, indicated that 70 per cent of all women in Guatemala were familiar with or had heard of some contraceptive method.

INCIDENCE OF ABORTION

Place	Year	Measurement	Coverage
National	1971	14.3 abortions/100 live births	HR

Note: PR = provider registration; SP = survey provider; SW = survey of women; HR = hospital admission records. For a detailed description of these abbreviations and information on sources of the data, see technical notes in the annex.

Source: The Population Policy Data Bank maintained by the Population Division of the Department for Economic and Social Information and Policy Analysis of the United Nations Secretariat. For additional sources, see list of references.

Guinea

ABORTION POLICY

Grounds on which abortion is permitted:

To save the life of the woman	Yes
To preserve physical health	Yes
To preserve mental health	Yes
Rape or incest	No
Foetal impairment	No
Economic or social reasons	No
Available on request	No

Additional requirements:

The concept of health within the context of the abortion provisions in the Penal Code of Guinea is not clearly defined. The written consent of two other physicians, in addition to the physician performing the abortion, is required. One of these physicians must be chosen from the court list of experts.

FERTILITY AND MORTALITY CONTEXT

Government's view on fertility level:	Too high
Government's intervention concerning fertility level:	To lower
Government's policy on contraceptive use:	Direct support provided
Percentage of currently married women using modern contraception (aged 15-49, 1987):	7
Total fertility rate (1990-1995):	7.0
Age-specific fertility rate (per 1,000 women aged 15-19, 1990-1995):	241
Government has expressed particular concern about:	
Morbidity and mortality resulting from induced abortion	Yes
Complications of child-bearing and childbirth	Yes
Maternal mortality rate (per 100,000 live births):	
National (1989)	900
Western Africa (around 1988)	760
Female life expectancy at birth (1990-1995):	45.0

BACKGROUND

Guinea was the first French colony to refuse, in 1958, to be integrated into the French African Community and to choose instead immediate independence. Nevertheless, the country inherited the legal framework of the former colonial authority.

Abortion legislation is based on article 317 of the Napoleonic Code of 1810, amended by the French Law-decree of 1939 and modified somewhat by the law of 1966. Abortion is legal if performed to preserve the life and physical and mental health of the pregnant woman. For all other reasons, abortion is generally illegal under the Criminal Code of Guinea. The written consent of two other physicians, in addition to the physician performing the abortion, is required. One of these physicians must be chosen from the court list of experts.

Any person suggesting, performing or attempting to perform an illegal abortion on a pregnant or supposedly pregnant woman is liable to imprisonment for a term ranging from one to two years and/or a fine of 4,000-40,000 CFA francs (CFAF). If the person habitually performs abortions, the penalty is increased to from one to three years and/or CFAF 4,000-60,000. Medical or paramedical personnel can, in addition, be suspended from the exercise of their profession for a period ranging from a minimum of five years to life. A woman inducing or attempting to induce her own miscarriage or allowing someone to do so is liable to imprisonment for a term ranging from 16 days to a year and a fine of from CFAF 3,600-15,000.

Induced abortion by means of herbal preparations has been noted among unmarried women. Illegal abortion is believed to be one of the causes of high maternal mortality rates, although little information is available. A test survey conducted at Conakry, the capital, indicated a maternal mortality rate of 900 deaths per 100,000 live births. A more recent survey, conducted at Conakry in 1990 and excluding non-resident women, estimated the maternal mortality rate at 564 per 100,000 live births. About 25 per cent of those deaths were caused by complications arising from abortion. Of the women who died at a medical facility following an abortion, 80 per cent had had an induced abortion.

Contraception is prohibited by the French law of 1920. Consequently, the importation, manufacture, advertisement, transportation, display, sale or distribution of pills, intra-uterine devices and condoms (except for health reasons) is forbidden. Although the Government views the fertility rate as being too high, a strong traditional pronatalist sentiment still exists among certain segments of the population.

Although a Population and Development Unit was established in 1984 within the Ministry of Planning, and the National Population Commission was established in 1990, a national population policy was still being formulated as of early 1992. Family planning has not yet been integrated into the overall health-care system, and no national maternal and child health programme existed as of 1992.

INCIDENCE OF ABORTION

Place	Year	Measurement	Coverage

Information not readily available.

Source: The Population Policy Data Bank maintained by the Population Division of the Department for Economic and Social Information and Policy Analysis of the United Nations Secretariat. For additional sources, see list of references.

Guinea-Bissau

ABORTION POLICY

Grounds on which abortion is permitted:

To save the life of the woman	Yes
To preserve physical health	No*
To preserve mental health	No*
Rape or incest	No*
Foetal impairment	No*
Economic or social reasons	No*
Available on request	No*

Additional requirements:

Abortion is legal when performed in a hospital within the first three months of pregnancy, with the consent of the spouse, or of the father, tutor or legal representative if the woman is unmarried.

---

* The Portuguese law forbidding abortion has not been repealed; however, the law is not enforced and abortion is largely tolerated.

FERTILITY AND MORTALITY CONTEXT

Government's view on fertility level:	Too high
Government's intervention concerning fertility level:	To lower
Government's policy on contraceptive use:	Direct support provided
Percentage of currently married women using modern contraception (aged 15-49):	..
Total fertility rate (1990-1995):	5.8
Age-specific fertility rate (per 1,000 women aged 15-19, 1990-1995):	189

Government has expressed particular concern about:
Morbidity and mortality resulting from induced abortion	Yes
Complications of child-bearing and childbirth	Yes

Maternal mortality rate (per 100,000 live births):
National (1986)	700
Western Africa (around 1988)	760

Female life expectancy at birth (1990-1995):	45.1

BACKGROUND

After independence, Guinea-Bissau retained Portuguese criminal law, which prohibits abortion. However, the Portuguese law of 1886, which contains a general ban on abortion, does not appear to be enforced and abortion practice is quite liberal. An abortion is allowed during the first three months of pregnancy and is available upon request. The consent of the woman's father, tutor or legal representative, or of her husband or companion, is required for the abortion to be performed. In special circumstances, however, it is possible for the pregnant woman to receive an abortion without the necessary consent. The expenses of legal abortion are covered by the Government. The intervention must be performed in a hospital.

Despite the tolerance of abortion in Guinea-Bissau, and direct governmental support for the provision of contraceptives, there is a high incidence of illegal abortion, particularly among adolescents. To reduce the number of induced abortions, the Government has developed information, education and communication programmes and has improved the distribution of family planning services throughout the country.

Development planning in Guinea-Bissau is still at its early stages, and population factors are not yet integrated into the planning process. The Government of Guinea-Bissau has adopted a primary health care approach, and family planning has been integrated into the maternal and child health programme as a means of spacing births and improving maternal and child health. The Government's approach to family planning has been highly cautious, however, reflecting the strong opposition of certain minorities.

INCIDENCE OF ABORTION

Place	Year	Measurement	Coverage

Information not readily available.

Source: The Population Policy Data Bank maintained by the Population Division of the Department for Economic and Social Information and Policy Analysis of the United Nations Secretariat. For additional sources, see list of references.

Guyana

Grounds on which abortion is permitted:

To save the life of the woman	Yes
To preserve physical health	Yes
To preserve mental health	Yes
Rape or incest	No
Foetal impairment	No
Economic or social reasons	No
Available on request	No

Additional requirements:

The authorization of a panel of physicians is required for performing an induced abortion.

FERTILITY AND MORTALITY CONTEXT

Government's view on fertility level:	Satisfactory
Government's intervention concerning fertility level:	No intervention
Government's policy on contraceptive use:	Direct support provided
Percentage of currently married women using modern contraception (aged 15-49, 1975):	28
Total fertility rate (1990-1995):	2.6
Age-specific fertility rate (per 1,000 women aged 15-19, 1990-1995):	61

Government has expressed particular concern about:
Morbidity and mortality resulting from induced abortion	Yes
Complications of child-bearing and childbirth	Yes

Maternal mortality rate (per 100,000 live births):
National (1984)	200
South America (around 1988)	220

Female life expectancy at birth (1990-1995):	68.0

BACKGROUND

Abortion is illegal under the Criminal Code in the laws of British Guiana (1954, cap. 10). Under sections 78-80 of the Code, any person found guilty of performing an induced abortion faces a penalty of life imprisonment. A woman inducing her own miscarriage may be imprisoned for up to 10 years, whereas the suppliers of equipment used to induce an abortion are subject to a five-year prison term.

In Guyana, although no explicit grounds are provided within the law on which abortion may legally be performed, as in many Commonwealth countries, justification for induced abortion has been derived from a ruling in the British case of *Rex* v. *Bourne*. In principle, the ruling provides that even where the law specifically forbids induced abortion without exception, the procedure may not be considered illegal if the purpose is to save the woman's life or to preserve her physical and mental health.

In 1987, the Government indicated that no substantial modifications had been made to the laws or regulations concerning induced abortion and that the level of induced abortion was not viewed as a matter of concern. The procedure does not appear to be authorized in the case of rape, incest or foetal impairment. Authorization for an induced abortion requires consultation with a physician or a panel of physicians. Abortion is reportedly subsidized by the Government.

Data from statistical sources registering the occurrence of abortion between 1971 and 1979 indicate a range of 17-26 abortion-related maternal deaths per 100,000 live births.

INCIDENCE OF ABORTION

Place	Year	Measurement	Coverage
National	1971	28 abortions/100 deliveries	HR

Notes: PR = provider registration; SP = survey provider; SW = survey of women; HR = hospital admission records. For a detailed description of these abbreviations and information on sources of the data, see technical notes in the annex.

Source: The Population Policy Data Bank maintained by the Population Division of the Department for Economic and Social Information and Policy Analysis of the United Nations Secretariat. For additional sources, see list of references.

Haiti

Grounds on which abortion is permitted:

To save the life of the woman	Yes
To preserve physical health	No*
To preserve mental health	No
Rape or incest	No*
Foetal impairment	No*
Economic or social reasons	No
Available on request	No

Additional requirements:

No information is readily available.

_____

* Official interpretation generally permits these grounds.

FERTILITY AND MORTALITY CONTEXT

Government's view on fertility level:	Too high
Government's intervention concerning fertility level:	To lower
Government's policy on contraceptive use:	Direct support provided
Percentage of currently married women using modern contraception (aged 15-49, 1989):	9
Total fertility rate (1990-1995):	4.8
Age-specific fertility rate (per 1,000 women aged 15-19, 1990-1995):	54

Government has expressed particular concern about:

Morbidity and mortality resulting from induced abortion	Yes
Complications of child-bearing and childbirth	Yes

Maternal mortality rate (per 100,000 live births):

National (1990)	600
Caribbean (around 1988)	260

Female life expectancy at birth (1990-1995):	58.3

BACKGROUND

The Haitian Penal Code prohibits abortion except to save the life of the pregnant woman. This provision, which is based on article 317 of the French Penal Code of 1810, states that anyone performing an abortion is liable to imprisonment for from three to nine years. If the abortion is performed by a medical professional, the penalty is hard labour.

In 1987, however, the Government reported that abortion was also allowed to preserve the pregnant woman's physical health and in cases of rape or incest or of foetal impairment, indicating possible flexibility in interpretation of the law. Nevertheless, as of 1992, it does not appear that any changes have been made in the abortion law.

Although the Government has often stated its concern with regard to the demographic situation in Haiti, it long abstained from integrating population issues into development plans or from formulating explicit population policies. The Division of Family Hygiene of the Public Health and Population Department was established in 1971 and inaugurated a national family planning programme in 1973. By the end of the 1970s, the sale of contraceptives was allowed in pharmacies and groceries. However, when the Haitian Institute of Statistics reported in 1975 that assumptions about high fertility in Haiti were not borne out by the results of the 1971 census, population policies appeared to be less imperative and the Government decided to focus instead on economic issues. After 1986, however, interest increased in integrating population variables into socio-economic planning. In 1986, Profamil, a private family planning association affiliated with the International Planned Parenthood Federation, was established and the National Population Council (CONAPO) was created. Several studies on contraceptive behaviour have been undertaken and a national population policy was awaiting parliamentary approval when the coup took place in 1991. It is expected that the process will eventually be resumed. A national census slated for 1992 has also been postponed.

The Government supports family planning and provides services through the Ministry of Health. Subsidized family planning services are officially available at government hospitals and dispensaries, although they are in short supply. Although the Government has expressed concern about the level of induced abortion, the poor hygienic conditions under which such interventions occur and the lack of competence of many of those performing them, the abortion issue has been eclipsed by the acute socio-economic problems of the country.

Nevertheless, the incidence of abortion in Haiti is believed to be relatively high, particularly in urban areas. National data on induced abortion are lacking, not only because abortion is illegal but because of the strong influence of the Catholic church on the issue of abortion. According to a national survey conducted in 1983, abortion had been used as a contraceptive method by 2 per cent of women nationwide and by 4 per cent of women at Port-au-Prince, while 59 per cent of the women surveyed were aware of abortion as a contraceptive method. Moreover, traditional medicine in Haiti is still frequently practised and at least 20 plants that supposedly have contraceptive and abortifacient properties are reported to be in use. Tests conducted on these herbs suggest that some of them have effective abortifacient effects mainly by bringing about uterine contractions.

Haiti

INCIDENCE OF ABORTION

Place	Year	Measurement	Coverage

Information not readily available.

Source: Population Policy Data Bank maintained by the Population Division of the Department for Economic and Social Information and Policy Analysis of the United Nations Secretariat. For additional sources, see list of references.

ABORTION POLICY

Grounds on which abortion is permitted:

To save the life of the woman	No
To preserve physical health	No
To preserve mental health	No
Rape or incest	No
Foetal impairment	No
Economic or social reasons	No
Available on request	No

Additional requirements:

Not applicable.

FERTILITY AND MORTALITY CONTEXT

Government's view on fertility level:	Satisfactory
Government's intervention concerning fertility level:	No intervention
Government's policy on contraceptive use:	Major restrictions
Percentage of currently married women using modern contraception (aged 15-49):	-
Total fertility rate (1985-1990):	..
Age-specific fertility rate (per 1,000 women aged 15-19, 1985-1990):	..

Government has expressed particular concern about:
Morbidity and mortality resulting from induced abortion -
Complications of child-bearing and childbirth -

Maternal mortality rate (per 100,000 live births):
National -
Developed countries (around 1988) 26

Female life expectancy at birth (1990-1995): ..

Holy See

The position of the Catholic church on abortion has been long-standing and consistent: the Holy See rejects abortion because it destroys the life of a developing human being. This opposition to abortion is on moral grounds. Sacred Scripture defines man as having been created in the image and likeness of God, taken from dust of the earth and carrying within him the divine breath of life. Thus, man is characterized by an immediacy with God that is proper to his being; man is *capax Dei* and because he lives under the personal protection of God, he is "sacred": "If anyone sheds the blood of man, by man shall his blood be shed; for in the image of God has man been made" (Genesis 9:6). According to the Catholic church, this statement of divine right does not permit exceptions: human life is untouchable because it is divine property.

The Holy See underscores the fact that life is a gift from God. It is a violation of the Divine Law, an offence against the dignity of the human person, a crime against life and an attempt against humanity to suppress the life of an innocent human being, whether it be foetus or embryo, child or adult, elderly, incurably sick or dying. The Holy See believes that an understanding of the sacred dignity of the human being leads one to attribute a value to all stages of life. The firm position of the Catholic church is that abortion, the destruction of life during its earliest stages of development, should not be permitted either as a demographic strategy or as a way of dealing with problems related to pregnancy.

Realizing that abortion is increasingly being performed with financial support from Governments and international organizations, the Holy See has appealed to all Governments and international organizations to affirm clearly and explicitly the value, inviolability and dignity of human life from the moment of conception, and to prohibit and exclude abortion as an element of family planning.

In a letter to bishops throughout the world, released 21 June 1991, Pope John Paul II called upon the bishops to promote respect for human life in the schools and seminaries, and to ensure that practices in Catholic hospitals and clinics should be "fully consonant with the nature of such institutions". As means permit, the bishops were urged to support projects that offer practical help to women or families experiencing difficulties. The bishops were also urged to encourage scientific reflection and legislative or political initiatives.

The Holy See views the widespread incidence of abortion as a war of the mighty against the weak. By deciding which human beings are or are not the subject of rights and by granting to some the power to violate the fundamental rights of others, the State not only contradicts the democratic ideal to which it appeals but allows the law of force to prevail over the force of law. The Holy See maintains that in the modern world, the respect for life is no longer a question of a purely individual morality but one of social morality, as States and international organizations become the grantors of abortion, pass the laws that authorize them and provide the wherewithal for those putting them into practice.

The position of the Holy See is that the human being is to be respected and treated as a person from the very moment of conception. From that same moment, one's rights as a person must be recognized; among them is the inviolable right of every innocent human being to life. The Holy See maintains that a new life begins at the time that the ovum is fertilized, a life which is neither that of the mother nor the father but is the life of a new human being with its own growth. In addition, the biological identity of a new human individual is already constituted at the time of fertilization. Thus, the Holy See believes that from the first moment of its existence, the embryo must be guaranteed the unconditional respect morally due to a human being in his spiritual and bodily totality.

Responding to the challenge of the abortion issue, the Holy See has insisted on the defence of life as a fundamental duty of every Christian; numerous papal statements have addressed the problem. The Congregation for the Doctrine of the Faith has published several important documents on the moral issues concerning respect for human life. In his 1991 address to the Extraordinary Consistory of Cardinals, Cardinal Joseph Ratzinger of Germany pointed out that any future Vatican document on the defence of human life should not only concern individual morality but should also address social and political morality. The various threats against human life could be confronted from five points of view: (*a*) a doctrinal approach could propose a solemn affirmation of the principle that the direct killing of an innocent human being is always a matter of grave sin; (*b*) a cultural approach would allow a denunciation of the anti-life ideology based on materialism and justified by utilitarianism; (*c*) a legislative approach would highlight the implicit presuppositions of various types of laws, showing that they are intrinsically immoral and clarifying the proper function of civil law in relation to the moral law; (*d*) a political approach could show how laws are always the implementation of a social plan and that the implicit intention of anti-life laws is basically totalitarian within a society and imperialistic on the part of developed countries seeking to contain third world countries on the pretext of demographic politics; and (*e*) a practical approach would make people aware of the evil involved in using certain abortifacient or contraceptive-abortifacient means to end innocent life.

In its recent universal catechism issued on 17 November 1992 to confront the new challenges posed by social, economic, political and scientific change today, the Catholic church reaffirmed its strong stand against abortion. The view of the church is that human life must be respected and protected from the moment of conception; from the beginning of existence, a human being should enjoy the rights of the individual, including the inviolable right to life. Thus, formal participation in abortion is considered a serious error.

INCIDENCE OF ABORTION

Place	Year	Measurement	Coverage

Not applicable.

Source: The Population Policy Data Bank maintained by the Population Division of the Department for Economic and Social Information and Policy Analysis of the United Nations Secretariat. For additional sources, see list of references.

Honduras

Grounds on which abortion is permitted:

To save the life of the woman	No*
To preserve physical health	No
To preserve mental health	No
Rape or incest	No
Foetal impairment	No
Economic or social reasons	No
Available on request	No

Additional requirements:

Consultation with a physician or a group of physicians is prerequisite to obtaining a legal abortion. The woman's consent, as well as that of her husband or closest relative, is also required.

---

* The Honduran Code of Medical Ethics, however, allows physicians to perform abortion on this ground.

FERTILITY AND MORTALITY CONTEXT

Government's view on fertility level:	Too high
Government's intervention concerning fertility level:	To lower
Government's policy on contraceptive use:	Direct support provided
Percentage of currently married women using modern contraception (aged 15-44, 1987):	33
Total fertility rate (1990-1995):	4.9
Age-specific fertility rate (per 1,000 women aged 15-19, 1990-1995):	100
Government has expressed particular concern about:	
Morbidity and mortality resulting from induced abortion	Yes
Complications of child-bearing and childbirth	Yes
Maternal mortality rate (per 100,000 live births):	
National (1983)	300
Central America (around 1988)	160
Female life expectancy at birth (1990-1995):	68.0

BACKGROUND

According to the Fundamental Law (Decree No. 94 of 25 June 1964), which established the Honduran Association of Physicians and set forth their code of medical ethics, a physician may perform an abortion only for therapeutic reasons. Written consent of the patient, her husband or her closest relative is required, together with the written opinion of a medical committee. The Fundamental Law represented a marginal liberalization, although not a modification, of the Penal Code of 1906, which deemed abortion to be illegal on all grounds.

In 1983, Honduras introduced two new articles in its Penal Code regarding abortion (Decree No. 144-83 of 26 September 1983), which were supposed to come into force in March 1985. Articles 130 and 131 allowed abortion in the case of rape or for eugenic reasons pending the consent of the woman and her husband. However, these articles were repealed in February 1985 before they came into force, on the grounds that they constituted a flagrant violation of the guarantees contained in articles 65, 67 and 68 of the Honduran Constitution. These articles stipulate that the right to life is inviolable and that the unborn child should be accorded the same rights as children that have been born.

Any person performing an illegal abortion with the pregnant woman's consent is subject to imprisonment for from two to three years. A woman wilfully inducing her own miscarriage is subject to the same penalty. However, if she acted in order to save her honour, the penalty is reduced to imprisonment for from six months to one year.

In 1987, the Government affirmed that Honduran women were widely limiting their fertility through the increasing use of contraception, with the vast majority choosing modern methods. Oral contraceptives and sterilization combined to account for over 70 per cent of total use. Notwithstanding the increase in contraception, induced abortion persists. The related increase in maternal morbidity has prompted the Government to express concern about the frequency of induced abortion.

INCIDENCE OF ABORTION

Place	Year	Measurement	Coverage
National	1971	22.2 abortions/100 live births	HR

Note: PR = provider registration; SP = survey provider; SW = survey of women; HR = hospital admission records. For a detailed description of these abbreviations and information on sources of the data, see technical notes in the annex.

Source: The Population Policy Data Bank maintained by the Population Division of the Department for Economic and Social Information and Policy Analysis of the United Nations Secretariat. For additional sources, see list of references.

Hungary

ABORTION POLICY

Grounds on which abortion is permitted:

To save the life of the woman	Yes
To preserve physical health	Yes
To preserve mental health	Yes
Rape or incest	Yes
Foetal impairment	Yes
Economic or social reasons	Yes
Available on request	No

Additional requirements:

A consultation with a nurse is compulsory to inform the pregnant woman on issues of contraception, as well as to provide assistance if the pregnancy is carried to term.

FERTILITY AND MORTALITY CONTEXT

Government's view on fertility level:	Too low
Government's intervention concerning fertility level:	To raise
Government's policy on contraceptive use:	Direct support provided
Percentage of currently married women using modern contraception (aged 15-39, 1986):	62
Total fertility rate (1990-1995):	1.8
Age-specific fertility rate (per 1,000 women aged 15-19, 1990-1995):	44
Government has expressed particular concern about:	
Morbidity and mortality resulting from induced abortion	No
Complications of child-bearing and childbirth	No
Maternal mortality rate (per 100,000 live births):	
National (1990)	21
Developed countries (around 1988)	26
Female life expectancy at birth (1990-1995):	74.3

BACKGROUND

Abortion was illegal in Hungary prior to 1952, as part of an effort by the Government to counter falling birth rates. However, two decrees, one in 1953 and the other in 1956, substantially liberalized the abortion law. Although the authorization of a special committee was needed in order to obtain an abortion, this requirement was never truly compulsory. If an applicant insisted on an abortion, the committee was required to allow it. In fact, from the early 1950s until the law was changed in 1973, a woman could have a pregnancy terminated within the first 12 weeks, with no further conditions.

Following a decree in 1973 (Ordinance No. 4), the previously liberal abortion policy in Hungary became more restrictive. Although abortion remained legal on social grounds, it was to be allowed only under the following conditions: if the woman was unmarried or separated; if she had inadequate housing; if she was aged 40 years or over; if the woman's husband was a regular soldier or was performing his military service; if either the woman or her husband were in prison; and for other exceptional social reasons. Furthermore, abortions were henceforth to be permitted only in authorized health-care establishments.

In 1982, Ordinance No. 3 of 10 February lowered the age limit from 40 to 35 years and provided that women were generally no longer required to seek the authorization of a committee. Even in exceptional situations in which authorization was required, mainly because of excess duration of the pregnancy, the chairman of the committee alone could grant the authorization.

In November and December 1988, respectively, Ordinance No. 76 of the Council of Ministers and Ordinance No. 15 of the Ministry of Social Affairs and Health declared that an abortion could be performed with the written request of the pregnant woman, if the required conditions were fulfilled. In the case of eugenic grounds, it was specified that pregnancy termination would be permitted: (a) during the first 12 weeks of the pregnancy if the probability of a genetic condition likely to cause a severe physical or mental handicap exceeded 10 per cent; (b) during 20 weeks of gestation (or 24 weeks where consideration of the application had been delayed by diagnostic examination) if the probability of a genetic condition likely to cause a handicap exceeded 50 per cent; and (c) irrespective of the length of the pregnancy in the case of malformation incompatible with viability.

The pregnant woman must always give consent in writing prior to the abortion. For a minor, the parents or guardian must grant authorization; and for a mentally incompetent woman, a legal representative must do so. Legal abortion is performed free of charge if authorized for health reasons or if the pregnancy resulted from rape or incest. Otherwise, the woman has to pay for the abortion. According to the Penal Code of 1988, a person performing an illegal abortion is subject to three years' imprisonment. If the guilty party is a physician, the penalty is five years, as it also is when performed without the woman's consent or if the procedure causes her serious injury or endangers her life. If the illegal abortion leads to the woman's death, the term of imprisonment can be up to eight years.

Ruling on the constitutionality of the abortion law in late 1991, the Constitutional Court requested the Parliament to formulate a new abortion law by December 1992, and at that time the Parliament did revise the abortion law. Under the new law, a woman can obtain an abortion up to the first 12 weeks of pregnancy if she states that the pregnancy has caused a serious crisis for her. An abortion is legal beyond the first trimester in certain circumstances, for example, if there is a misdiagnosis of the pregnancy, if the woman is under age 18 or in cases of genetic or teratogenic risk. The new law also introduces a compulsory consultation with a nurse, who must inform the pregnant woman of the conditions and effects of abortion, as well as of the possibilities for assistance if the choice is made to carry the pregnancy to term. An abortion performed for medical reasons is free of charge; otherwise, the fee is 5,000 florints (Ft). This fee can be reduced according to the economic status of the family.

Hungary

Place	Year	Measurement	Coverage
National	1960	76.4 abortions/1,000 women aged 15-44	PR
National	1965	80.0 abortions/1,000 women aged 15-44	PR
National	1970	83.8 abortions/1,000 women aged 15-44	PR
National	1975	41.5 abortions/1,000 women aged 15-44	PR
National	1980	35.6 abortions/1,000 women aged 15-44	PR
National	1985	36.6 abortions/1,000 women aged 15-44	PR
National	1986	37.5 abortions/1,000 women aged 15-44	PR
National	1987	37.8 abortions/1,000 women aged 15-44	PR
National	1988	39.0 abortions/1,000 women aged 15-44	PR
National	1989	39.5 abortions/1,000 women aged 15-44	PR
National	1990	40.0 abortions/1,000 women aged 15-44	PR

Note: PR = provider registration; SP = survey provider; SW = survey of women; HR = hospital admission records. For a detailed description of these abbreviations and information on sources of the data, see technical notes in the annex.

Source: Population Policy Data Bank maintained by the Population Division of the Department for Economic and Social Information and Policy Analysis of the United Nations Secretariat. For additional sources, see list of references.

ABORTION POLICY

Grounds on which abortion is permitted:

To save the life of the woman	Yes
To preserve physical health	Yes
To preserve mental health	Yes
Rape or incest	Yes
Foetal impairment	Yes
Economic or social reasons	Yes
Available on request	No

Additional requirements:

A written report from two physicians is necessary. In the case of non-agreement, the request must be submitted for decision by a three-member committee. For social grounds, certification of a physician and a social worker is required.

FERTILITY AND MORTALITY CONTEXT

Government's view on fertility level:	Satisfactory
Government's intervention concerning fertility level:	No intervention
Government's policy on contraceptive use:	Direct support provided
Percentage of currently married women using modern contraception (aged 15-49):	..
Total fertility rate (1990-1995):	2.2
Age-specific fertility rate (per 1,000 women aged 15-19, 1990-1995):	31
Government has expressed particular concern about:	
Morbidity and mortality resulting from induced abortion	No
Complications of child-bearing and childbirth	No
Maternal mortality rate (per 100,000 live births):	
National (1989)	-
Developed countries (around 1988)	26
Female life expectancy at birth (1990-1995):	80.8

Iceland

The law of 22 May 1975 liberalized induced abortion in Iceland, permitting it on a broad variety of grounds. In addition to life, mental and physical health, and criminal or eugenic reasons, this statute lists a number of social factors as grounds for abortion. Requiring certification by a physician and a social worker, these social factors—which are beyond the control of the pregnant woman and which are deemed to make the birth of a child too difficult for the woman and her immediate family—include the fact that the woman has given birth to several children at frequent intervals and only a short time has elapsed since the previous birth; that the woman lives in difficult family circumstances due to the presence of many young children or to the serious ill health of other persons in the household; that the woman cannot look after a child satisfactorily because of her youth or lack of maturity; or that the woman's or her partner's physical or mental illness seriously impedes their capacity to care for or to rear a child.

Any woman that applies for an abortion in Iceland is required to receive counselling with regard to the social assistance that is available to her. The abortion, if carried out, must be performed in an approved hospital. Following the abortion, the woman must receive counselling concerning contraceptive use before she leaves the hospital and must return later for a medical examination and further counselling.

By law, abortion in Iceland must be performed during the first 16 weeks of pregnancy. However, this limit does not apply in cases where the mother's life or health is in jeopardy or if there is foetal deformity. Written authorization from the committee approving the abortion is obligatory in such situations.

A person who performs an abortion in violation of the law is subject to from five to seven years of imprisonment.

INCIDENCE OF ABORTION

Place	Year	Measurement	Coverage
National	1960	1.6 abortions/1,000 women aged 15-44	PR
National	1965	1.8 abortions/1,000 women aged 15-44	PR
National	1970	2.4 abortions/1,000 women aged 15-44	PR
National	1975	6.0 abortions/1,000 women aged 15-44	PR
National	1980	10.7 abortions/1,000 women aged 15-44	PR
National	1985	12.8 abortions/1,000 women aged 15-44	PR
National	1986	12.3 abortions/1,000 women aged 15-44	PR
National	1987	12.0 abortions/1,000 women aged 15-44	PR
National	1988	11.6 abortions/1,000 women aged 15-44	PR
National	1989	11.5 abortions/1,000 women aged 15-44	PR
National	1990	12.1 abortions/1,000 women aged 15-44	PR

Note: PR = provider registration; SP = survey provider; SW = survey of women; HR = hospital admission records. For a detailed description of these abbreviations and information on sources of the data, see technical notes in the annex.

Source: The Population Policy Data Bank maintained by the Population Division of the Department for Economic and Social Information and Policy Analysis of the United Nations Secretariat. For additional sources, see list of references.

ABORTION POLICY

Grounds on which abortion is permitted:

To save the life of the woman	Yes
To preserve physical health	Yes
To preserve mental health	Yes
Rape or incest	Yes
Foetal impairment	Yes
Economic or social reasons	No*
Available on request	No

Additional requirements:

Contraceptive failure on the part of the wife or husband constitutes valid grounds for legal abortion. Unless a medical emergency exists, a legal abortion must be performed during the first 20 weeks of gestation by a registered physician in a hospital established or maintained by the Government or in a facility approved by specific legislation. A second opinion is required in cases where the duration of the pregnancy is between 12 and 20 weeks, except in urgent cases. In general, the consent of the pregnant woman is required before the performance of an abortion, while written consent of her guardian must be obtained for a minor (defined as under age 18) or a mentally retarded woman.

---

* Abortion on this ground may be considered under health grounds.

FERTILITY AND MORTALITY CONTEXT

Government's view on fertility level:	Too high
Government's intervention concerning fertility level:	To lower
Government's policy on contraceptive use:	Direct support provided
Percentage of currently married women using modern contraception (aged 15-44, 1988):	39
Total fertility rate (1990-1995):	3.9
Age-specific fertility rate (per 1,000 women aged 15-19, 1990-1995):	57
Government has expressed particular concern about:	
Morbidity and mortality resulting from induced abortion	Yes
Complications of child-bearing and childbirth	Yes
Maternal mortality rate (per 100,000 live births):	
National (1984)	460
Southern Asia (around 1988)	570
Female life expectancy at birth (1990-1995):	60.7

India

BACKGROUND

The Medical Termination of Pregnancy Act of 1971, which went into effect on 1 April 1972, significantly liberalized abortion laws in India. Prior to enactment of the legislation, the Indian Penal Code (Act No. 45 of 1860) permitted abortion only when it was justified to save the life of the woman. Article 312 of the Penal Code provided that any person performing an illegal abortion was subject to imprisonment for three years and/or a fine; if the woman was "quick with child", the punishment was imprisonment for up to seven years and a fine. The same penalty applied to a woman that wilfully induced her own miscarriage.

The Medical Termination of Pregnancy Act of 1971 essentially nullified article 312. Under the new Act, a pregnancy can be terminated if it involves risk to the life or grave injury to the physical or mental health of the pregnant woman or if the pregnancy is likely to result in the birth of a child suffering from serious physical or mental abnormalities. The law also permits the termination of a pregnancy resulting from rape or from failure of any contraceptive method used either by the woman or her husband for the purpose of limiting the number of children. In determining whether continuance of the pregnancy would involve a risk of injury to the health of the mother, the law allows the physician to take into account the woman's actual or reasonably foreseeable socio-economic environment.

A pregnancy may be terminated only within the first 20 weeks of gestation. As required by law, when the length of the pregnancy has not exceeded 12 weeks, a physician need not seek another opinion before performing the abortion; when the pregnancy exceeds 12 weeks but does not exceed 20 weeks, two physicians must give approval for the abortion, unless a medical emergency exists. Termination of a pregnancy by any person other than a registered physician is a punishable offence.

An abortion can be performed only in a hospital established by the Government or in a facility approved by specific legislation, except in urgent cases. A legal abortion is free of charge if it is performed in a government hospital, but it is at the patient's expense if performed in a non-governmental institution. Consent of the woman or written consent of the guardian of a minor or a mentally retarded woman is required before performance of an abortion.

The Medical Termination of Pregnancy Act of 1971 was enacted by the Indian Government with the intention of reducing the incidence of illegal abortion and consequent maternal mortality and morbidity. However, according to government data, only about 1 million abortions were performed annually under these laws. Implementation of the new abortion statutes has been slow and geographically uneven; abortion services are often inaccessible and women are reluctant to utilize those services because of the lack of anonymity and confidentiality. Therefore, the number of illegal or unregistered abortions performed by medical or non-medical practitioners is still very high. According to various estimates, the number of abortions performed outside approved facilities varies between 2 million and 6 million per annum. It has been observed that the women that make use of hospital facilities for the medical termination of pregnancy are mostly educated, from an urban middle-income family, married and between 20 and 30 years of age. In contrast, the women admitted to public hospitals with complications from illegal septic abortions are largely illiterates from poorer segments of the population. These observations are consistent with other findings indicating that the level of awareness of the legality of the procedure is fairly low, and the existing facilities for the legal medical termination of pregnancy are either not available or are not utilized by many high-risk women who seek illegal abortions.

The Indian Government has repeatedly emphasized that the medical termination of pregnancy should not be viewed as a method of family planning for the individual or as a method of reducing the national birth rate. However, most women that have obtained an abortion tend to have at least two living children and to be non-users of contraception. Indeed, one study estimated that up to 80 per cent of abortion patients were not using any contraceptive method. The Government and voluntary family planning organizations have therefore been attempting to promote acceptance of post-abortion contraception. In addition to the other effective contraceptive methods that are recommended, sterilization and insertion of an intra-uterine device have become increasingly popular.

The strong preference for sons under patriarchal traditions and the availability of inexpensive prenatal diagnostic techniques have resulted in an increased use of prenatal gender tests in India, even among the rural poor. Some private clinics provide such a test and then offer an induced abortion if the parents are dissatisfied with the sex of the foetus. Although there are no reliable figures on the incidence of this practice, highly distorted sex ratios in regions where such practices are believed to be common suggest that a significant number of female foetuses are aborted annually. In response, at least one state government has passed laws to regulate the use of prenatal diagnostic techniques in an attempt to stop their abuse in encouraging the abortion of foetuses.

Despite the liberalization of the abortion law, unsafe abortions have contributed to the high rates of maternal mortality in India. It is estimated that unsafe abortions account for 20 per cent of maternal deaths in India. In contrast, it has been reported that maternal deaths associated with induced abortions performed in hospital facilities for medical termination of pregnancy are negligible. In order to reduce illegal abortions and maternal mortality and morbidity, the Government has made an effort to encourage greater use of contraception and to further publicize the abortion law, as well as to improve the availability of facilities for medical termination of pregnancy.

INCIDENCE OF ABORTION

Place	Year	Measurement	Coverage
National	1977	1.9 abortions/1,000 women aged 15-44	PR
National	1985	3.6 abortions/1,000 women aged 15-44	PR
National	1986	3.5 abortions/1,000 women aged 15-44	PR
National	1987	3.4 abortions/1,000 women aged 15-44	PR
National	1988	3.3 abortions/1,000 women aged 15-44	PR
National	1989	3.3 abortions/1,000 women aged 15-44	PR

Note: PR = provider registration; SP = survey provider; SW = survey of women; HR = hospital admission records. For a detailed description of these abbreviations and information on sources of the data, see technical notes in the annex.

Source: The Population Policy Data Bank maintained by the Population Division of the Department for Economic and Social Information and Policy Analysis of the United Nations Secretariat. For additional sources, see list of references.

Indonesia

ABORTION POLICY

Grounds on which abortion is permitted:

To save the life of the woman	Yes
To preserve physical health	No
To preserve mental health	No
Rape or incest	No
Foetal impairment	No
Economic or social reasons	No
Available on request	No

Additional requirements:

The medical procedure must be performed by a health worker possessing the necessary skills and authority, under the guidance of an expert team. Consent of the pregnant woman, her husband or her family for the procedure is necessary and it must be performed in an approved health-care facility.

FERTILITY AND MORTALITY CONTEXT

Government's view on fertility level:	Too high
Government's intervention concerning fertility level:	To lower
Government's policy on contraceptive use:	Direct support provided
Percentage of currently married women using modern contraception (aged 15-49, 1991):	47
Total fertility rate (1990-1995):	3.1
Age-specific fertility rate (per 1,000 women aged 15-19, 1990-1995):	43
Government has expressed particular concern about:	
Morbidity and mortality resulting from induced abortion	No
Complications of child-bearing and childbirth	Yes
Maternal mortality rate (per 100,000 live births):	
National (1987)	400
South-eastern Asia (around 1988)	340
Female life expectancy at birth (1990-1995):	64.5

BACKGROUND

Modelled on the conservative Dutch Criminal Code, the Indonesian Criminal Code, enacted on 1 January 1918 by the Dutch colonial Government, was directed to ending the traditional abortion procedures performed throughout the country. The Criminal Code generally forbids and makes illegal the performance of induced abortion. Consequently, under section 348 of the Criminal Code, any person performing an induced abortion can be imprisoned for five and one-half years. Under section 346 of the Code, a woman causing herself to miscarry may be imprisoned for up to four years. In addition, sections 349-350 of the Code provide for harsher penalties, including the revocation of the right to practise for a medical practitioner that performs an abortion. In 1992, however, a new health law was passed which modified the Criminal Code, expressly allowing "certain medical procedures" in an effort to save the mother's life and/or her foetus.

A considerable number of Indonesian women are believed to seek termination of unwanted pregnancies. Due to the restrictive nature of the laws on induced abortion, most women wanting to terminate a pregnancy usually go to a traditional practitioner (*dukun*), despite the associated risk of infection arising from unsanitary conditions and practices and the possibility of serious complications arising from an incomplete abortion.

Since the early 1970s, there have been continuing attempts in Indonesia to reform the laws concerning abortion. These efforts have been spearheaded by members of the legal and medical professions, as well as by women's organizations that seek to reduce morbidity and mortality associated with clandestine abortions. As a result of these efforts, in 1977 the Government established an interdepartmental committee with members drawn from the Departments of Health, Religion and Justice, the Police Service, the Attorney General's Office, academic institutions and related associations of health professionals, with the mandate of drafting a bill of law concerning abortion. The committee's draft bill of 1989 on Pregnancy Termination for Health Considerations was passed into law in September 1992 by a narrow margin. The new health law specifies that "in the case of emergency and with the purpose of saving the life of a pregnant woman or her foetus, it is permissible to carry out certain medical procedures". The abortion must be approved by a multidisciplinary committee, must have the consent of the pregnant woman or of her husband if she is unable to give her consent and must be performed by an obstetrician-gynaecologist in an approved facility. What impact the new law will have is not clear, given that prior to its passage, under an informal understanding reached in the 1970s between the Chief Justice of the High Court and medical professionals, abortions performed on broad health grounds would not be prosecuted. Although it has been reported that the intent of the new law was to codify that understanding, the performance of abortions on health grounds may be inhibited, because abortions are now permitted only if the woman's life is threatened.

Although the laws in Indonesia with regard to induced abortion are relatively restrictive, they are not strictly enforced. Because it is a criminal offence to perform an induced abortion and because officially acknowledged cases of abortions are usually classified as spontaneous abortions, it is difficult to determine accurately the incidence of abortion in Indonesia. It has been estimated that as many as one in every five pregnancies may end in abortion. From hospital and clinic records, it is apparent that the incidence of abortion has not decreased despite the country's laws. Most abortions are performed during the first 12 weeks of pregnancy. Complications from induced abortion continue to be a major cause of death among women of reproductive age and contribute to the high maternal mortality rate in Indonesia.

The family planning movement was begun by the Indonesia Planned Parenthood Association, which was established in 1957. In 1967, the Government became a signatory to the Declaration on Population, a high-level statement endorsed by a number of Heads of States in Asia, which states that family planning is a basic human right. Since 1969, family planning has been a national programme that has been included as part of the Government's five-year national development plans (REPELITA). A Contraceptive Prevalence Survey conducted in 1987 showed that nearly half of currently married women in Indonesia were using contraceptives. Among women with two or more children, 60 per cent were using contraceptives. Over half of all women with zero parity or only one child responded that the ideal family size was two children.

Indonesia

Increasingly, women in Indonesia with more than three children have been opting for long-term contraceptives, such as the intra-uterine device (IUD), Norplant or sterilization. However, voluntary sterilization is not encouraged. Although induced abortion is not permitted, except to save the life of the woman, menstrual regulation, which was begun at the Teaching Hospital of the University of Indonesia in 1973, is available. Qualified physicians are permitted to offer menstrual regulation services.

INCIDENCE OF ABORTION

Place	Year	Measurement	Coverage
Jakarta	1972	18.3 abortions/100 deliveries	HR
Jakarta	1975	39.6 abortions/100 deliveries	HR

Note: PR = provider registration; SP = survey provider; SW = survey of women; HR = hospital admission records. For a detailed description of these abbreviations and information on sources of the data, see technical notes in the annex.

Source: The Population Policy Data Bank maintained by the Population Division of the Department for Economic and Social Information and Policy Analysis of the United Nations Secretariat. For additional sources, see list of references.

ABORTION POLICY

Grounds on which abortion is permitted:

To save the life of the woman	Yes
To preserve physical health	No
To preserve mental health	No
Rape or incest	No
Foetal impairment	No
Economic or social reasons	No
Available on request	No

Additional requirements:

Authorization for an abortion requires consultation with a professional or a panel of professionals.

FERTILITY AND MORTALITY CONTEXT

Government's view on fertility level:	Too high
Government's intervention concerning fertility level:	To lower
Government's policy on contraceptive use:	Direct support provided
Percentage of currently married women using modern contraception (aged 15-49):	..
Total fertility rate (1990-1995):	6.0
Age-specific fertility rate (per 1,000 women aged 15-19, 1990-1995):	106
Government has expressed particular concern about:	
Morbidity and mortality resulting from induced abortion	No
Complications of child-bearing and childbirth	Yes
Maternal mortality rate (per 100,000 live births):	
National (1985)	120
Southern Asia (around 1988)	570
Female life expectancy at birth (1990-1995):	67.8

Iran (Islamic Republic of)

Before 1973, induced abortion was illegal in the Islamic Republic of Iran, except in cases of extreme therapeutic necessity. Article 182 of the criminal law indicated a prison term of from one to three years for a pregnant woman who took any kind of medication without the prescription of a physician or used any instrument with the intention of inducing an abortion. However, if the woman had done so on the orders of her husband, she was considered innocent, and her husband received the specified punishment. Article 183 of the criminal law indicated that a person performing an abortion could be sentenced to prison with hard labour for a period of 3-10 years unless it could be proved that the action had been taken to save the life of the mother. The law also specified a prison term for a person taking violent action with the intention of causing an abortion or causing an abortion by prescribing any type of medication or herb or using any type of instrument.

In 1973, induced abortion was legalized in Iran. In 1976, an amendment to section 3 of article 42 of the Civil Penal Code permitted a physician to perform an abortion if: (a) the couple were able to provide evidence of social or medico-social grounds for an abortion; (b) the abortion was performed during the first trimester; (c) written permission of the parents was obtained and; (d) there was no danger to the health of the mother from the procedure. In the event that the pregnant woman or her husband was insane, the law required written permission of the legal guardian of the insane partner. If the woman was unmarried, her own consent was sufficient. For a woman in the process of suing for a divorce, the consent of her husband was required. In the case of an abortion for medical purposes, the physician had to obtain the endorsed opinion of two other qualified physicians. In such cases, the written consent of the woman alone was considered to be sufficient. The law also required that the abortion be performed in a fully equipped hospital or clinic.

After the revolution in 1979, abortion was once again made illegal on most grounds. Abortion is currently prohibited on all grounds except to save the life of the pregnant woman. In such cases, authorization for an abortion requires consultation with a professional or a panel of professionals.

Studies undertaken in Iran before the legalization of abortion in 1973 indicated induced abortion was found among the higher socio-economic groups. Those studies also suggested that regardless of the legal restrictions, induced abortion was widely accepted and practised by persons in those groups. The lower socio-economic groups, on the other hand, did not have access to such means and the incidence of abortion was low. Another study conducted in 1970 found that about 15 per cent of all family planning acceptors at Teheran and in five major provinces of Iran had had at least one abortion. That study also showed that the frequency of abortion increased with family size. In a similar study conducted among teachers attending the Obstetrics and Gynaecology Clinic in 1969/70, it was found that almost 30 per cent of the respondents had had at least one abortion, with the highest incidence (60 per cent) occurring in age group 30-34.

Following the change of Government in 1979, the performance of most abortions, as well as family planning activities, was discontinued. In 1984, however, the Supreme Council for Policy Making in Health, Curative Services and Medical Education recommended the use of legitimately approved methods of contraception in order to improve the welfare of women and children. In 1989, concerned about the consequences of high rates of population growth and high fertility for national development, the Government adopted a population policy calling for improving contraceptive access and subsidizing contraception and sterilization, with the aim of reducing the growth rate to 2.3 per cent per annum by the year 2011. In 1991, the Government discontinued certain benefits (such as subsidized food rations and maternity leave) for the fourth child. Television programming was used to provide information on contraception and family planning. The goal of the Five-Year Economic, Social and Cultural Development Plan for the period 1989-1993 is to reduce the total fertility rate to four children per woman by the year 2011. The Government has proposed to raise levels of contraceptive use to 24 per cent of women of child-bearing age by 1993 and to prevent 1 million unwanted births. To reach these goals, the Plan recommends the repeal of "all regulations which encourage population growth" and the adoption of "measures in conformity with national birth control policies".

INCIDENCE OF ABORTION			
Place	*Year*	*Measurement*	*Coverage*

Information not readily available.

Source: The Population Policy Data Bank maintained by the Population Division of the Department for Economic and Social Information and Policy Analysis of the United Nations Secretariat. For additional sources, see list of references.

Iraq

ABORTION POLICY

Grounds on which abortion is permitted:

To save the life of the woman	Yes
To preserve physical health	Yes
To preserve mental health	Yes
Rape or incest	Yes
Foetal impairment	Yes
Economic or social reasons	No
Available on request	No

Additional requirements:

Approval from two physicians is needed in order to obtain a legal abortion. The written consent of the pregnant woman's husband is also necessary.

FERTILITY AND MORTALITY CONTEXT

Government's view on fertility level:	Too low
Government's intervention concerning fertility level:	To raise
Government's policy on contraceptive use:	No support provided
Percentage of currently married women using modern contraception (aged <50, 1989):	10
Total fertility rate (1990-1995):	5.7
Age-specific fertility rate (per 1,000 women aged 15-19, 1990-1995):	59
Government has expressed particular concern about:	
Morbidity and mortality resulting from induced abortion	No
Complications of child-bearing and childbirth	No
Maternal mortality rate (per 100,000 live births):	
National	..
Western Asia (around 1988)	280
Female life expectancy at birth (1990-1995):	67.5

BACKGROUND

Although abortion is not permitted on request in Iraq, it is authorized to save the life of a pregnant woman, to preserve her physical or mental health, in the case of rape or incest and for eugenic reasons. The intervention requires a recommendation from two medical specialists and written consent from the pregnant woman's husband.

Women and non-medical personnel that violate the abortion law in Iraq may be imprisoned for a period of one year and be required to pay a fine. A physician performing an illegal abortion may receive a longer prison term and pay a larger fine.

In keeping with the Government's goal of promoting rapid population growth in Iraq, women are paid full wages while on maternity leave, with the expressed aim of encouraging all women to have a minimum of four children. Furthermore, until recently, access to modern contraceptives in Iraq was restricted.

After the Gulf crisis, the Ministry of Health removed the embargo on contraceptives and thereafter permitted the sale of contraceptives in Iraq without restriction. The embargo was removed in spite of a study that indicated that the infant mortality rate in Iraq had at least trebled in the aftermath of the crisis, civil strife and international sanctions. One study estimated that, compared with the period prior to the crisis, as many as 170,000 more children would die each year from disease and from the "catastrophic" breakdown of the health-care system.

INCIDENCE OF ABORTION

Place	Year	Measurement	Coverage

Information not readily available.

Source: The Population Policy Data Bank maintained by the Population Division of the Department for Economic and Social Information and Policy Analysis of the United Nations Secretariat. For additional sources, see list of references.

Ireland

ABORTION POLICY

Grounds on which abortion is permitted:

To save the life of the woman	Yes
To preserve physical health	No
To preserve mental health	No
Rape or incest	No
Foetal impairment	No
Economic or social reasons	No
Available on request	No

Additional requirements:

Information is not readily available.

FERTILITY AND MORTALITY CONTEXT

Government's view on fertility level:	Satisfactory
Government's intervention concerning fertility level:	To maintain
Government's policy on contraceptive use:	No support provided
Percentage of currently married women using modern contraception (aged 15-49):	..
Total fertility rate (1990-1995):	2.1
Age-specific fertility rate (per 1,000 women aged 15-19, 1990-1995):	15

Government has expressed particular concern about:

Morbidity and mortality resulting from induced abortion	No
Complications of child-bearing and childbirth	No

Maternal mortality rate (per 100,000 live births):

National (1989)	4
Developed countries (around 1988)	26

Female life expectancy at birth (1990-1995):	78.1

BACKGROUND

Abortion in Ireland is ruled largely by the British Offences Against the Person Act of 1861, which prohibits the voluntary termination of pregnancy in any circumstance. In September 1983, a referendum was approved which inserted stronger language into the Constitution and guaranteed that the Government would defend the life of the unborn. Although this amendment was intended to ban abortion completely in Ireland, it was interpreted in February 1992 by the Supreme Court as allowing abortion in limited circumstances.

In February 1992, in a case that attracted international attention, a 14-year-old Irish rape victim was prevented by the High Court from travelling to England to obtain an abortion. The Supreme Court overturned the High Court decision, ruling that the girl could travel to England for an abortion. In its decision, the Supreme Court ruled that the life of the girl was endangered by a situation of emotional distress which could lead her to commit suicide. This interpretation now stands as the law of the land.

The outcome of this case had important implications for the Maastricht Treaty for European Unity, which was to be voted upon by Ireland in a referendum later in 1992. In negotiating the Treaty, the Irish Government had succeeded in having language inserted into the Treaty insulating Ireland from European Community interference with its abortion law. Because of the public outcry over the February abortion case, the Government quickly moved to amend the Treaty to allow women to travel abroad for abortion and to receive information on abortion in Ireland. It feared that if the Treaty was not amended, it would be defeated in the referendum and Ireland would lose important benefits promised by the Treaty.

The Government also promised a referendum on three proposed amendments to article 40.3.3 of the Constitution relating to abortion. In the referendum, which was held in November 1992, the freedoms to travel abroad and to obtain information in Ireland about abortion services abroad were approved, while the third question on the referendum, which would have reversed the 1992 Supreme Court decision, was not approved, therefore leaving the legal situation of abortion in Ireland unchanged. The Government is expected to take legislative action in the near future that would take into account the ruling of the Supreme Court.

The referendum of November 1992 was the culmination of a series of judicial rulings which have fuelled the debate on the abortion issue in Ireland. In 1986, the Irish High Court deemed unlawful the counselling activities of two Dublin-based organizations that put pregnant women in contact with clinics abroad for the purpose of obtaining an abortion or abortion counselling. Such activities were interpreted as implying encouragement of pregnancy termination. This decision was upheld by the Supreme Court in 1987. In 1989, the Supreme Court granted an injunction against a counselling group to prevent it from distributing a guide containing information on the availability of abortion services in the United Kingdom. In 1991, the European Court of Justice ruled that even though the provision of abortion was a service, the counselling group was not protected by guarantees of the free flow of goods and services within the European Community, because the counselling group was not asked by specific service providers to distribute such information and thus was not directly working for them. This decision opened the possibility for clinics abroad to advertise directly and to provide information on abortion services. Based on the results of the November 1992 referendum, the provision of such information is now permitted.

The dependence of Ireland upon neighbouring countries for abortion services, contraception and counselling has raised concern among its partners in the European Community. As a result, the Government of Ireland has come under pressure to modify its position. The number of Irish women having an abortion abroad has been increasing sharply, from 122 women in 1969 to 3,700 in 1983 and to an estimated 4,000 women per annum subsequently. It is estimated that 4,063 Irish women travelled to the United Kingdom to obtain an abortion in 1990.

The provision of contraceptives in Ireland has aroused considerable controversy in the country. For example, the Irish Family Planning Association opened a clinic in Dublin in 1969, which operated only semi-

Ireland

legally, as contraception was forbidden by the law until a Supreme Court decision in 1973 ruled that, on the basis of a right to marital privacy, it was unconstitutional to ban the importation of contraceptives and allowed adults to import and possess contraceptives. The decision did not nullify sections of the law, however, forbidding the sale of contraceptives. In 1979, the Health (Family Planning) Act was enacted by Parliament. It allowed the importation and sale of contraceptives only by pharmacists and by prescription. In 1985, an amendment to the Act enlarged the categories of persons allowed to sell contraceptives, also authorizing medical practitioners, employees of health boards and family planning services that were approved by the Ministry of Health and Social Services, and employees of hospitals that provided maternity services or services for the treatment of sexually transmitted diseases. The Act also allowed persons over 18 years of age to buy condoms and spermicides without prescription. Other contraceptives are still sold in Ireland only by prescription. Because of the rise in the incidence of sexually transmitted diseases, a new law on contraceptives, which permits the distribution of condoms in vending machines, was approved by Parliament in June 1993.

INCIDENCE OF ABORTION

Place	Year	Measurement	Coverage[a]
National	1975	2.6 abortions/1,000 women aged 15-44	SP
National	1976	2.9 abortions/1,000 women aged 15-44	SP
National	1977	3.5 abortions/1,000 women aged 15-44	SP
National	1978	3.8 abortions/1,000 women aged 15-44	SP
National	1979	4.2 abortions/1,000 women aged 15-44	SP
National	1980	4.8 abortions/1,000 women aged 15-44	SP
National	1981	5.2 abortions/1,000 women aged 15-44	SP
National	1982	5.2 abortions/1,000 women aged 15-44	SP
National	1983	5.0 abortions/1,000 women aged 15-44	SP
National	1984	5.3 abortions/1,000 women aged 15-44	SP
National	1985	5.2 abortions/1,000 women aged 15-44	SP
National	1986	5.2 abortions/1,000 women aged 15-44	SP
National	1987	4.8 abortions/1,000 women aged 15-44	SP
National	1988	5.0 abortions/1,000 women aged 15-44	SP
National	1989	4.9 abortions/1,000 women aged 15-44	SP
National	1990	5.4 abortions/1,000 women aged 15-44	SP

Note: PR = provider registration; SP = survey provider; SW = survey of women; HR = hospital admission records. For a detailed description of these abbreviations and information on sources of the data, see technical notes in the annex.

[a] Based only on numbers of abortions obtained in England and Wales by residents of Ireland; excluding an unknown number of residents of Ireland that gave an address in England.

Source: Population Policy Data Bank maintained by the Population Division of the Department for Economic and Social Information and Policy Analysis of the United Nations Secretariat. For additional sources, see list of references.

ABORTION POLICY

Grounds on which abortion is permitted:

To save the life of the woman	Yes
To preserve physical health	Yes
To preserve mental health	Yes
Rape or incest	Yes
Foetal impairment	Yes
Economic or social reasons	No
Available on request	No

Additional requirements:

An abortion must be performed by a physician in a recognized medical institution, with the written consent of the pregnant woman. A legal abortion requires the approval of a committee composed of two physicians and a social worker. The committee members must be appointed by the director of the hospital where the abortion will be performed, or by the Minister of Health or a person empowered by him if the procedure is to be performed in another recognized medical institution.

FERTILITY AND MORTALITY CONTEXT

Government's view on fertility level:	Too low
Government's intervention concerning fertility level:	To raise
Government's policy on contraceptive use:	Direct support provided
Percentage of currently married women using modern contraception (aged 15-49):	..
Total fertility rate (1990-1995):	2.9
Age-specific fertility rate (per 1,000 women aged 15-19, 1990-1995):	23
Government has expressed particular concern about:	
Morbidity and mortality resulting from induced abortion	Yes
Complications of child-bearing and childbirth	No
Maternal mortality rate (per 100,000 live births):	
National (1989)	7
Western Asia (around 1988)	280
Female life expectancy at birth (1990-1995):	78.4

Israel

Before the creation of the State of Israel in 1948, abortion legislation in Palestine was based on the British Offences Against the Person Act of 1861. A woman inducing her own abortion was liable to imprisonment for seven years, while any person performing an illegal abortion could be imprisoned for 14 years. In practice, however, the law was not strictly enforced. In 1948, the Government of Israel also adopted the British Act of 1861. How narrowly the Act was interpreted was unclear, however, because a District Court at Haifa ruled in 1952 that induced abortion was permissible on medical grounds.

In 1977, the grounds on which a legal abortion could be performed in Israel were extended. The Criminal Law Amendment (Interruption of Pregnancy) of 31 January 1977 permitted abortion if the continuation of the pregnancy would endanger the woman's life or cause her physical or mental harm, or if the woman was under 17 or over 40 years of age. Abortion was permitted if the pregnancy resulted from rape, incest or extramarital sexual intercourse, or if the foetus was suspected to have a physical or mental malformation. Abortion was also legal if the continuation of the pregnancy would cause grave harm to the woman or her existing children owing to difficult family or social circumstances which prevailed in the woman's environment.

The Law of 1977 abolished any penalties that were previously imposed on a woman inducing her own abortion. The penalty imposed on a person performing an induced abortion was also reduced from 14 to 5 years of imprisonment or a fine.

An abortion requires the approval of a three-member committee consisting of a social worker and two physicians, one of whom must be an obstetrician/gynaecologist. The committee is required to give its approval in writing and must set out the grounds justifying the abortion. The written consent of the pregnant woman is required, after the physical and mental risks and consequences involved in the procedure have been explained to her. The law also states that a minor does not require her guardian's consent. An abortion must be performed by a physician in an approved medical institution.

The law was further amended in 1979 to repeal the clause permitting abortion on broad social and economic grounds. Although abortion is still legal on extended medical grounds, segments of the Israeli population have proposed that the abortion law be further restricted. Both moral and political reasons have been voiced against liberalized abortion legislation. Some believe that destroying a foetus is equivalent to murder and that it is immoral to take the life of the unborn.

The law does not specify a gestational limit for having an abortion, nor is parental consent required for minors. The costs of the abortion for minors and women who have an abortion on medical grounds are usually covered by the social insurance system. Otherwise, the woman pays the equivalent of $150-200, depending upon the hospital.

The recent large influx of Soviet Jews to Israel—over 300,000 in 1990 and 1991—suggests that requests for abortion services may increase by as much as 24 per cent, given the widespread use of abortion in the former USSR. Israel may have to expand both family planning services and the medical committees entitled to grant a legal abortion. Current regulations establish that only the medical committees based throughout the country at 28 public and private hospitals have the power to authorize an abortion.

It is estimated that the abortion rate in Israel was fairly stable from 1979 to 1987. However, the rates reported during this period may underestimate the actual rates because significant numbers of illegal abortions may have been unreported. Data obtained by the Central Bureau of Statistics in 1988 show that a majority (59 per cent) of abortion applicants were married, 33 per cent were single and the remainder were widowed or divorced. Most women (44 per cent) had applied for an abortion because they had conceived out of wedlock. Other reasons given by committees for approving an abortion were danger to the woman's life (25 per cent) and a suspected birth defect (20 per cent). Estimates of illegal abortions suggest that between 2,000 and 5,000 were performed during the 1980s, or from 12 to 25 per cent of the total. Most of these abortions were performed on healthy married women.

INCIDENCE OF ABORTION

Place	Year	Measurement	Coverage
National	1982	19.1 abortions/1,000 women aged 15-44	PR
National	1983	18.2 abortions/1,000 women aged 15-44	PR
National	1984	21.4 abortions/1,000 women aged 15-44	PR
National	1985	20.3 abortions/1,000 women aged 15-44	PR
National	1986	18.8 abortions/1,000 women aged 15-44	PR
National	1987	16.0 abortions/1,000 women aged 15-44	PR
National	1988	15.6 abortions/1,000 women aged 15-44	PR
National	1989	15.2 abortions/1,000 women aged 15-44	PR
National	1990	14.9 abortions/1,000 women aged 15-44	PR

Note: PR = provider registration; SP = survey provider; SW = survey of women; HR = hospital admission records. For a detailed description of these abbreviations and information on sources of the data, see technical notes in the annex.

Source: The Population Policy Data Bank maintained by the Population Division of the Department for Economic and Social Information and Policy Analysis of the United Nations Secretariat. For additional sources, see list of references.

Italy

Grounds on which abortion is permitted:

To save the life of the woman	Yes
To preserve physical health	Yes
To preserve mental health	Yes
Rape or incest	Yes
Foetal impairment	Yes
Economic or social reasons	Yes
Available on request	No

Additional requirements:

A one-week reflection period is imposed unless the situation is one of urgency. A certificate attesting to the pregnancy and the request for termination must be issued by a physician and signed by both the woman and the physician. If the pregnant woman is under age 18, parental authorization is required. After the first three months of pregnancy, abortion is allowed only if the foetus has a genetic deficiency or to preserve the physical and mental health of the mother. An abortion must be performed in a public hospital or authorized private facility.

FERTILITY AND MORTALITY CONTEXT

Government's view on fertility level:	Too low
Government's intervention concerning fertility level:	To raise
Government's policy on contraceptive use:	Direct support provided
Percentage of currently married women using modern contraception (aged 18-44, 1979):	32
Total fertility rate (1990-1995):	1.3
Age-specific fertility rate (per 1,000 women aged 15-19, 1990-1995):	10
Government has expressed particular concern about:	
Morbidity and mortality resulting from induced abortion	No
Complications of child-bearing and childbirth	Yes
Maternal mortality rate (per 100,000 live births):	
National (1988)	8
Developed countries (around 1988)	26
Female life expectancy at birth (1990-1995):	80.3

BACKGROUND

The provisions of the Penal Code of 1930, which prohibited the advertisement and practice of any type of contraception and abortion, were the subject of prolonged debate among the various political parties in Italy. In 1971, the provisions relating to the prohibition on advertising or inciting the use of contraceptives were repealed. In 1975, the provisions of the Civil Code relating to family and the status of women were revised (among other things, divorce was legalized), and a law establishing family planning counselling centres and permitting them to dispense contraceptive information and services was enacted. Also in 1975, a judgement of the Constitutional Court enlarged the grounds on which abortion was permitted from the narrow ground of saving the mother's life to those of health. Lastly, on 22 May 1978, Law No. 194, which liberalized abortion was approved.

According to the new law, abortion is legal during the first 90 days of pregnancy when the continuation of the pregnancy or childbirth would seriously endanger the physical or mental health of the pregnant woman, taking into account her state of health, her economic, social or family situation, the circumstances under which conception occurred or the likelihood that the child would be born with abnormalities or malformations. A woman that desires to have her pregnancy interrupted on any of the grounds given above must apply to a physician, who, after a medical examination, must inform her of possible alternatives and of the availability of social welfare facilities. If the woman persists in her request to terminate the pregnancy, the physician must issue a certificate, signed by himself and by the woman, attesting to her pregnancy and her request. Following a reflection period of seven days, the woman may present herself with the certificate to an authorized medical facility to obtain the requested intervention. The reflection period is not required in urgent cases, such as those involving a threat to the woman's life. If the pregnant woman is under age 18, parental authorization is required, unless there are serious reasons rendering this impossible or inadvisable. In this case, and if the parents refuse to give their consent, the magistrate responsible for guardianship matters can issue the necessary authorization.

After the first trimester of pregnancy, abortion is allowed only to save the woman's life or when the mother's physical or mental health is endangered (such as by foetal impairment). Penalties may be levied on the person performing the abortion and on the woman when the termination of pregnancy occurs outside of the legal provisions.

An abortion must be performed in a public hospital or authorized private facility and is free of charge. Medical and paramedical personnel that are opposed to abortion on moral or religious grounds can declare in advance their conscientious objection and be exempted from performing or assisting in the performance of an abortion.

The law adopted in 1978 was viewed as one of the most liberal abortion laws in Western Europe. The new law, in fact, provides such broad grounds on which abortion is permitted that it has been interpreted by some as allowing abortion on request—although the law does not specifically contain such a provision—because it is the woman herself who attests that she is in one of the situations described by the law and the primary role of the physician is to certify the existence of a pregnancy.

In practice, however, the situation is very different, and it varies considerably from one region of the country to another. The conscience clause is partially responsible for many of the difficulties in availability of services. Moreover, a major reason is the strong influence of the Holy See. When Law No. 194 was approved, the Holy See immediately issued a warning that any person performing an abortion and any woman obtaining an abortion would be excommunicated. Owing to the political pressure exerted by the Catholic church on members of the Christian Democratic Party and the fear of some physicians that their medical practice would consist largely of the performance of abortions, nearly 70 per cent of physicians in Italy and a majority of other health-care professionals have invoked the conscience clause. The situation is more

Italy

dramatic in southern Italy, where in some regions the proportion of physicians resorting to the conscience clause exceeds 90 per cent. In many smaller hospitals, there are no personnel willing to perform an abortion.

Because of the high proportion of gynaecologists that are conscientious objectors and the lack of hospital facilities, in some areas of Italy the delay between the issuance of a certificate and the intervention is at least three weeks. In addition, not all areas have family planning centres, as provided by the law of 1975. Sex education programmes are not provided in schools and the Government has no special programmes for family planning; two thirds of the women nationwide either do not use contraceptives or depend upon less reliable traditional methods.

The number of legal abortions in Italy has steadily declined since 1982, while adolescent pregnancy and illegal abortions, particularly among unmarried adolescents (two out of three of whom live in central or southern Italy), have been increasing. The incidence of illegal abortion remains controversial; during the 1980s, the number of illegal abortions was estimated at between 220,000 and 800,000 per annum.

INCIDENCE OF ABORTION

Place	Year	Measurement		Coverage
National	1979	15.9	abortions/1,000 women aged 15-44	PR
National	1980	18.7	abortions/1,000 women aged 15-44	PR
National	1981	18.7	abortions/1,000 women aged 15-44	PR
National	1982	19.6	abortions/1,000 women aged 15-44	PR
National	1983	19.5	abortions/1,000 women aged 15-44	PR
National	1984	18.4	abortions/1,000 women aged 15-44	PR
National	1985	16.8	abortions/1,000 women aged 15-44	PR
National	1986	16.0	abortions/1,000 women aged 15-44	PR
National	1987	15.3	abortions/1,000 women aged 15-44	PR
National	1990	12.7	abortions/1,000 women aged 15-44	PR

Note: PR = provider registration; SP = survey provider; SW = survey of women; HR = hospital admission records. For a detailed description of these abbreviations and information on sources of the data, see technical notes in the annex.

Source: Population Policy Data Bank maintained by the Population Division of the Department for Economic and Social Information and Policy Analysis of the United Nations Secretariat. For additional sources, see list of references.

ABORTION POLICY

Grounds on which abortion is permitted:

To save the life of the woman	Yes
To preserve physical health	Yes
To preserve mental health	Yes
Rape or incest	No*
Foetal impairment	No*
Economic or social reasons	No
Available on request	No

Additional requirements:

The spouse's consent is required. In order to perform an abortion on the grounds of mental health, foetal impairment, rape or incest, the approval of two specialists must be obtained.

_____

* Legal interpretation generally permits these grounds.

FERTILITY AND MORTALITY CONTEXT

Government's view on fertility level:	Too high
Government's intervention concerning fertility level:	To lower
Government's policy on contraceptive use:	Direct support provided
Percentage of currently married women using modern contraception (aged 15-49, 1988-1989):	51
Total fertility rate (1990-1995):	2.4
Age-specific fertility rate (per 1,000 women aged 15-19, 1990-1995):	87.4
Government has expressed particular concern about:	
Morbidity and mortality resulting from induced abortion	Yes
Complications of child-bearing and childbirth	Yes
Maternal mortality rate (per 100,000 live births):	
National (1984)	26
Caribbean (around 1988)	260
Female life expectancy at birth (1990-1995):	75.8

Jamaica

Abortion is illegal in Jamaica under the British Offences Against the Person Act of 1861, derived from common law. However, the judicial decision of 1938, *Rex* v. *Bourne*, has been applied in Jamaica since 1975, permitting abortion in order to preserve the physical and mental health of the woman. The approval of two specialists is required to perform an abortion on the grounds of mental health, rape or incest, or foetal impairment. Any person procuring or attempting to procure an illegal abortion, regardless of whether the woman is with child, is subject to life imprisonment or to imprisonment for not less than three years, with or without hard labour.

Although there were only a few hundred legal abortions in Jamaica during the 1970s, illegal abortion was widespread. Indeed, it is estimated that there were from 10,000 to 20,000 illegal abortions during that period. According to data for 1977, 20 per cent of all gynaecological beds in Jamaican hospitals were occupied by patients suffering from the effects of an illegal abortion, whereas 7.5 per cent of all maternal deaths were attributed to septic abortion. Evidence supports the fact that women from lower income households generally have more dangerous types of abortion and suffer a higher rate of complications than women from higher income households.

Physicians in Jamaica are usually hesitant to perform an abortion, as the law affords them no real protection, and many of them fear the possibility of prosecution. A survey conducted in 1973 found that 84 per cent of all physicians and 88 per cent of nurses and midwives in Jamaica favoured a more liberal abortion law. The majority of survey respondents supported offering the provision of abortions under the auspices of the National Family Planning Board, particularly as a backup method in the event of contraceptive failure.

A study in 1989 indicated that pregnancy-related deaths in Jamaica are more than twice the official figure. However, although liberalization of the current abortion law has been a topic of debate in Jamaica since the 1970s and the Government is concerned about the large number of women treated for septic abortion, there had been no changes in the law as of 1992.

The Government of Jamaica was one of the first in the Latin American and Caribbean area to adopt a policy designed to decrease the rate of population growth. The Jamaican Family Planning Association was established in 1956. Ten years later, the National Family Planning Programme was initiated and was placed under the authority of the semi-autonomous National Family Planning Board.

Place	Year	Measurement	Coverage

Information not readily available.

Source: The Population Policy Data Bank maintained by the Population Division of the Department for Economic and Social Information and Policy Analysis of the United Nations Secretariat. For additional sources, see list of references.

ABORTION POLICY

Grounds on which abortion is permitted:

To save the life of the woman	Yes
To preserve physical health	Yes
To preserve mental health	Yes*
Rape or incest	Yes
Foetal impairment	No
Economic or social reasons	Yes
Available on request	No

Additional requirements:

Induced abortions are allowed only within the first 24 weeks of gestation. All legal abortions must be performed within medical facilities at the discretion of a physician designated by a local medical association. The consent of the woman or her spouse is required, while the consent of a mentally retarded woman can be given by her guardian. When the pregnancy is a result of rape or incest, the abortion can be performed without the legal consent of the woman.

---

* Permission for an abortion on this ground must be considered in conjunction with other grounds.

FERTILITY AND MORTALITY CONTEXT

Government's view on fertility level:	Too low
Government's intervention concerning fertility level:	No intervention
Government's policy on contraceptive use:	Direct support provided
Percentage of currently married women using modern contraception (aged 15-49, 1990):	52
Total fertility rate (1990-1995):	1.7
Age-specific fertility rate (per 1,000 women aged 15-19, 1990-1995):	4
Government has expressed particular concern about:	
Morbidity and mortality resulting from induced abortion	No
Complications of child-bearing and childbirth	Yes
Maternal mortality rate (per 100,000 live births):	
National (1990)	9
Developed countries (around 1988)	26
Female life expectancy at birth (1990-1995):	81.6

Japan

In 1948, with the introduction of the Eugenic Protection Law (No. 156 of 13 July), abortion was liberalized in Japan. Previously, abortion had been considered a criminal act under a code derived from the French legal system adopted in 1880. Article 212 of the Japanese Criminal Code (Law No. 45 of 1907) generally prohibited all induced abortions except when they were judged to be absolutely necessary from a medical standpoint to save the life of the mother. Any person performing an illegal abortion was subject to imprisonment for up to two years. A woman wilfully inducing her own miscarriage might be imprisoned for up to one year. Physicians and pharmacists that performed an abortion were subject to harsher penalties.

Before and during the Second World War, the Japanese Government favoured population growth. It maintained a restrictive attitude towards abortion and discouraged the practice of birth control. The National Eugenic Law of 1940, which provided the legal basis for the performance of induced abortion and sterilization, was promulgated with the overall purpose of enforcing official restrictions on abortion. The law reaffirmed that abortion was legal only on therapeutic grounds.

In the years immediately following the Second World War, Japan was faced with a serious imbalance between a rapidly growing population and a war-shattered economy. The need to limit family size became increasingly apparent and there was a high incidence of illegally induced abortion. The Government responded by promoting family planning through the methods then available, which were mostly traditional, and by legalizing abortion. The Eugenic Protection Law, under the jurisdiction of the Public Health Bureau, was enacted to "prevent the increase of the number of defective progeny from the eugenic point of view and also to protect the life and health of the mother". Article 14 of the Law permits termination of pregnancy on the ground of maternal health protection if a woman's health might be affected seriously by continuation of the pregnancy or by delivery. It also permits an abortion on eugenic grounds when the husband or a relative within the fourth degree suffered from mental illness or from hereditary physical or mental diseases. Pregnancy due to violence can be terminated on humanitarian grounds. In all instances, abortions are confined to the first 24 weeks of gestation.

Under the law, an abortion may be performed only in a medical facility by a physician specializing in obstetrics and gynaecology that has been designated by the local medical association. The consent of the woman or her spouse is required. The sole consent of the person in question is sufficient if the father cannot be identified or disappears after conception has occurred, or if the spouse fails to declare his or her intention. If the woman who is to undergo the abortion is insane or mentally retarded, the consent may be given by the woman's guardian.

The Eugenic Protection Law has undergone several amendments, which have modified the provisions of article 212 of the Criminal Code. Most importantly, the amendment of 1949 (Law No. 154 of 31 May) added economic considerations to the legal justifications for abortion. A further amendment in 1952 (Law No. 141 of 17 May) eliminated the need to apply for committee authorization to perform an abortion, with the sole requirements being the physician's discretion and the consent of the relevant person.

With the liberalized law, abortion became the primary mode of fertility control in Japan. Abortion played a significant role during the early years of the overall fertility decline, with contraception subsequently playing a greater role. According to health authorities, the number of induced abortions in Japan continued to increase after the 1948 law was enacted. A peak was reached in 1955, when more than 1,170,000 abortions were reported against about 1,731,000 officially registered live births. Thereafter, the number of induced abortions gradually decreased. As of 1983, slightly over 567,000 cases—about half of the number of abortions that were performed in 1955—were reported.

The vast majority of abortions in Japan have been performed under the maternal health protection indication, which is in effect a combination of medical and socio-economic reasons. Nearly all abortions have occurred within the first trimester. In contrast to the general declining trend in the total incidence of abortion, the number of abortions obtained by women with low parity and by teenagers has been increasing since the late 1970s. As reported by one study in 1990, pregnancies among adolescents in Japan occur at a rate of about 22 per 1,000, and most of them end in abortion.

The high incidence of abortion in Japan is believed to be due in part to government restrictions on contraceptive use. Oral contraception has been illegal in Japan. It may be obtained from physicians, however, for the control of irregular menstrual cycles and for other medical purposes but not for birth control. In March 1992, the Japanese Government reaffirmed its position concerning the long-term ban on birth control pills because, in its view, their use "would discourage the use of condoms and lead to an epidemic of AIDS". The intra-uterine device was legalized in Japan only in 1974 after its effectiveness and safety had been proved abroad. The National Survey on Family Planning in Japan conducted in 1986 found that about 80 per cent of contraceptive users relied upon the condom. The survey results also demonstrated a relatively high rate of contraceptive failure; about 31 per cent of the women surveyed had undergone one or more abortions.

INCIDENCE OF ABORTION

Place	Year	Measurement	Coverage
National	1950-1954	40.7 abortions/1,000 women aged 15-44	PR
National	1955-1959	52.2 abortions/1,000 women aged 15-44	PR
National	1960-1964	41.9 abortions/1,000 women aged 15-44	PR
National	1965-1969	30.3 abortions/1,000 women aged 15-44	PR
National	1970	28.0 abortions/1,000 women aged 15-44	PR
National	1971	28.2 abortions/1,000 women aged 15-44	PR
National	1972	27.6 abortions/1,000 women aged 15-44	PR
National	1973	26.3 abortions/1,000 women aged 15-44	PR
National	1974	25.5 abortions/1,000 women aged 15-44	PR
National	1975	25.2 abortions/1,000 women aged 15-44	PR
National	1976	24.9 abortions/1,000 women aged 15-44	PR
National	1977	24.1 abortions/1,000 women aged 15-44	PR
National	1978	23.3 abortions/1,000 women aged 15-44	PR
National	1979	23.1 abortions/1,000 women aged 15-44	PR
National	1980	22.5 abortions/1,000 women aged 15-44	PR
National	1981	22.6 abortions/1,000 women aged 15-44	PR
National	1982	22.5 abortions/1,000 women aged 15-44	PR
National	1983	21.5 abortions/1,000 women aged 15-44	PR
National	1984	21.4 abortions/1,000 women aged 15-44	PR
National	1985	20.6 abortions/1,000 women aged 15-44	PR
National	1986	19.8 abortions/1,000 women aged 15-44	PR
National	1987	18.6 abortions/1,000 women aged 15-44	PR
National	1988	15.6 abortions/1.000 women aged 15-44	PR
National	1989	14.9 abortions/1,000 women aged 15-44	PR
National	1990	14.5 abortions/1,000 women aged 15-44	PR

Note: PR = provider registration; SP = survey provider; SW = survey of women; HR = hospital admission records. For a detailed description of these abbreviations and information on sources of the data, see technical notes in the annex.

Source: The Population Policy Data Bank maintained by the Population Division of the Department for Economic and Social Information and Policy Analysis of the United Nations Secretariat. For additional sources, see list of references.

Jordan

ABORTION POLICY

Grounds on which abortion is permitted:

To save the life of the woman	Yes
To preserve physical health	Yes
To preserve mental health	Yes
Rape or incest	No
Foetal impairment	No
Economic or social reasons	No
Available on request	No

Additional requirements:

An abortion procedure on any of the approved grounds must be certified by two licensed physicians. Written consent to the abortion is required either from the woman or from someone with legal authority to act on her behalf. A legal abortion must be performed in a licensed facility.

FERTILITY AND MORTALITY CONTEXT

Government's view on fertility level:	Too high
Government's intervention concerning fertility level:	To lower
Government's policy on contraceptive use:	Direct support provided
Percentage of currently married women using modern contraception (aged 15-49, 1990):	27
Total fertility rate (1990-1995):	5.7
Age-specific fertility rate (per 1,000 women aged 15-19, 1990-1995):	61
Government has expressed particular concern about:	
Morbidity and mortality resulting from induced abortion	Yes
Complications of child-bearing and childbirth	Yes
Maternal mortality rate (per 100,000 live births):	
National	..
Western Asia (around 1988)	280
Female life expectancy at birth (1990-1995):	69.8

BACKGROUND

Abortion is prohibited in Jordan under the Penal Code. However, under Public Health Law No. 21 of 1971 (section 62(a)), abortion is legal for medical reasons. A therapeutic abortion must be approved by two physicians and may not be performed beyond 120 days of gestation; otherwise, it is considered *haram* (unlawful) under Islamic laws.

Under Criminal Law No. 1,487 of 1 May 1960, any person performing an illegal abortion can be imprisoned for from one to three years. The sentence for a medical practitioner performing an abortion is increased by one third. A woman inducing her own miscarriage may be punished by imprisonment for from six months to three years. It appears that abortion can be obtained for reasons other than those officially approved. Under article 324 of the Penal Code, a woman who procures a miscarriage to protect her honour and any person committing the crimes stated in articles 322-323 to protect the honour of a descendant or relative to the third degree is subject to a reduced penalty. Reputation and family honour are therefore considered mitigating circumstances for an abortion. This provision may allow abortion on grounds that are otherwise disallowed, such as rape and incest.

Although the laws in Jordan with regard to induced abortion are relatively restrictive, they are broadly interpreted with considerable discretion. It has been observed that the effect of induced abortion on fertility is significant, compared with the effect in a number of other countries in the region. Most unsafe abortions are performed by midwives. Consequently, training courses have been introduced to remove some of the dangers associated with traditional birth practices. International assistance is being provided to improve and expand maternal and child health programmes and to broaden the range of modern contraceptives that are available in the country.

Reliable statistics on abortion are not readily available. However, one estimate puts the induced abortion rate at one per 1,000 deliveries. The major reasons for having an abortion are believed to be: illness of the mother; having too many children; unwanted new child; complicated childbirth; and being an unmarried mother.

INCIDENCE OF ABORTION

Place	Year	Measurement	Coverage

Information not readily available.

Source: The Population Policy Data Bank maintained by the Population Division of the Department for Economic and Social Information and Policy Analysis of the United Nations Secretariat. For additional sources, see list of references.

Kazakhstan

ABORTION POLICY

Grounds on which abortion is permitted:

To save the life of the woman	Yes
To preserve physical health	Yes
To preserve mental health	Yes
Rape or incest	Yes
Foetal impairment	Yes
Economic or social reasons	Yes
Available on request	Yes

Additional requirements:

An abortion requires the consent of the pregnant woman; it is authorized if performed by a licensed physician in a hospital or other recognized medical institution. Abortion is available on request during the first 12 weeks of gestation. Thereafter, induced abortion is available within 28 weeks from conception on judicial, genetic, vital, broad medical and social grounds, as well as for personal reasons if authorized by a commission of local physicians.

FERTILITY AND MORTALITY CONTEXT

Government's view on fertility level:	Satisfactory
Government's intervention concerning fertility level:	To maintain
Government's policy on contraceptive use:	Direct support provided
Percentage of currently married women using modern contraception (aged 15-49, 1990):	22
Total fertility rate (1985-1990):	3.0
Age-specific fertility rate (per 1,000 women aged 15-19, 1985-1990):	43
Government has expressed particular concern about:	
Morbidity and mortality resulting from induced abortion	Yes
Complications of child-bearing and childbirth	Yes
Maternal mortality rate (per 100,000 live births):	
National (1990)	54.8
Developed countries (around 1988)	26
Female life expectancy at birth (1985-1990):	73.6

BACKGROUND

As was the case with all of the former Soviet republics, Kazakhstan, known prior to 1992 as the Kazakh Soviet Socialist Republic, was subject to the abortion legislation and regulations of the former Union of Soviet Socialist Republics. As a result, abortion practices in Kazakhstan were similar to those throughout the former USSR.

The description given below pertains to the situation in Kazakhstan prior to independence.

The Soviet law of 27 June 1936 prohibited induced abortion in most circumstances, permitting it only for eugenic reasons. Physicians and non-medical personnel that performed abortions in hospitals or as part of an out-patient service were subject to a maximum of three years in prison. A husband, relative or physician who pressured a woman into having an abortion could be sentenced to a maximum of two years in prison. The pregnant woman could be prosecuted by public trial and/or required to pay a large fine.

In a decree of 23 November 1955, the Soviet Government repealed the prohibition of abortion. Regulations issued in 1956 and subsequently in 1982 specified that abortions could be performed during the first 12 weeks of gestation, although not less than six months after a woman's previous abortion. An abortion was considered illegal if not performed in a hospital or if the person performing the abortion did not have an advanced medical education. The maximum penalty for an illegal abortion was set at eight years in a labour camp.

In 1974, the Ministry of Public Health of the USSR published a document entitled "On the side-effects and complications of oral contraceptives", in which the mass use of oral contraception was de facto prohibited. On 5 June 1987, in Order No. 757, the Ministry of Public Health legalized and officially permitted the provision of early vacuum aspirations in any clinic regardless of the place of residence of the woman. Vacuum aspiration had been the method of induced abortion provided during the first 20 days of pregnancy with the obligatory diagnosis of pregnancy.

During the 1980s, the Ministry of Public Health continued its efforts to decrease the number of illegal abortions by formally broadening the grounds on which abortions were legal and increasing their availability. Most of the later changes were not followed by a simultaneous increase in actual de facto accessibility of abortion services. On 31 December 1987, the Ministry of Public Health published Order No. 1342, which permits induced abortion during the first 28 weeks of gestation on judicial, genetic, broad medical and social grounds (for example, more than five children in the family), as well as on demand with the special authorization of a commission of local physicians.

The high incidence of abortion has been attributed to a number of factors, including shortages of high-quality modern contraceptives and reliance upon less reliable traditional methods, a lack of knowledge among couples of contraception and of the detrimental health consequences of frequent abortions and the absence of adequate training for physicians, nurses, teachers and other specialists. In 1989, the availability of condoms in the entire former Soviet Union amounted to only 11 per cent of demand; intra-uterine devices (IUDs), 30 per cent; and pills, 2 per cent. Data from the All-Union sample survey of contraceptive use conducted in 1990 indicate that in Kazakhstan, 22 per cent of all women aged 15-49 regularly used contraception, 8 per cent sometimes used contraception, 55 per cent did not use any contraceptive method and 9 per cent knew nothing about contraception. IUD is the most commonly used method of contraception.

In 1989, a total of 83,228 induced abortions were registered in Kazahkstan, giving an abortion rate of 86.3 per 1,000 women aged 15-49 years, one of the highest rates in the former Soviet Union. The actual figure is much higher, because this total does not include most abortions performed in departmental health services and commercial clinics, early vacuum aspirations and self-induced abortions. In 1988, 3.3 per cent of all induced abortions were performed on primigravidae and 8 per cent of all induced abortions were

Kazakhstan

vacuum aspirations. In 1989, illegal abortions calculated on the basis of their registered complications accounted for 28.8 per cent of all abortions among primigravidae. Among women under age 17, they accounted for 24 per cent of all induced abortions. Up to 91 per cent of all deaths due to abortion were the result of illegal abortion.

Maternal mortality rates in Kazakhstan were 55.6 and 48.6 per 100,000 births in 1980 and 1988, respectively, one of the highest rates in the former Soviet Union; in 1988, 18 per cent of all maternal deaths were due to criminal abortion.

INCIDENCE OF ABORTION

Place	Year	Measurement	Coverage
National	1970	125.6 abortions/1,000 women aged 15-49	PR
National	1975	108.7 abortions/1,000 women aged 15-49	PR
National	1980	99.2 abortions/1,000 women aged 15-49	PR
National	1985	90.7 abortions/1,000 women aged 15-49	PR
National	1988	88.3 abortions/1,000 women aged 15-49	PR
National	1989	86.3 abortions/1,000 women aged 15-49	PR
National	1990	85.4 abortions/1,000 women aged 15-49	PR

Note: PR = provider registration; SP = survey provider; SW = survey of women; HR = hospital admission records. For a detailed description of these abbreviations and information on sources of the data, see technical notes in the annex.

Source: Population Policy Data Bank maintained by the Population Division of the Department for Economic and Social Information and Policy Analysis of the United Nations Secretariat. For additional sources, see list of references.

ABORTION POLICY

Grounds on which abortion is permitted:

To save the life of the woman	Yes
To preserve physical health	No
To preserve mental health	No
Rape or incest	No
Foetal impairment	No
Economic or social reasons	No
Available on request	No

Additional requirements:

An abortion must be performed by a certified physician, with the consent of the woman and her spouse. Two medical opinions, one of which must be from the physician who has treated the woman and the other from a psychiatrist, are required before the abortion is performed. The abortion must also be performed in a hospital.

FERTILITY AND MORTALITY CONTEXT

Government's view on fertility level:	Too high
Government's intervention concerning fertility level:	To lower
Government's policy on contraceptive use:	Direct support provided
Percentage of currently married women using modern contraception (aged 15-49, 1988-1989):	18
Total fertility rate (1990-1995):	6.3
Age-specific fertility rate (per 1,000 women aged 15-19, 1990-1995):	142
Government has expressed particular concern about:	
Morbidity and mortality resulting from induced abortion	Yes
Complications of child-bearing and childbirth	Yes
Maternal mortality rate (per 100,000 live births):	
National (1977)	168
Eastern Africa (around 1988)	680
Female life expectancy at birth (1990-1995):	60.8

Kenya

In Kenya, the Penal Code of 1973 (chapter 63, sections 158-160) generally prohibits abortion. Section 240 of the Penal Code, however, specifies that a person is not criminally responsible if an abortion is performed to save the life of the pregnant woman. Two medical opinions are required before the abortion is performed—one from the physician who has treated the woman and the other from a psychiatrist. The abortion must be performed by a licensed physician and requires the consent of the pregnant woman and her husband if she is married.

Any person performing an illegal abortion may be imprisoned for up to 13 years, whereas a woman wilfully inducing her own abortion may be imprisoned for up to seven years. Any person that supplies any object or substance, knowing that it will be used to perform an abortion, may be imprisoned for up to three years. Section 244 of the Penal Code also bans the advertisement of drugs and/or appliances that can be used to induce an abortion. Prior to the independence of Kenya in 1963, abortion laws were strictly enforced. For example, a physician was convicted of manslaughter in 1959 for performing a therapeutic abortion on a woman who subsequently died (*Mehar Singh Bansel* v. *R*).

Although official abortion statistics are not readily available, hospital-based studies have shown that illegal abortion is a serious and growing health concern in Kenya. Data obtained from hospitals throughout the country between 1988 and 1989 show that over half of all gynaecological admissions were due to abortion. During the 1970s and the early 1980s, the Kenyatta National Hospital admitted between 2,000 and 3,000 abortion cases per annum, whereas the figure exceeded 10,000 admissions by 1990. Various studies have also shown that there is a high incidence of abortion among adolescent female students, who resort to illegal abortion to avoid expulsion from school.

A large proportion of maternal deaths in Kenya are due to illegal abortion. In a retrospective study carried out at the Kenyatta National Hospital between 1978 and 1987, it was found that abortion was the most important determinant of maternal death, accounting for over 20 per cent of all those deaths. Due to the serious consequences of induced abortion, the Kenya Medical Association recommended the liberalization of the abortion laws in 1986.

Although Kenya has one of the oldest family planning programmes in sub-Saharan Africa (initiated in 1967), the country has had low contraceptive use rates and has until recently sustained one of the highest fertility levels on the continent. However, recent data indicate that the demographic picture may be changing. For example, the Kenya Demographic and Health Survey conducted in 1989 indicates that the total fertility rate declined from 8.1 children per woman in 1977 to 6.7 in 1989, whereas the contraceptive prevalence rate among currently married women increased from 7 to 27 per cent over the same period. These changes have been attributed to the increasing cost of educating children and to the greater availability of family planning information and services. The Government's target is to reduce the population growth rate from 3.3 per cent per annum in 1989 to 2.5 per cent by the year 2000 and to reduce the total fertility rate from 7.7 in 1984 to 5.0 by 2000.

Place	Year	Measurement	Coverage
Information not readily available.			

Source: The Population Policy Data Bank maintained by the Population Division of the Department for Economic and Social Information and Policy Analysis of the United Nations Secretariat. For additional sources, see list of references.

ABORTION POLICY

Grounds on which abortion is permitted:

To save the life of the woman	Yes
To preserve physical health	No
To preserve mental health	No
Rape or incest	No
Foetal impairment	No
Economic or social reasons	No
Available on request	No

Additional requirements:

Information is not readily available.

FERTILITY AND MORTALITY CONTEXT

Government's view on fertility level:	Too high
Government's intervention concerning fertility level:	To lower
Government's policy on contraceptive use:	Direct support provided
Percentage of currently married women using modern contraception (aged 15-49):	..
Total fertility rate (1990-1995):	..
Age-specific fertility rate (per 1,000 women aged 15-19, 1990-1995):	..
Government has expressed particular concern about:	
Morbidity and mortality resulting from induced abortion	..
Complications of child-bearing and childbirth	..
Maternal mortality rate (per 100,000 live births):	
National	..
Oceania (around 1988)	600
Female life expectancy at birth (1990-1995):	..

Kiribati

BACKGROUND

According to the Penal Code of Kiribati, it is a felony to cause the death of a child before it has an existence independent of the mother, except when the act is done in good faith to preserve the life of the mother. Thus, induced abortion is generally illegal.

The goal of the Government of Kiribati is to reduce the fertility level in order to lower population growth and to improve maternal and child health and family well-being. The Government hopes to achieve a total fertility rate of 2.0 children per woman by the year 2000. Most methods of family planning are available. However, as there are no pharmacies in Kiribati, contraceptives are distributed only by prescription through government hospitals and clinics. A non-governmental agency, the Christian Family Life Centre, provides family planning services that emphasize "natural family planning". The law prohibiting the advertisement and sale of contraceptives has not been repealed.

INCIDENCE OF ABORTION

Place	Year	Measurement	Coverage

Information not readily available.

Source: The Population Policy Data Bank maintained by the Population Division of the Department for Economic and Social Information and Policy Analysis of the United Nations Secretariat. For additional sources, see list of references.

ABORTION POLICY

Grounds on which abortion is permitted:

To save the life of the woman	Yes
To preserve physical health	Yes
To preserve mental health	Yes
Rape or incest	No
Foetal impairment	Yes
Economic or social reasons	No
Available on request	No

Additional requirements:

Except in urgent cases, an abortion may be performed only in public hospitals after a medical committee, composed of three specialists under the chairmanship of a specialist in gynaecology and obstetrics, has processed the application. An abortion is allowed if it is established that the child if born will suffer from a grave and incurable physical or mental deficiency. The consent of both the woman and her husband must be obtained. The hospital director must be notified before the abortion is performed.

FERTILITY AND MORTALITY CONTEXT

Government's view on fertility level:	Satisfactory
Government's intervention concerning fertility level:	To raise
Government's policy on contraceptive use:	No support provided
Percentage of currently married women using modern contraception (aged <50, 1987):	27
Total fertility rate (1990-1995):	3.7
Age-specific fertility rate (per 1,000 women aged 15-19, 1990-1995):	49
Government has expressed particular concern about:	
Morbidity and mortality resulting from induced abortion	No
Complications of child-bearing and childbirth	No
Maternal mortality rate (per 100,000 live births):	
National (1987)	2
Western Asia (around 1988)	280
Female life expectancy at birth (1990-1995):	77.5

Kuwait

The Criminal Code of Kuwait (Law No. 46 of 23 November 1960) generally prohibited abortion, although it provided that abortion was legal if performed by an obstetrician and not by a general physician, in order to save the life of the mother. With the enactment of article 12 of Law No. 25 of 1981, Kuwait became one of the first countries in the region to permit abortion during the first four months of pregnancy on less restrictive grounds. Abortion is currently permitted if the continuation of the pregnancy would place the health of the mother in serious danger or if there is proof that the foetus will be born with a serious physical malformation or mental deficiency which cannot be expected to be cured.

Ministerial Decree No. 55 of 1984 was issued to implement the law of 1981. It requires that, except in urgent cases, an abortion must be performed in a government hospital which has a gynaecology and obstetrics department. If the woman is not already at the government hospital nearest her usual residence, she should be referred to it and should bring a detailed report of her case and the reasons for the requested abortion. In the event that the woman cannot be transferred to the nearest government hospital without endangering her life, an abortion may be performed in a private hospital which is approved by the Ministry of Public Health.

The abortion must be approved by a medical commission consisting of three specialized physicians under the chair of a specialist in gynaecology and obstetrics who is at least a departmental head. The decision of the committee must be unanimous. An ordinance issued by the Minister of Public Health sets forth the conditions to be fulfilled by the medical commission and the formal procedures to be observed with respect to the operation. The hospital director must be notified before the abortion is performed. The consent of the pregnant woman and her husband, or of any person standing *in loco parentis* in the absence of the latter, is required. This foregoing procedure does not apply to cases of inevitable, incomplete, septic or retarded abortions, or to cases of extra-uterine or ovarian pregnancy.

According to Law No. 46 of 23 November 1960, any person performing an abortion is subject to imprisonment for up to 10 years, and/or a fine. Physicians, pharmacists and midwives that commit the offence are liable to harsher penalties. A woman wilfully inducing her own miscarriage is subject to imprisonment for up to five years and a fine. Any person that supplies instruments for abortion, knowing that they will be used for that purpose, is subject to imprisonment for up to three years and a fine.

Although Ministerial Decree No. 55 of 1984 requires that the Ministry of Public Health be notified in all abortion cases, no comprehensive data on the incidence of abortion and on mortality due to abortion are readily available. One study reports that between 1969 and 1980, there were 49,066 abortions recorded in the maternity hospital. Another study, conducted to review abortion cases in the special abortion ward of the Kuwait Maternity Hospital during the period 1973-1977, found that the incidence of accidental uterine perforation was extremely low among the abortion cases admitted to the hospital and that the maternal mortality rate related to abortion was much lower than that for delivery cases.

The Government does not consider the level of induced abortion and complications associated with induced abortion to be a matter of concern. It is generally recognized that maternal mortality in Kuwait is among the lowest in the world, and maternal mortality associated with abortion is negligible.

There is no active family planning programme in Kuwait. The Government provides incentives for child-bearing among Kuwaiti nationals. However, access to contraceptive methods is permitted. In practice, contraceptives and family planning advice are available in the free government health clinics.

INCIDENCE OF ABORTION

Place	Year	Measurement	Coverage
National	1969-1973	23.9 abortions/100 live births	HR
National	1973-1977	20.0 abortions/100 deliveries	HR

Note: PR = provider registration; SP = survey provider; SW = survey of women; HR = hospital admission records. For a detailed description of these abbreviations and information on sources of the data, see technical notes in the annex.

Source: The Population Policy Data Bank maintained by the Population Division of the Department for Economic and Social Information and Policy Analysis of the United Nations Secretariat. For additional sources, see list of references.

Kyrgyzstan

ABORTION POLICY

Grounds on which abortion is permitted:

To save the life of the woman	Yes
To preserve physical health	Yes
To preserve mental health	Yes
Rape or incest	Yes
Foetal impairment	Yes
Economic or social reasons	Yes
Available on request	Yes

Additional requirements:

An abortion requires the consent of the pregnant woman; it is authorized if performed by a licensed physician in a hospital or other recognized medical institution. Abortion is available on request during the first 12 weeks of gestation. Thereafter, induced abortion is available within 28 weeks from conception on judicial, genetic, vital, broad medical and social grounds, as well as for personal reasons if authorized by a commission of local physicians.

FERTILITY AND MORTALITY CONTEXT

Government's view on fertility level:	Satisfactory
Government's intervention concerning fertility level:	To maintain
Government's policy on contraceptive use:	Direct support provided
Percentage of currently married women using modern contraception (aged 15-49, 1990):	25
Total fertility rate (1985-1990):	4.0
Age-specific fertility rate (per 1,000 women aged 15-19, 1985-1990):	41
Government has expressed particular concern about:	
Morbidity and mortality resulting from induced abortion	Yes
Complications of child-bearing and childbirth	Yes
Maternal mortality rate (per 100,000 live births):	
National (1990)	52.9
Developed countries (around 1988)	26
Female life expectancy at birth (1985-1990):	71.8

BACKGROUND

As was the case with all of the former Soviet republics, Kyrgyzstan, known prior to 1992 as the Kirgizian Soviet Socialist Republic, was subject to the abortion legislation and regulations of the former Union of Soviet Socialist Republics. As a result, abortion practices in Kyrgyzstan were similar to those throughout the former USSR.

The description given below pertains to the situation in Kyrgyzstan prior to independence.

The Soviet law of 27 June 1936 prohibited induced abortion in most circumstances, permitting it only for eugenic reasons. Physicians and non-medical personnel that performed abortions in hospitals or as part of an out-patient service were subject to a maximum of three years in prison. A husband, relative or physician who pressured a woman into having an abortion could be sentenced to a maximum of two years in prison. The pregnant woman could be prosecuted by public trial and/or be required to pay a large fine.

In a decree of 23 November 1955, the Soviet Government repealed the prohibition of abortion. Regulations issued in 1956 and subsequently in 1982 specified that abortions could be performed during the first 12 weeks of gestation, although not less than six months after a woman's previous abortion. An abortion was considered illegal if not performed in a hospital or if the person performing the abortion did not have an advanced medical education. The maximum penalty for an illegal abortion was set at eight years in a labour camp.

In 1974, the Ministry of Public Health of the USSR published a document entitled "On the side-effects and complications of oral contraceptives", in which the mass use of oral contraception was de facto prohibited. On 5 June 1987, in Order No. 757, the Ministry of Public Health legalized and officially permitted the provision of early vacuum aspirations in any clinic regardless of the place of residence of the woman. Vacuum aspiration had been the method of induced abortion provided during the first 20 days of pregnancy with the obligatory diagnosis of pregnancy.

During the 1980s, the Ministry of Public Health continued its efforts to decrease the number of illegal abortions by formally broadening the grounds on which abortions were legal and increasing their availability. Most of the later changes were not followed by a simultaneous increase in actual de facto accessibility of abortion services. On 31 December 1987, the Ministry of Public Health published Order No. 1342, which permits induced abortion during the first 28 weeks of gestation on judicial, genetic, broad medical and social grounds (for example, more than five children in the family), as well as on demand with the special authorization of a commission of local physicians.

The high incidence of abortion has been attributed to a number of factors, including shortages of high-quality modern contraceptives and reliance upon less reliable traditional methods, a lack of knowledge among couples of contraception and of the detrimental health consequences of frequent abortions and the absence of adequate training for physicians, nurses, teachers and other specialists. In 1989, the availability of condoms in the entire former Soviet Union amounted to only 11 per cent of demand; intra-uterine devices, 30 per cent; and pills, 2 per cent. Data from the All-Union sample survey of contraceptive use conducted in 1990 indicate that in Kyrgyzstan, 24.6 per cent of all women aged 15-49 years regularly used contraception, 6 per cent sometimes used contraception, 51.3 per cent did not use any contraceptive method and 13 per cent knew nothing about contraception. Sample survey data for 1988 show that in the city of Frunze (now Bishkek), of every 100 contraceptive users, 40 per cent used condoms, 16 per cent used the vaginal douche method, 15 per cent used spermicides and 10 per cent practised coitus interruptus.

In 1989, a total of 87,212 induced abortions were registered in Kyrgyzstan, giving an abortion rate of 86.5 per 1,000 women aged 15-49 years, one of the highest rates in the former Soviet Union. The actual figure is much higher because this total does not include most abortions performed in departmental health

Kyrgyzstan

services and commercial clinics, early vacuum aspirations and self-induced abortions. In 1988, 2.8 per cent of all induced abortions were performed on primigravidae, and 28 per cent of all induced abortions were vacuum aspirations. In 1989, illegal abortions, calculated on the basis of their registered complications, accounted for 26.4 per cent of all abortions and 40 per cent of all abortions among primigravidae. Among women under age 17, they accounted for 15 per cent of all induced abortions.

Maternal mortality rates in Kyrgyzstan were 49.4 and 53.8 per 100,000 births in 1980 and 1988, respectively, one of the highest rates in the former Soviet Union; in 1988, 10 per cent of all maternal deaths were due to criminal abortion.

INCIDENCE OF ABORTION

Place	Year	Measurement	Coverage
National	1970	102.5 abortions/1,000 women aged 15-49	PR
National	1975	84.1 abortions/1,000 women aged 15-49	PR
National	1980	76.6 abortions/1,000 women aged 15-49	PR
National	1985	73.8 abortions/1,000 women aged 15-49	PR
National	1988	80.3 abortions/1,000 women aged 15-49	PR
National	1989	86.5 abortions/1,000 women aged 15-49	PR
National	1990	76.3 abortions/1,000 women aged 15-49	PR

Note: PR = provider registration; SP = survey provider; SW = survey of women; HR = hospital admission records. For a detailed description of these abbreviations and information on sources of the data, see technical notes in the annex.

Source: Population Policy Data Bank maintained by the Population Division of the Department for Economic and Social Information and Policy Analysis of the United Nations Secretariat. For additional sources, see list of references.

ABORTION POLICY

Grounds on which abortion is permitted:

To save the life of the woman	Yes
To preserve physical health	No
To preserve mental health	No
Rape or incest	No
Foetal impairment	No
Economic or social reasons	No
Available on request	No

Additional requirements:

Special approval from the Ministry of Health is required.

FERTILITY AND MORTALITY CONTEXT

Government's view on fertility level:	Satisfactory
Government's intervention concerning fertility level:	No intervention
Government's policy on contraceptive use:	Indirect support provided
Percentage of currently married women using modern contraception (aged 15-49):	..
Total fertility rate (1990-1995):	6.7
Age-specific fertility rate (per 1,000 women aged 15-19, 1990-1995):	51

Government has expressed particular concern about:
Morbidity and mortality resulting from induced abortion ..
Complications of child-bearing and childbirth Yes

Maternal mortality rate (per 100,000 live births):
National (1991) 300
South-eastern Asia (around 1988) 340

Female life expectancy at birth (1990-1995): 52.5

Lao People's Democratic Republic

The Criminal Code of the Lao People's Democratic Republic is the Law of 21 November 1922, which was extensively amended by Law-ordinance No. 237 of 12 August 1965. Under this law, abortion is illegal, except when the life of the mother is endangered by the pregnancy. Abortion is reportedly punishable by imprisonment for a period of 5-10 years.

Due to substantial emigration and low population density, the Government of the Lao People's Democratic Republic had pursued a pronatalist population stance. However, the Five-Year Development Plan for the period 1991-1995, promulgated by the Fifth Party Congress in March 1991, recognizes that demographic growth must be compatible with economic development in order to improve people's well-being and emphasizes the need for comprehensive public-health services, including maternal and child health (MCH) and birth-spacing services. The Plan also recognizes that large families can have a negative impact on the health of women and children and can impair women's contribution to economic development.

In 1988, the Government endorsed birth-spacing as a means of improving maternal and child health and subsequently legalized the sale and distribution of contraceptives. In 1990, the Ministry of Public Health began to provide birth-spacing services on a very limited basis in the MCH units of two main hospitals at Vientiane and in one or two MCH units in the provinces, in order to improve maternal and child health and to discourage illegal abortions. These services, however, are operating at a very low level and offer only a limited range of contraceptives. Contraceptives are available through commercial outlets to those who can afford them, particularly in the capital. Data on contraceptive prevalence and knowledge do not exist except for one very limited Knowledge, Attitude and Practice (KAP) survey undertaken in a relatively prosperous section of Vientiane, where three quarters of those interviewed did not know of a single method of contraception. Anecdotal evidence and the high level of fertility suggest that contraceptive prevalence is likely to be well below 10 per cent. There have been no qualitative studies on issues relating to reproductive health and birth-spacing practices. It is believed that there is an unmet demand for birth-spacing services, as evidenced by the high incidence of complications following induced abortion and the frequent requests for sterilization at hospitals.

Information on mortality is not readily available in the Lao People's Democratic Republic. However, there is general recognition that the health conditions and mortality levels, including maternal mortality, are highly unfavourable. The reduction of mortality through the provision of maternal and child health care throughout the country is a priority on the Government's agenda.

INCIDENCE OF ABORTION

Place	Year	Measurement	Coverage

Information not readily available.

Source: The Population Policy Data Bank maintained by the Population Division of the Department for Economic and Social Information and Policy Analysis of the United Nations Secretariat. For additional sources, see list of references.

ABORTION POLICY

Grounds on which abortion is permitted:

To save the life of the woman	Yes
To preserve physical health	Yes
To preserve mental health	Yes
Rape or incest	Yes
Foetal impairment	Yes
Economic or social reasons	Yes
Available on request	Yes

Additional requirements:

The abortion must be performed in a hospital or other authorized health-care facility. After the first trimester of pregnancy, special authorization is required for an abortion.

FERTILITY AND MORTALITY CONTEXT

Government's view on fertility level:	Too low
Government's intervention concerning fertility level:	To raise
Government's policy on contraceptive use:	Direct support provided
Percentage of currently married women using modern contraception (aged 15-49, 1990):	19
Total fertility rate (1990-1995):	2.0
Age-specific fertility rate (per 1,000 women aged 15-19, 1990-1995):	43
Government has expressed particular concern about:	
Morbidity and mortality resulting from induced abortion	Yes
Complications of child-bearing and childbirth	Yes
Maternal mortality rate (per 100,000 live births):	
National (1990)	23.7
Developed countries (around 1988)	26
Female life expectancy at birth (1990-1995):	75.7

Latvia

As was the case with all of the former Soviet republics, Latvia, known prior to 1992 as the Latvian Soviet Socialist Republic, was subject to the abortion legislation and regulations of the former Union of Soviet Socialist Republics. As a result, abortion practices in Latvia were similar to those throughout the former USSR.

The description given below pertains to the situation in Latvia prior to independence.

The Soviet law of 27 June 1936 prohibited induced abortion in most circumstances, permitting it only for eugenic reasons. Physicians and non-medical personnel that performed abortions in hospitals or as part of an out-patient service were subject to a maximum of three years in prison. A husband, relative or physician who pressured a woman into having an abortion could be sentenced to a maximum of two years in prison. The pregnant woman could be prosecuted by public trial and/or be required to pay a large fine.

In a decree of 23 November 1955, the Soviet Government repealed the prohibition of abortion. Regulations issued in 1956 and subsequently in 1982 specified that abortions could be performed during the first 12 weeks of gestation, although not less than six months after a woman's previous abortion. An abortion was considered illegal if not performed in a hospital or if the person performing the abortion did not have an advanced medical education. The maximum penalty for an illegal abortion was set at eight years in a labour camp.

In 1974, the Ministry of Public Health of the USSR published a document entitled "On the side-effects and complications of oral contraceptives", in which the mass use of oral contraception was de facto prohibited. On 5 June 1987, in Order No. 757, the Ministry of Public Health legalized and officially permitted the provision of early vacuum aspirations in any clinic regardless of the place of residence of the woman. Vacuum aspiration had been the method of induced abortion provided during the first 20 days of pregnancy with the obligatory diagnosis of pregnancy.

During the 1980s, the Ministry of Public Health continued its efforts to decrease the number of illegal abortions by formally broadening the grounds on which abortions were legal and increasing their availability. Most of the later changes were not followed by a simultaneous increase in actual de facto accessibility of abortion services. On 31 December 1987, the Ministry of Public Health published Order No. 1342, which permits the provision of induced abortion during the first 28 weeks of gestation on judicial, genetic, broad medical and social grounds (for example, more than five children in the family), as well as on demand with the special authorization of a commission of local physicians.

The high incidence of abortion has been attributed to a number of factors, including shortages of high-quality modern contraceptives and reliance upon less reliable traditional methods, a lack of knowledge among couples of contraception and of the detrimental health consequences of frequent abortions and the absence of adequate training for physicians, nurses, teachers and other specialists. In 1989, the availability of condoms in the entire former Soviet Union amounted to only 11 per cent of demand; intra-uterine devices (IUDs), 30 per cent; and pills, 2 per cent of demand. Data from the All-Union sample survey of contraceptive use conducted in 1990 indicate that in Latvia, 18.6 per cent of all women aged 15-49 regularly used contraception, 12.9 per cent sometimes used contraception, 57.8 per cent did not use any contraception at all and 5.1 per cent knew nothing about contraception.

In 1989, a total of 48,957 induced abortions were registered in Latvia, giving an abortion rate of 75.0 per 1,000 women aged 15-49 years, in the medium range among the former Soviet republics. The actual figure is much higher, because this total does not include most abortions performed in departmental health services and commercial clinics, early vacuum aspirations and self-induced abortions. In 1988, 7.1 per cent of all induced abortions were performed on primigravidae, and almost none were performed on women under age 17; of the total, 1.6 per cent were done by early vacuum aspiration. In 1989, illegal abortions, calculated on the basis of their registered complications, accounted for 13.9 per cent of all abortions and 23.9 per cent of all abortions among primigravidae. Among women under age 17, they accounted for 23.4 per cent of all induced abortions, and up to 100 per cent of all causes of deaths from all abortions.

Maternal mortality rates in Latvia were 25.3 and 29.1 per 100,000 births in 1980 and 1988, respectively, one of the lowest rates in the former Soviet Union; in 1988, 25 per cent of all maternal deaths were due to criminal abortion.

Population issues have been given increasing attention in Latvia since 1976 when, for the first time in the USSR, a Council for dealing with population problems was established at the republic level. The programme, entitled "The population of Latvia in 1986-2000", was a constituent part of the Latvian economic and social development plan for that period. The intent of the programme was, among other things, to reach replacement-level fertility. The Government increased its assistance and grants to families with children and enhanced the prestige of parenthood and the family. As a result, during the 1980s, the rate of natural increase rose significantly—from 1 per 1,000 in 1979 to 4 per 1,000 during the period 1983-1989. During the period 1989-1991, however, due to the economic and political crisis related to the independence process, there was again a decline in fertility, as well as a deterioration of health conditions. In addition, the crisis had a negative effect on the various population programmes in Latvia, which were not able to function normally during that period.

The new Government, concerned about the decline in fertility, has established several programmes to improve health and social indicators. One such programme, "Population of Latvia", is directly related to population issues and is intended to encourage a higher birth rate.

INCIDENCE OF ABORTION

Place	Year	Measurement	Coverage
National	1975	91.4 abortions/1,000 women aged 15-49	PR
National	1980	92.5 abortions/1,000 women aged 15-49	PR
National	1985	88.7 abortions/1,000 women aged 15-49	PR
National	1988	83.3 abortions/1,000 women aged 15-49	PR
National	1989	75.0 abortions/1,000 women aged 15-49	PR
National	1990	70.0 abortions/1,000 women aged 15-49	PR

Note: PR = provider registration; SP = survey of provider; SW = survey of women; HR = hospital admission records; C = complete; I = incomplete. For a detailed description of these abbreviations and information on sources of the data, see technical notes in the annex.

Source: Population Policy Data Bank maintained by the Population Division of the Department for Economic and Social Information and Policy Analysis of the United Nations Secretariat. For additional sources, see list of references.

Lebanon

Grounds on which abortion is permitted:

To save the life of the woman	Yes
To preserve physical health	No
To preserve mental health	No
Rape or incest	No
Foetal impairment	No
Economic or social reasons	No
Available on request	No

Additional requirements:

Before an abortion can be performed to save the life of a woman, it must be certified by two physicians, in addition to the one performing the abortion. The consent of the woman is required before an abortion can be performed, except when her life is in danger and she is unconscious or unable to give the required consent.

FERTILITY AND MORTALITY CONTEXT

Government's view on fertility level:	Satisfactory
Government's intervention concerning fertility level:	No intervention
Government's policy on contraceptive use:	Direct support provided
Percentage of currently married women using modern contraception (aged 15-49, 1971):	23
Total fertility rate (1990-1995):	3.1
Age-specific fertility rate (per 1,000 women aged 15-19, 1990-1995):	44
Government has expressed particular concern about: Morbidity and mortality resulting from induced abortion	..
Complications of child-bearing and childbirth	..
Maternal mortality rate (per 100,000 live births): National	..
Western Asia (around 1988)	280
Female life expectancy at birth (1990-1995):	70.5

102

BACKGROUND

Articles 539-546 of the Penal Code of 1 March 1943 (put into effect on 1 October 1943) made abortion illegal in Lebanon in all circumstances. The provision of information for the purpose of propagating or facilitating abortion could be punished by imprisonment for from two months to two years and a fine. The same penalties could be imposed on a person selling, displaying or holding for the purpose of selling those objects which could produce an abortion. Abortion with consent or self-induced abortion by the pregnant woman was punishable by imprisonment for from six months to three years. A longer sentence was imposed if a death occurred. Abortion performed without consent was punishable by a prison term of at least five years; if death resulted, the term was increased to not less than 10 years. These penalties were applied even if the woman was not pregnant when subjected to the abortive practice. A person performing an abortion to save the honour of a descendant or relative to the second degree, as well as a woman inducing her own abortion to save her honour, was subject to a reduced penalty. Physicians, surgeons, midwives, chemists, pharmacists or their employees performing an abortion were subject to harsher penalties. In addition, persons performing an abortion could be prohibited from practising their profession or activity, and the place of business could also be closed.

Presidential Decree (No. 13187) of 20 October 1969, although once again affirming that abortion is illegal, permits an abortion when it is the only means of saving the life of the pregnant woman. The consent of the woman is required before the intervention is performed, except when she is in a very dangerous condition and unconscious. In the latter case, when an abortion is necessary to save the life of the pregnant woman, the physician is allowed to perform the abortion in spite of the opposition of her husband or relatives. Under the Decree, the attending physician or surgeon is required to consult two physicians, who must jointly give their approval by signing, after medical examination and consultation, four copies of a statement to the effect that it is possible to save the life of the mother only through abortion. A record containing a statement of the facts, excluding the name of the patient, must be sent to the President of the Physician's Association.

No national statistics on the incidence of induced abortion in Lebanon are readily available. Some earlier studies based on hospital records conducted in the early 1970s, however, show that the most important cause of maternal death in Lebanon was complications resulting from induced abortion, including infection, haemorrhage, perforation of the uterus and acute renal failure.

The Government of Lebanon acknowledges that major population problems associated with large families and inadequate spacing of births exist among certain subgroups of the population but, in general, considers population growth to be satisfactory. Non-governmental family planning services have largely been offered by the Lebanon Family Planning Association. Since the late 1970s, the Government has become increasingly involved in providing direct support to family planning services. In 1979, the Municipality of Beirut signed an agreement with the Lebanon Family Planning Association to integrate the activities of the voluntary organization into local government programmes. Under this agreement, the Association provides its services as an integral part of the overall family welfare services rendered by the municipal centres and the municipality provides some financial support to the Association.

In 1983, an amendment to the Penal Code of 1 March 1943 repealed articles 537 and 538. These two articles, which were based on the French anticontraception law of 1920, prohibited the use of contraceptives. In the same year, the Ministry of Health made a decision to allocate funds for family planning services, including sterilization, which is not regulated by state law. Prior to that time, the Penal Code had prohibited, under penalties of imprisonment and a fine, advertising or publishing any information about contraceptives, as well as the sale of contraceptives. In practice, however, there existed an almost uncontrolled trade in contraceptives in Lebanon. Several types of contraceptives were designated as pharmaceuticals and were commonly sold in pharmacies without prescription. Pills were also distributed free of charge by the Family Planning Association at its headquarters and clinics. The initial permission for the Family Planning

Lebanon

Association to import contraceptives was obtained from the Minister of Health in 1969, who granted the Association an exception to import 25,000 boxes of the contraceptive Eugynon, which was provided on a complimentary basis by the International Planned Parenthood Federation, on the condition that it would be distributed free of charge by the Association clinics. The Family Planning Association requested the special approval on the grounds that the pill would be used "for the regulation of the menstrual cycle of women". Since then, the Ministry of Health has approved the importation of all types of contraceptive pills, classifying them as pharmaceuticals rather than as contraceptives.

A Ministerial Decision of the Minister of Health and Social Affairs of 19 January 1984 established the National Population Council of Lebanon. This decision marked an attempt by the Government to monitor population trends and their impact on development and to motivate the general public to become aware of population issues. However, the continuing regional and internal conflicts in Lebanon have hindered family planning efforts both by the Government and by the voluntary family planning organizations.

INCIDENCE OF ABORTION

Place	Year	Measurement	Coverage

Information not readily available.

Source: The Population Policy Data Bank maintained by the Population Division of the Department for Economic and Social Information and Policy Analysis of the United Nations Secretariat. For additional sources, see list of references.

ABORTION POLICY

Grounds on which abortion is permitted:

To save the life of the woman	Yes
To preserve physical health	No
To preserve mental health	No
Rape or incest	No
Foetal impairment	No
Economic or social reasons	No
Available on request	No

Additional requirements:

Information is not readily available.

FERTILITY AND MORTALITY CONTEXT

Government's view on fertility level:	Too high
Government's intervention concerning fertility level:	To lower
Government's policy on contraceptive use:	Direct support provided
Percentage of currently married women using modern contraception (aged 15-49, 1977):	2
Total fertility rate (1990-1995):	4.7
Age-specific fertility rate (per 1,000 women aged 15-19, 1990-1995):	80
Government has expressed particular concern about:	
Morbidity and mortality resulting from induced abortion	Yes
Complications of child-bearing and childbirth	Yes
Maternal mortality rate (per 100,000 live births):	
National (1973)	1,600
Southern Africa (around 1988)	270
Female life expectancy at birth (1990-1995):	63.0

Lesotho

There is no statutory abortion law in Lesotho. Instead, abortion is a matter of common law, which was patterned after Roman-Dutch law. Under this law, abortion is prohibited except when performed to save the life of the pregnant woman. The Regulation of Advertisements Proclamation of 1953 (No. 60, section 3) prohibits the advertisement of items that could be used to procure an abortion. However, the Proclamation excludes from criminal liability those persons publishing advertisements in technical journals circulated among medical practitioners, chemists, pharmacists and hospital managers. No details exist about the penalties for transgressing the law nor are any procedural requirements available.

Although abortion figures are not readily available in Lesotho, a study conducted in 1981 by the Faculty of Law of the University of Lesotho indicates that abortion is a common phenomenon. The report documents the fact that Basotho women frequently request an abortion from medical personnel and that some women seek a clandestine abortion in neighbouring South Africa. The study also provides criminal statistics from the Office of Commissioner of Police which suggest that self-induced and other illegal abortions are frequently reported to the police and that some cases have been subject to prosecution. Despite the recognition that abortion is a serious health issue in Lesotho, a National Symposium held at Maseru in 1974 and a national survey conducted between 1978 and 1979 found that the majority of the Basotho people did not wish to liberalize the abortion law. The general view has been that unwanted pregnancies should be prevented through contraception rather than abortion.

The Government of Lesotho views population growth as a potential constraint to development because of the scarce resources of the country and an economy that is heavily dependent upon remittances from migrant workers in South Africa. In the Fourth Five-Year Development Plan (1986/87-1990/91) the Government indicated that its objective was to decrease the population growth rate from 2.6 to 2 per cent per annum and to increase the contraceptive prevalence rate from less than 10 to 25 per cent by the year 2000. The Government has taken several measures to achieve these demographic goals. In 1987, it established the Population and Manpower Division within the Ministry of Planning, Economic and Manpower Development to conduct and coordinate population research, to create awareness of the impact of population growth on social and economic well-being and to help formulate a comprehensive population policy.

Family planning services in Lesotho are primarily provided by the Ministry of Health, the Private Health Association of Lesotho and the Lesotho Planned Parenthood Association. Although the Government has indicated its desire to reduce the population growth rate and has initiated some important programme activities, these activities have been limited by a shortage of contraceptives, the unwillingness of church-funded programmes to provide methods of family planning other than natural methods, inadequate personnel and training, poor communication and cultural factors limiting the adoption of a small family norm.

INCIDENCE OF ABORTION

Place	Year	Measurement	Coverage

Information not readily available.

Source: The Population Policy Data Bank maintained by the Population Division of the Department for Economic and Social Information and Policy Analysis of the United Nations Secretariat. For additional sources, see list of references.

ABORTION POLICY

Grounds on which abortion is permitted:

To save the life of the woman	Yes
To preserve physical health	Yes
To preserve mental health	Yes
Rape or incest	Yes
Foetal impairment	Yes
Economic or social reasons	No
Available on request	No

Additional requirements:

No abortion can be performed unless two physicians, one of whom may be the physician performing the abortion, certify to the circumstances that justify the intervention. Certificates from the two physicians must be submitted to the hospital where the procedure will be performed or to the Minister of Health if the abortion is not to be performed in a hospital. If the pregnancy resulted from rape or incest, the certificates must also be submitted to the County Attorney or the police before the abortion is performed. Failure to comply with any of these requirements gives rise to the presumption that the abortion is unjustified.

FERTILITY AND MORTALITY CONTEXT

Government's view on fertility level:	Too high
Government's intervention concerning fertility level:	To lower
Government's policy on contraceptive use:	Direct support provided
Percentage of currently married women using modern contraception (aged 15-49, 1986):	5
Total fertility rate (1990-1995):	6.8
Age-specific fertility rate (per 1,000 women aged 15-19, 1990-1995):	230
Government has expressed particular concern about:	
Morbidity and mortality resulting from induced abortion	Yes
Complications of child-bearing and childbirth	Yes
Maternal mortality rate (per 100,000 live births):	
National	..
Western Africa (around 1988)	760
Female life expectancy at birth (1990-1995):	57.0

Liberia

The Liberian Penal Law of 1979 (section 16.3) provides that abortion is prohibited except when continuation of the pregnancy would gravely impair the physical or mental health of the mother, or if it is believed that the child would be born with severe physical or mental defects or that the pregnancy resulted from rape, incest or other felonious intercourse. Intercourse with a girl under 16 years of age is deemed felonious for the purpose of the law.

Two physicians, one of whom may be the physician performing the abortion, must certify in writing as to the circumstances that justify the procedure. Certificates from the two physicians must be submitted in advance to the hospital where the abortion is to be performed or to the Minister of Health if the abortion is not to be performed in a hospital. The certificates must also be submitted to the County Attorney or the police if the pregnancy resulted from felonious intercourse. Failure to comply with any of these requirements gives rise to the presumption that the abortion was unjustified.

There are various penalties for failing to comply with the law. Any person performing an illegal abortion commits a felony of the third degree or a felony of the second degree if the pregnancy exceeds 24 weeks. A woman whose pregnancy exceeds 24 weeks commits a felony of the third degree if she purposely induces her own abortion, or if she uses instruments, drugs or violence upon herself for the purpose of inducing an abortion. A person that assists a woman to use instruments, drugs or violence upon herself for the purpose of inducing her own abortion commits a felony of the third degree regardless of whether the pregnancy exceeds 24 weeks. If, by representing that the purpose is to perform an abortion, a person performs an act designed to cause abortion even though the woman is not pregnant or the abortionist does not believe she is pregnant, that person is considered to have committed a felony of the third degree. The law further provides that these regulations do not apply to the prescription, administration or distribution of drugs or other substances for avoiding pregnancy, whether by preventing implantation of a fertilized ovum or by any other method that operates before, at or immediately after fertilization.

The Government of Liberia has expressed concern about the high incidence of illegal abortion. The Government has explicitly stated that the reduction of illegal abortion is one of the major goals of the family planning programme. Illegal abortions are particularly common among urban adolescent women. A survey conducted at Monrovia in 1984, among young women aged 14-21 years, found that over 50 per cent of students and 20 per cent of non-students that had ever been pregnant had had an induced abortion.

Family planning services are operated by the Ministry of Health and Social Welfare and the Family Planning Association of Liberia. Access to contraception is permitted to adolescents regardless of marital status. The Government's target is to provide contraceptives by the year 2000 to all couples and individuals desiring to use them. Contraceptive use is currently very low in Liberia. In 1986, the Liberia Demographic and Health Survey found that only 6 per cent of women of reproductive age were using modern methods of contraception.

INCIDENCE OF ABORTION

Place	Year	Measurement	Coverage

Information not readily available.

Source: The Population Policy Data Bank maintained by the Population Division of the Department for Economic and Social Information and Policy Analysis of the United Nations Secretariat. For additional sources, see list of references.

Libyan Arab Jamahiriya

ABORTION POLICY

Grounds on which abortion is permitted:

To save the life of the woman	Yes
To preserve physical health	No
To preserve mental health	No
Rape or incest	No
Foetal impairment	No
Economic or social reasons	No
Available on request	No

Additional requirements:

A physician that considers that continuation of the pregnancy would endanger the woman's life must submit the case to another specialist in gynaecology and obstetrics. If both physicians are in agreement, they must prepare a formal report, which includes the consent of the pregnant woman or that of her legal representative if she is a minor.

FERTILITY AND MORTALITY CONTEXT

Government's view on fertility level:	Satisfactory
Government's intervention concerning fertility level:	No intervention
Government's policy on contraceptive use:	No support provided
Percentage of currently married women using modern contraception (aged 15-49):	..
Total fertility rate (1990-1995):	6.4
Age-specific fertility rate (per 1,000 women aged 15-19, 1990-1995):	110
Government has expressed particular concern about:	
Morbidity and mortality resulting from induced abortion	..
Complications of child-bearing and childbirth	..
Maternal mortality rate (per 100,000 live births):	
National (1978)	80
Northern Africa (around 1988)	360
Female life expectancy at birth (1990-1995):	65.0

BACKGROUND

Abortion is generally illegal in the Libyan Arab Jamahiriya under the Penal Code of 1953. Any person causing an abortion is subject to imprisonment for at least six months. A woman who induces her own miscarriage is liable to the same penalty. However, the Health Law of 13 December 1973 (No. 166), although stating that a physician shall refrain from prescribing any abortifacient substances and shall not in any circumstances perform an abortion, asserts that a specialist in gynaecology may perform an abortion if the specialist believes on technical grounds that the abortion is necessary to safeguard the life of the pregnant woman. In those cases, the physician must obtain an opinion of a specialist in gynaecology and obstetrics approving the abortion. The pregnant woman, or her legal representative if she is a minor, must consent to the intervention.

Since the discovery of oil in the 1950s, the Government has used its substantial oil revenues to improve socio-economic conditions. The Libyan Arab Jamahiriya has made significant progress in expanding health and educational facilities. The decline in mortality coupled with continuing high fertility has produced high population growth rates. Nevertheless, the country has found it necessary to import foreign labour to satisfy the labour demands of the economy. The labour shortages in the Libyan Arab Jamahiriya have been aggravated by low female participation rates.

Although the Government provides child allowances, free education, health care, subsidized housing and social security, and supports maternal and child health programmes, family planning does not receive official governmental support. The importation of modern contraceptives was still illegal and the sale of contraceptives prohibited until the mid 1980s. The desire to plan fertility is increasing and couples are in the process of changing their reproductive behaviour, paralleling the rise in women's education. As a result of the increase in demand, contraceptive services are available in the private sector.

INCIDENCE OF ABORTION

Place	Year	Measurement	Coverage

Information not readily available.

Source: The Population Policy Data Bank maintained by the Population Division of the Department for Economic and Social Information and Policy Analysis of the United Nations Secretariat. For additional sources, see list of references.

Liechtenstein

ABORTION POLICY

Grounds on which abortion is permitted:

To save the life of the woman	Yes
To preserve physical health	Yes
To preserve mental health	Yes
Rape or incest	No
Foetal impairment	No
Economic or social reasons	No
Available on request	No

Additional requirements:

An induced abortion must be performed by a physician, with the consent of the pregnant woman. The physician must determine that a danger actually exists to the life or the physical or mental health of the pregnant woman.

FERTILITY AND MORTALITY CONTEXT

Government's view on fertility level:	Satisfactory
Government's intervention concerning fertility level:	No intervention
Government's policy on contraceptive use:	No support provided
Percentage of currently married women using modern contraception (aged 15-49):	..
Total fertility rate (1990-1995):	..
Age-specific fertility rate (per 1,000 women aged 15-19, 1990-1995):	..
Government has expressed particular concern about:	
Morbidity and mortality resulting from induced abortion	No
Complications of child-bearing and childbirth	No
Maternal mortality rate (per 100,000 live births):	
National	..
Developed countries (around 1988)	26
Female life expectancy at birth (1990-1995):	..

BACKGROUND

In Liechtenstein, under the legal code of 24 June 1987, the only legal grounds for performing an induced abortion are to preserve the life or the physical or mental health of the pregnant woman. The only other legal ground for performing an abortion is if the pregnant woman has not, at any time, been married to the man who impregnated her and was not fourteen years of age at the time of conception. The induced abortion must be performed by a physician with the consent of the woman. The physician must determine that a danger to the pregnant woman's life or to her physical or mental health actually exists. If the abortion is performed without the consent of the woman, the physician can be imprisoned for up to three years; and should the procedure lead to her death, the physician can be imprisoned for six months to five years. However, in circumstances where it is impossible to obtain the consent of the woman because of imminent danger to her life, the physician is exempt from punishment if the abortion is performed without first obtaining her consent. A woman inducing her own miscarriage can be imprisoned for up to one year. Publicly advertising abortion services is prohibited under the law and is punishable by a prison term of up to one year or a fine.

Liechtenstein, with an estimated population of about 28,000 in 1990, does not pursue any demographic policies intended to modify rates of population growth or fertility. The Government provides neither direct nor indirect support for modern methods of contraception.

INCIDENCE OF ABORTION

Place	Year	Measurement	Coverage

Information not readily available.

Source: The Population Policy Data Bank maintained by the Population Division of the Department for Economic and Social Information and Policy Analysis of the United Nations Secretariat. For additional sources, see list of references.

Lithuania

ABORTION POLICY

Grounds on which abortion is permitted:

To save the life of the woman	Yes
To preserve physical health	Yes
To preserve mental health	Yes
Rape or incest	Yes
Foetal impairment	Yes
Economic or social reasons	Yes
Available on request	Yes

Additional requirements:

The intervention must be performed in a hospital or other authorized health-care facility. After the first trimester of pregnancy, special authorization is required for an abortion.

FERTILITY AND MORTALITY CONTEXT

Government's view on fertility level:	Satisfactory
Government's intervention concerning fertility level:	To raise
Government's policy on contraceptive use:	Direct support provided
Percentage of currently married women using modern contraception (aged 15-49, 1990):	12
Total fertility rate (1990-1995):	2.0
Age-specific fertility rate (per 1,000 women aged 15-19, 1990-1995):	35
Government has expressed particular concern about:	
Morbidity and mortality resulting from induced abortion	Yes
Complications of child-bearing and childbirth	Yes
Maternal mortality rate (per 100,000 live births):	
National (1990)	22.9
Developed countries (around 1988)	26
Female life expectancy at birth (1990-1995):	77.4

As was the case with all of the former Soviet republics, Lithuania, known prior to 1992 as the Lithuanian Soviet Socialist Republic, was subject to the abortion legislation and regulations of the former Union of Soviet Socialist Republics. As a result, abortion practices in Lithuania were similar to those throughout the former USSR.

The description given below pertains to the situation in Lithuania prior to independence.

The Soviet law of 27 June 1936 prohibited induced abortion in most circumstances, permitting it only for eugenic reasons. Physicians and non-medical personnel that performed abortions in hospitals or as part of an out-patient service were subject to a maximum of three years in prison. A husband, relative or physician who pressured a woman into having an abortion could be sentenced to a maximum of two years in prison. The pregnant woman could be prosecuted by public trial and/or be required to pay a large fine.

In a decree of 23 November 1955, the Soviet Government repealed the prohibition of abortion. Regulations issued in 1956 and subsequently in 1982 specified that abortions could be performed during the first 12 weeks of gestation, although not less than six months after a woman's previous abortion. An abortion was considered illegal if not performed in a hospital or if the person performing the abortion did not have an advanced medical education. The maximum penalty for an illegal abortion was set at eight years in a labour camp.

In 1974, the Ministry of Public Health of the USSR published a document entitled "On the side-effects and complications of oral contraceptives", in which the mass use of oral contraception was de facto prohibited. On 5 June 1987, in Order No. 757, the Ministry of Public Health legalized and officially permitted the provision of early vacuum aspirations in any clinic regardless of the place of residence of the woman. Vacuum aspiration had been the method of induced abortion provided during the first 20 days of pregnancy with the obligatory diagnosis of pregnancy.

During the 1980s, the Ministry of Public Health continued its efforts to decrease the number of illegal abortions by formally broadening the grounds on which abortions were legal and increasing their availability. Most of the later changes were not followed by a simultaneous increase in actual de facto accessibility of abortion services. On 31 December 1987, the Ministry of Public Health published Order No. 1342, which permits induced abortion during the first 28 weeks of gestation on judicial, genetic, broad medical and social grounds (for example, more than five children in the family), as well as on demand with the special authorization of a commission of local physicians.

The high incidence of abortion has been attributed to a number of factors, including shortages of high-quality modern contraceptives and reliance upon less reliable traditional methods, a lack of knowledge among couples of contraception and of the detrimental health consequences of frequent abortions and the absence of adequate training for physicians, nurses, teachers and other specialists. In 1989, the availability of condoms in the entire former Soviet Union amounted to only 11 per cent of demand; intra-uterine devices (IUDs), 30 per cent; and pills, 2 per cent. Data from the All-Union sample survey of contraceptive use conducted in 1990 indicate that in Lithuania, 12 per cent of all women aged 15-49 years regularly used contraception, 7.4 per cent sometimes used contraception, 68.7 per cent did not use any contraceptive method and 6.5 per cent knew nothing about contraception.

In 1989, a total of 50,117 induced abortions were registered in Lithuania, giving an abortion rate of 54.3 per 1,000 women aged 15-49 years, in the medium range of rates among the former Soviet republics. The actual figure is much higher, because this total does not include most abortions performed in departmental health services, commercial clinics, early vacuum aspirations and self-induced abortions. In 1988, 12.2 per cent of all induced abortions were performed on primigravidae. No early vacuum aspirations were recorded in 1988. In 1989, illegal abortions, calculated on the basis of their registered complications, accounted for

Lithuania

14.5 per cent of all abortions and 27.3 per cent of all abortions among primigravidae. Among women under age 17, they accounted for 16.6 per cent of all induced abortions. The Government is concerned about the high level of induced abortion and the possibility of restricting abortion was being discussed.

Maternal mortality rates in Lithuania were 27.0 and 19.4 per 100,000 births in 1980 and 1988, respectively, one of the lowest rates in the former Soviet Union. In 1988, 27.3 per cent of all maternal deaths were due to criminal abortion.

Concerned about the decline in total fertility—the total fertility rate for the period 1990-1995 is estimated to be 2.0 births per woman—Lithuania enacted a series of measures in 1989 to help women with children participate in labour-market activities.

INCIDENCE OF ABORTION

Place	Year	Measurement	Coverage
National	1975	53.0 abortions/1,000 women aged 15-49	PR
National	1980	50.9 abortions/1,000 women aged 15-49	PR
National	1985	46.3 abortions/1,000 women aged 15-49	PR
National	1988	59.4 abortions/1,000 women aged 15-49	PR
National	1989	54.3 abortions/1,000 women aged 15-49	PR
National	1990	30.1 abortions/1,000 women aged 15-49	PR

Note: PR = provider registration; SP = survey provider; SW = survey of women; HR = hospital admission records. For a detailed description of these abbreviations and information on sources of the data, see technical notes in the annex.

Source: Population Policy Data Bank maintained by the Population Division of the Department for Economic and Social Information and Policy Analysis of the United Nations Secretariat. For additional sources, see list of references.

ABORTION POLICY

Grounds on which abortion is permitted:

To save the life of the woman	Yes
To preserve physical health	Yes
To preserve mental health	Yes
Rape or incest	Yes
Foetal impairment	Yes
Economic or social reasons	Yes
Available on request	No

Additional requirements:

Certification by a physician other than the one performing the abortion is required for all grounds. The woman must give written agreement. A one-week reflection period is required and the pregnant woman must be given an information booklet in which options other than abortion are explained. An abortion must be performed in a hospital or other approved facility.

FERTILITY AND MORTALITY CONTEXT

Government's view on fertility level:	Too low
Government's intervention concerning fertility level:	To raise
Government's policy on contraceptive use:	No support provided
Percentage of currently married women using modern contraception (aged 15-49):	..
Total fertility rate (1990-1995):	1.6
Age-specific fertility rate (per 1,000 women aged 15-19, 1990-1995):	13
Government has expressed particular concern about:	
Morbidity and mortality resulting from induced abortion	Yes
Complications of child-bearing and childbirth	Yes
Maternal mortality rate (per 100,000 live births):	
National (1989)	-
Developed countries (around 1988)	26
Female life expectancy at birth (1990-1995):	79.1

Luxembourg

The legal framework with regard to abortion was liberalized in Luxembourg in 1978, a few years later than similar liberalization occurred in other Western European countries. Due to the overall conservatism in Luxembourg, the liberalized law was enacted by only a small margin.

Prior legislation on the interruption of pregnancy in Luxembourg was based on the Napoleonic Penal Code of 1810 (adopted in 1879), which provided severe punishment for the performer of the abortion and for the pregnant woman. The defence of necessity applied but was not formally provided. A Law of 15 November 1978 repealed the provision of the 1879 Code and legalized abortion in certain circumstances.

Abortion is legal during the first 12 weeks of gestation in the following circumstances (section 353 of the Penal Code, as amended): when the continuation of the pregnancy is likely to endanger the physical or mental health of the pregnant woman; when there is a strong likelihood that the child will be born with a serious disease, serious malformation or considerable mental defects; when the pregnancy resulted from rape; when the living conditions that may result from the birth of a child are likely to endanger the physical or mental health of the pregnant woman.

The woman is required to consult a gynaecologist or an obstetrician and to give her consent in writing to the abortion, except when her life is in danger, she is a minor or she is not able to manifest her will. In these cases, an ad hoc legal representative is required to give consent.

Additional requirements are a one-week waiting period in order to allow the woman to reflect on her decision and a physician's certification concerning the existence of the circumstances listed above. Subject to these conditions, the abortion may be covered by government insurance plans. The woman must also be provided with a booklet containing information on contraception, voluntary sterilization, government allowances, adoption and the risks associated with abortion.

Beyond the 12-week period, the law permits abortion only for reasons of physical malformation or serious mental defects or on therapeutic grounds. In such cases, two qualified physicians are required to attest that a serious threat exists to the woman or the child. A physician is not required to perform an abortion except when the life of the pregnant woman is in jeopardy. If the woman does not give her consent, the person performing the abortion is liable to imprisonment (article 348 of the Penal Code). An abortion must be performed in a hospital or other approved facility.

In regard to illegal abortion, a person interrupting a pregnancy with the consent of the pregnant woman is subject to imprisonment for from two to five years and a fine of 2,501-250,000 Luxembourg francs (Lux F). The pregnant woman undergoing the illegal abortion is subject to a fine of Lux F 2,500-20,000. A woman "in a situation of distress" is not considered to have committed an offence (sections 350- 351 of the Penal Code, as amended). Given that "distress" is not defined, the law has been liberally interpreted.

Despite the passage of a more liberal abortion law, there has been some reluctance on the part of physicians in Luxembourg to perform abortions, in part due to the prevailing religious conservatism. Physicians generally perform an abortion only in special circumstances, such as when the woman is well known to them or when the woman's situation is particularly difficult. Given that most hospitals in the country are private and belong to religious orders, many physicians have preferred to send women to family planning centres where information on abortion services abroad can be obtained.

INCIDENCE OF ABORTION

Place	Year	Measurement	Coverage

Information not readily available.

Source: The Population Policy Data Bank maintained by the Population Division of the Department for Economic and Social Information and Policy Analysis of the United Nations Secretariat. For additional sources, see list of references.

Madagascar

Grounds on which abortion is permitted:

To save the life of the woman	Yes
To preserve physical health	No
To preserve mental health	No
Rape or incest	No
Foetal impairment	No
Economic or social reasons	No
Available on request	No

Additional requirements:

The attending physician must consult with two additional physicians, one of whom must be taken from a list of experts provided by the Court. The physician must attest to the fact that the life of the woman cannot be saved by any means other than the intervention contemplated.

FERTILITY AND MORTALITY CONTEXT

Government's view on fertility level:	Too high
Government's intervention concerning fertility level:	To lower
Government's policy on contraceptive use:	Indirect support provided
Percentage of currently married women using modern contraception (aged 15-49, 1985):	2
Total fertility rate (1990-1995):	6.6
Age-specific fertility rate (per 1,000 women aged 15-19, 1990-1995):	125

Government has expressed particular concern about:

Morbidity and mortality resulting from induced abortion	Yes
Complications of child-bearing and childbirth	Yes

Maternal mortality rate (per 100,000 live births):

National (1990)	350-400
Eastern Africa (around 1988, estimate)	680

Female life expectancy at birth (1990-1995):	57

BACKGROUND

According to the Penal Code inherited from the former French colonial rulers, abortion is generally illegal in Madagascar, although it is permitted to save the life of the woman. In all other circumstances, any person performing or attempting to perform an abortion is subject to imprisonment for from one to five years and to a fine of 90,000-180,000 Malagasy francs (FMG). These penalties are increased to 5-10 years of imprisonment and up to FMG 3.6 million in fines for persons that habitually perform abortions. Medical and paramedical personnel are subject, in addition, to suspension from the practice of their profession for a minimum of five years to life. A woman inducing her own miscarriage is subject to imprisonment for from six months to two years and to a fine of FMG 18,000-360,000.

The French anticontraception law of 1920 is still in force in Madagascar. This law prohibits the importation, manufacture, sale or distribution and advertisement of contraceptives, and makes them available only in pharmacies by prescription for health reasons.

Until the 1980s, the Government's attitude with regard to population issues, including family planning, was one of non-intervention and essentially one of opposition, because of the firm belief that the resources of the country were still largely unexploited. However, a non-governmental organization affiliated with the International Planned Parenthood Federation, Fianakaviana Sambatra (FISA, meaning "happy family"), was founded in 1967 and progressively gained recognition, assisting the Government in a number of population-related activities.

Beginning in the 1980s, the worsening economic situation in Madagascar led to greater attention to population matters. In 1984, the Government appointed a Parliamentary Committee for population and development and established the Ministry of Population, Social Affairs, Youth and Sports. FISA began openly to provide family planning services, in collaboration with the new Ministry. In 1986, the Population and Development Unit was established within the Ministry of Planning. A national population and development conference was held in 1987, which sparked research into the linkages between population and development, culminating in the national population policy adopted by the Parliament in January 1991. In that document, the reduction of fertility is a major goal, to be achieved by expanding access to family planning information and services through a national family planning programme.

Wider availability of contraceptives also is being pursued as a means of decreasing maternal and infant mortality and morbidity. A significant proportion of maternal deaths in Madagascar are attributable to induced abortion; an estimated 16 per cent of reported maternal deaths in hospitals are due to complications resulting from abortion, while in rural areas it is estimated that some 40 per cent of maternal mortality is related to complications from abortion.

INCIDENCE OF ABORTION

Place	Year	Measurement	Coverage

Information not readily available.

Source: Population Policy Data Bank maintained by the Population Division of the Department for Economic and Social Information and Policy Analysis of the United Nations Secretariat. For additional sources, see list of references.

Malawi

ABORTION POLICY

Grounds on which abortion is permitted:

To save the life of the woman	Yes
To preserve physical health	Yes
To preserve mental health	No
Rape or incest	No
Foetal impairment	No
Economic or social reasons	No
Available on request	No

Additional requirements:

Authorization must be obtained following consultation with a professional. Permission of the spouse is, in theory, required.

FERTILITY AND MORTALITY CONTEXT

Government's view on fertility level:	Too high
Government's intervention concerning fertility level:	To lower
Government's policy on contraceptive use:	Direct support provided
Percentage of currently married women using modern contraception (aged 15-49, 1984):	1
Total fertility rate (1990-1995):	7.6
Age-specific fertility rate (per 1,000 women aged 15-19, 1990-1995):	249

Government has expressed particular concern about:

Morbidity and mortality resulting from induced abortion	Yes
Complications of child-bearing and childbirth	Yes

Maternal mortality rate (per 100,000 live births):

National (1987)	167
Eastern Africa (around 1988)	680

Female life expectancy at birth (1990-1995):	44.9

BACKGROUND

In Malawi, the Penal Code of 1930 prohibits abortion except to preserve the life of the pregnant woman (chapter 7, sections 149-151). Despite the existence of the British *Bourne* case (1938), which allows abortion on physical and mental grounds, the Government asserts that only the preservation of life and physical health constitutes legal grounds for termination of pregnancy in Malawi.

Any person performing an illegal abortion is subject to up to 14 years in prison. A woman inducing her own miscarriage or consenting to an illegal abortion may be imprisoned for up to seven years. Anyone that unlawfully supplies or procures any instrument, knowing that it is intended to be used to perform an illegal abortion, is guilty of a felony and is liable to imprisonment for three years.

The Government of Malawi considers its rates of population growth and fertility to be unsatisfactory and too high. However, it has long abstained from formulating a policy of explicit intervention to modify fertility or population growth. The Government has introduced several measures to improve the levels of living and the quality of life of its population, including programmes to encourage child-spacing, decrease mortality and adjust social and economic factors, including measures to improve the status of women.

The Government has emphasized birth-spacing as a means of improving the health and welfare of its population. Indeed, when the family planning programme was introduced in 1982, its chief objective was to encourage birth-spacing. In September 1987, the ruling party adopted a resolution calling for birth-spacing as a national policy. However, the Government's position was that the programme should encourage and facilitate families to space children and should not interfere with their right to have the number of children they desire.

Subsequently, the Government decided to address the fertility issue more directly and it has begun to draft a comprehensive population policy with the explicit aim of reducing fertility and population growth. The Government's goals are to strengthen the national child-spacing programme; to increase the availability of family planning services, which are provided by the Ministry of Health through the maternal and child health programme; and to increase the contraceptive prevalence rate by 1996 from the current low level of 3 per cent.

The Government has also expressed its concern about the level of induced abortion and adolescent pregnancies and is strengthening its information and educational programmes. In fact, the level of induced abortion is believed to be quite high. In 1981, it was reported that 17 per cent of maternal deaths were due to complications from septic abortion.

INCIDENCE OF ABORTION

Place	Year	Measurement	Coverage

Information not readily available.

Source: Population Policy Data Bank maintained by the Population Division of the Department for Economic and Social Information and Policy Analysis of the United Nations Secretariat. For additional sources, see list of references.

Malaysia

ABORTION POLICY

Grounds on which abortion is permitted:

To save the life of the woman	Yes
To preserve physical health	Yes
To preserve mental health	Yes
Rape or incest	No
Foetal impairment	Yes
Economic or social reasons	No
Available on request	No

Additional requirements:

Third-party authorization by a medical professional is required. The legal period allowed is 120 days and the woman's consent is required.

FERTILITY AND MORTALITY CONTEXT

Government's view on fertility level:	Too high
Government's intervention concerning fertility level:	To lower
Government's policy on contraceptive use:	Direct support provided
Percentage of currently married women using modern contraception (aged 15-49, 1984):	30
Total fertility rate (1990-1995):	3.6
Age-specific fertility rate (per 1,000 women aged 15-19, 1990-1995):	29
Government has expressed particular concern about:	
Morbidity and mortality resulting from induced abortion	Yes
Complications of child-bearing and childbirth	Yes
Maternal mortality rate (per 100,000 live births):	
National (1985)	40
South-eastern Asia (around 1988)	340
Female life expectancy at birth (1990-1995):	73.0

BACKGROUND

Under section 312 of the Penal Code of Malaysia, which was in effect until amended in 1989, the only ground for having an abortion was to save the life of the woman. A national fertility and family survey found that a majority of the women surveyed (71 per cent) endorsed abortion on the grounds of rape or incest; 54.3 per cent endorsed it if the woman was unmarried, 52.2 per cent for health reasons and 34.5 per cent for economic and social reasons.

In April 1989, section 312 of Act 727 of the Penal Code was amended substantially to permit abortion if the performing physician is of the opinion, formed "in good faith", that continuation of the pregnancy constitutes risk to the "mental and physical health of the pregnant woman, greater than if the pregnancy were terminated".

Abortion in Malaysia is free of charge if it is performed in a government hospital. Third-party authorization by a physician is required, and the legal period allowed is 120 days. The pregnant woman's consent is required and penalties for the person performing the abortion depend upon the presence or absence of this consent.

During the early stages of pregnancy, both the person performing an unauthorized abortion and the woman may be subject to three years in prison and/or a fine. In the later stages of pregnancy (after 120 days), both may be sentenced to up to seven years in prison and be liable for a fine. A person performing an unauthorized abortion without the woman's consent is subject to 20 years of imprisonment and/or a fine. If an unauthorized abortion causes the woman's death, the prison term for the person who performed the procedure may be extended by 10 years if the woman's consent was previously obtained or by 20 years if it was not obtained.

Information on the incidence of abortion is not readily available. A report issued prior to the 1989 amendment of section 312 of the Penal Code estimated an abortion ratio of one in three live births. In addition, induced abortion ratios per 100 pregnancies have reportedly more than doubled, with ratios in urban areas three times as high as in rural areas.

Citing the advantages of a larger population in providing both an expanded domestic market and a reservoir of labour resources, the Government promulgated a revised population policy in 1984, which sought to decelerate the tempo of the decline in the fertility rate and to stabilize population size at about 70 million by the year 2100.

Under the new programme, the family is being promoted as the basic unit of society. The "total family concept" calls for greater emphasis on parenting, child development, marriage and family counselling and for the provision of child-care facilities to allow women to combine parenting with labour-market activities. At the same time, the Government reported that, according to family planning surveys, a sizeable proportion of the couples that did not want additional children were not practising contraception and that many couples were relying upon inefficient traditional methods. The Government concluded that the situation called for greater educational efforts to bring those unserved target groups into the programme.

Malaysia has over 25 years of history of family planning. In 1966, the Malaysian Parliament passed the National Family Planning Act and established the National Family Planning Board to formulate policies and methods for the promotion and spread of family planning practices in the country. In 1976, the Employment Ordinance of 1955, which provided for a maternity leave and allowance for a period of 60 days, was amended to disallow a maternity allowance to a woman with three or more children.

A comprehensive family planning programme was formulated as part of the Sixth Malaysian Development Plan for the period 1991-1995. It is to be implemented by various governmental and

Malaysia

non-governmental agencies. Both the Ministry of Health and the Malaysian Federation of Family Planning Associations disseminate information and family planning services to both men and women.

INCIDENCE OF ABORTION

Place	Year	Measurement	Coverage
National	1985	7.0 abortions/1,000 women aged 15-44	PR
National	1986	6.8 abortions/1,000 women aged 15-44	PR
National	1987	6.5 abortions/1,000 women aged 15-44	PR
National	1988	6.4 abortions/1,000 women aged 15-44	PR

Note: PR = provider registration; SP = survey of provider; SW = survey of women; HR = hospital admission records. For a detailed description of these abbreviations and information on sources of the data, see technical notes in the annex.

Source: Population Policy Data Bank maintained by the Population Division of the Department for Economic and Social Information and Policy Analysis of the United Nations Secretariat. For additional sources, see list of references.

ABORTION POLICY

Grounds on which abortion is permitted:

To save the life of the woman	Yes
To preserve physical health	Yes
To preserve mental health	No
Rape or incest	No
Foetal impairment	No
Economic or social reasons	No
Available on request	No

Additional requirements:

Abortion is allowed only for certified medical reasons. The consent of the spouse is required.

FERTILITY AND MORTALITY CONTEXT

Government's view on fertility level:	Too high
Government's intervention concerning fertility level:	To lower
Government's policy on contraceptive use:	Direct support provided
Percentage of currently married women using modern contraception (aged 15-49):	..
Total fertility rate (1990-1995):	6.2
Age-specific fertility rate (per 1,000 women aged 15-19, 1990-1995):	64

Government has expressed particular concern about:
Morbidity and mortality resulting from induced abortion   ..
Complications of child-bearing and childbirth   Yes

Maternal mortality rate (per 100,000 live births):
National (1989)   480
Southern Asia (around 1988)   570

Female life expectancy at birth (1990-1995):   62.0

Maldives

Abortion is not allowed in Maldives except for certified medical reasons. The consent of the spouse is required.

The Government is concerned about balancing population growth and economic and ecological pressures. All methods of contraception are legal, and the Government supports and promotes family planning services. At first, the main focus of the Government's policy was birth-spacing in order to improve maternal and child health. In 1992, the Government established targets for fertility and contraceptive prevalence. It has also developed educational programmes on population issues, in particular family planning.

INCIDENCE OF ABORTION

Place	Year	Measurement	Coverage

Information not readily available.

Source: The Population Policy Data Bank maintained by the Population Division of the Department for Economic and Social Information and Policy Analysis of the United Nations Secretariat. For additional sources, see list of references.

ABORTION POLICY

Grounds on which abortion is permitted:

To save the life of the woman	Yes
To preserve physical health	No
To preserve mental health	No
Rape or incest	No
Foetal impairment	No
Economic or social reasons	No
Available on request	No

Additional requirements:

Information is not readily available.

FERTILITY AND MORTALITY CONTEXT

Government's view on fertility level:	Too high
Government's intervention concerning fertility level:	To lower
Government's policy on contraceptive use:	Direct support provided
Percentage of currently married women using modern contraception (aged 15-49, 1987):	1
Total fertility rate (1990-1995):	7.1
Age-specific fertility rate (per 1,000 women aged 15-19, 1990-1995)	199
Government has expressed particular concern about:	
Morbidity and mortality resulting from induced abortion	Yes
Complications of child-bearing and childbirth	Yes
Maternal mortality rate (per 100,000 live births):	
National (1987)	1,750-2,900
Western Africa (around 1988)	760
Female life expectancy at birth (1990-1995):	47.6

Mali

Article 170 of the Penal Code of Mali (Law No. 99 of 3 August 1961) contains a general prohibition of abortion. However, the Penal Code also includes the explicit general provision of the defence of necessity, exonerating persons from certain crimes if they acted to defend themselves or other persons. This provision has been construed in some instances to apply to situations involving a serious threat to a pregnant woman's health and, in particular, to her life. Health reasons have also been interpreted to include cases of foetal impairment.

The penalty in Mali for performing or attempting to perform an abortion is imprisonment for a term ranging from one to five years. The person performing the abortion may also incur a fine of 20,000-1,000,000 CFA francs (CFAF) and face a sentence of 1-10 years of *interdiction de sejour* (exile). The law provides a similar penalty for a woman inducing or attempting to induce her own miscarriage.

In 1972, Mali became the first francophone country in Western Africa to repeal the French law of 31 July 1920, which prohibited the advertisement, sale or distribution of contraceptives. Mali was also the first country in francophone Africa to accept and legalize family planning as an integral part of its effort to protect the health of mothers and children through longer intervals between births.

A family planning association (Association malienne pour la promotion et la protection de la famille, an affiliate of the International Planned Parenthood Federation), which was established in 1972, focuses on information, education and communication activities in regard to family planning. Government-sponsored clinics located at Bamako, the capital city, in the regional capitals and main towns and in all 46 districts, offer family planning services, including the distribution of contraceptives. A population policy formulated by the Government was officially adopted in 1991.

Among its objectives, the national population policy is directed to reducing population growth and fertility. The goal is to attain a 60 per cent contraceptive prevalence rate by the year 2020, which, it is hoped, will lower the incidence of induced abortion. It considers induced abortion to be a consequence of the unmet demand for contraceptives.

The demand for family planning services remains partially unmet owing to, among other things, the Government's policy of limiting the authorization to distribute hormonal contraceptives to physicians and midwives (who are the only health-care personnel receiving family planning training) and of restricting the prescription of contraceptives to married women that have spousal consent.

The number of abortions performed in Mali has been increasing. Although still relatively small, the number was sufficient for the Government to express concern about their impact on medical resources.

INCIDENCE OF ABORTION

Place	Year	Measurement	Coverage

Information not readily available.

Source: The Population Policy Data Bank maintained by the Population Division of the Department for Economic and Social Information and Policy Analysis of the United Nations Secretariat. For additional sources, see list of references.

Malta

Grounds on which abortion is permitted:

To save the life of the woman	No
To preserve physical health	No
To preserve mental health	No
Rape or incest	No
Foetal impairment	No
Economic or social reasons	No
Available on request	No

Additional requirements:

Information is not readily available.

FERTILITY AND MORTALITY CONTEXT

Government's view on fertility level:	Satisfactory
Government's intervention concerning fertility level:	No intervention
Government's policy on contraceptive use:	No support provided
Percentage of currently married women using modern contraception (aged 15-49):	..
Total fertility rate (1990-1995):	2.1
Age-specific fertility rate (per 1,000 women aged 15-19, 1990-1995):	12
Government has expressed particular concern about:	
Morbidity and mortality resulting from induced abortion	No
Complications of child-bearing and childbirth	No
Maternal mortality rate (per 100,000 live births):	
National (1990)	0
Developed countries (around 1988)	26
Female life expectancy at birth (1990-1995):	78.2

BACKGROUND

Abortion is forbidden in Malta in all circumstances.

The penalty for abortion in Malta is from 18 months to three years of imprisonment for the person performing the abortion, as well as for the consenting woman. The punishment is severe if a physician performs the abortion.

Family planning has been gaining increased acceptance in Malta over the years. Under the Press Law of 1974, the ban on the advertisement of contraceptives was lifted. In the following year, the prohibition of the importation of contraceptives was repealed. The Government provides no support for family planning activities.

INCIDENCE OF ABORTION

Place	Year	Measurement	Coverage

Information not readily available.

Source: The Population Policy Data Bank maintained by the Population Division of the Department for Economic and Social Information and Policy Analysis of the United Nations Secretariat. For additional sources, see list of references.

Marshall Islands

Grounds on which abortion is permitted:

To save the life of the woman	Yes
To preserve physical health	Yes
To preserve mental health	Yes
Rape or incest	No
Foetal impairment	No
Economic or social reasons	No
Available on request	No

Additional requirements:

An abortion requires spousal consent. In addition, counselling services must be provided prior to the abortion, and the woman must sign a consent form stating that she will utilize family planning services after the abortion.

FERTILITY AND MORTALITY CONTEXT

Government's view on fertility level:	Too high
Government's intervention concerning fertility level:	To lower
Government's policy on contraceptive use:	Direct support provided
Percentage of currently married women using modern contraception (aged 15-49):	..
Total fertility rate (1990-1995):	..
Age-specific fertility rate (per 1,000 women aged 15-19, 1990-1995):	..
Government has expressed particular concern about:	
Morbidity and mortality resulting from induced abortion	..
Complications of child-bearing and childbirth	..
Maternal mortality rate (per 100,000 live births):	
National	..
Oceania (around 1988)	600
Female life expectancy at birth (1990-1995):	..

BACKGROUND

In the Marshall Islands, abortion is permitted to save the life of the pregnant woman or to preserve her physical or mental health. An abortion can only be performed after the woman receives counselling and signs a form indicating that she will utilize family planning services following the abortion. Abortions are performed by a limited number of physicians, as a number of physicians are reluctant to perform the procedure.

The country has a tradition of concern for the economic limitations of a fragile atoll environment and the need to control population growth. In 1982, a Leadership Seminar on Population Education helped raise awareness of the population problems facing the Marshall Islands. The principal problems identified were: a population growth rate of 3.2 per cent per annum; an uneven geographical distribution of population; and a highly skewed age distribution, with over 50 per cent of the population under age 15, resulting in a heavy dependency ratio. As a result of the seminar, in September 1982, the Government established the Task Force on Population Awareness to address those population problems. A national population policy, which was approved in 1990, addresses the problems of high population growth, the poor health conditions of mothers and children and the high rates of adolescent fertility.

INCIDENCE OF ABORTION

Place	Year	Measurement	Coverage

Information not readily available.

Source: The Population Policy Data Bank maintained by the Population Division of the Department for Economic and Social Information and Policy Analysis of the United Nations Secretariat. For additional sources, see list of references.

Mauritania

ABORTION POLICY

Grounds on which abortion is permitted:

To save the life of the woman	Yes
To preserve physical health	No
To preserve mental health	No
Rape or incest	No
Foetal impairment	No
Economic or social reasons	No
Available on request	No

Additional requirements:

The attending physician must consult with two additional physicians, one of whom must be taken from a list of experts provided by the court. The physician must attest that the life of the woman cannot be saved by any means other than the intervention contemplated.

FERTILITY AND MORTALITY CONTEXT

Government's view on fertility level:	Satisfactory
Government's intervention concerning fertility level:	No intervention
Government's policy on contraceptive use:	Indirect support provided
Percentage of currently married women using modern contraception (aged 15-49, 1990):	1
Total fertility rate (1990-1995):	6.5
Age-specific fertility rate (per 1,000 women aged 15-19, 1990-1995):	160
Government has expressed particular concern about:	
Morbidity and mortality resulting from induced abortion	Yes
Complications of child-bearing and childbirth	Yes
Maternal mortality rate (per 100,000 live births):	
National	..
Western Africa (around 1988)	760
Female life expectancy at birth (1990-1995):	49.7

BACKGROUND

Although the Penal Code of Mauritania was modified in 1983, the article concerning abortion is directly derived from the Napoleonic Code of 1810 and from the French law of 1939. Abortion is generally illegal and any person performing, attempting to perform, or suggesting an abortion is subject to imprisonment for a period of from one to five years and a fine of 10,000-200,000 ouguiyas (UM). For persons that routinely perform abortions, the penalty is increased to 5-10 years of imprisonment and a fine of UM 100,000-400,000. A woman who induces her own miscarriage or consents to an abortion is liable to a prison term of from six months to two years and a fine of UM 5,000-60,000. Medical and paramedical personnel may be suspended from the practice of their profession either permanently or for a minimum period of five years. In addition, a court may decide on exile (*interdiction de séjour*) for the offender.

The criminal law of 1972 expressly recognizes the defence of necessity where the woman's life is seriously at risk. In this instance, the abortion may be performed if the attending physician consults with two additional physicians, one of whom must be chosen from a list of experts provided by the court. The physician must attest to the fact that the life of the woman cannot be saved by any means other than the intervention contemplated. The Government reported in 1987 that abortion was allowed in the case of rape or incest, although no legislative evidence is available to support that statement.

The French anticontraception law of 31 July 1920 is still in force in Mauritania. According to this law, the importation, manufacture, sale, advertisement or transport of contraceptives is prohibited.

Until recently, the Government's policy with regard to population issues has been focused on increasing population size, because the country was considered to be underpopulated, with one of the lowest overall population densities in the world. The Government therefore did not intervene to modify the high rate of fertility. For the first time, the Fourth Economic and Social Development Plan, 1981-1985, included an analysis of demographic factors. The Government stopped implementing the Plan, however, when the economic crisis in Mauritania worsened because of the effects of prolonged drought. Nevertheless, the idea began to spread that one of the causes of the intensifying process of desertification was the increase of population pressure on natural resources. Moreover, there was growing sentiment that a healthy population was more likely to contribute to the development process.

The year 1986 was a turning-point in the Government's appraisal of the demographic situation. At the Meeting on Family Health, held in July 1986, the Director of Islamic Orientation stated that Islam allowed family planning by natural methods and permitted the use of modern methods of contraception for therapeutic reasons. During the First Family Planning Seminar, held in December 1986, initial steps were taken for the preparation of a national family planning policy.

Given the very high rates of infant and maternal mortality in Mauritania, the Government decided to integrate family planning activities into maternal and child health services and began to allow the use of contraceptives. The spacing of births is currently viewed as a means of improving the health of mothers and children, avoiding the negative effects of abrupt weaning and preventing risks related to early or late pregnancies. Nevertheless, the Government remains very cautious and has not yet approved an explicit family planning policy.

Although the number of desired children in Mauritania is still very high, demand for contraceptive services has existed and has partially been satisfied either abroad, in neighbouring Senegal or by "under the counter" sales. Currently, contraceptives are available in pharmacies in Mauritania. Surveys show a very low rate of contraceptive prevalence, although it is probably underestimated, owing to the sensitiveness of the issue.

Mauritania

Abortion seems to be uncommon, although "abortion tourism"—that is, women from Mauritania travelling abroad to obtain an abortion—has been reported. Social and religious reasons, however, generally persuade the woman to have the unwanted child. As a result, the phenomenon of abandoned children appears to be widespread, especially among unmarried women. Because it is very difficult for an unmarried mother in Mauritania to find a husband, these women often conceal the delivery and subsequently abandon the child.

INCIDENCE OF ABORTION

Place	Year	Measurement	Coverage

Information not readily available.

Source: The Population Policy Data Bank maintained by the Population Division of the Department for Economic and Social Information and Policy Analysis of the United Nations Secretariat. For additional sources, see list of references.

ABORTION POLICY

Grounds on which abortion is permitted:

To save the life of the woman	No[*]
To preserve physical health	No
To preserve mental health	No
Rape or incest	No
Foetal impairment	No
Economic or social reasons	No
Available on request	No

Additional requirements:

The intervention must by approved by the Solicitor General.

---

[*] Legal interpretation generally permits this ground.

FERTILITY AND MORTALITY CONTEXT

Government's view on fertility level:	Satisfactory
Government's intervention concerning fertility level:	To maintain
Government's policy on contraceptive use:	Direct support provided
Percentage of currently married women using modern contraception (aged 15-49, 1985):	46
Total fertility rate (1990-1995):	2.1
Age-specific fertility rate (per 1,000 women aged 15-19, 1990-1995):	39
Government has expressed particular concern about:	
Morbidity and mortality resulting from induced abortion	Yes
Complications of child-bearing and childbirth	Yes
Maternal mortality rate (per 100,000 live births):	
National (1987)	99.2
Eastern Africa (around 1988)	680
Female life expectancy at birth (1990-1995):	73.5

Mauritius

BACKGROUND

The legal framework for abortion in Mauritius is a result of the interaction of French and English law. The French ruled Mauritius from 1721 to 1810, while the British ruled from 1810 until independence was attained in 1968. The provisions of the Penal Code are derived directly from the French Napoleonic Penal Code of 1810 and from the British Offences against the Person Act of 1861. The pertinent article relating to abortion was not modified by the 1938 revision of the Penal Code of Mauritius.

Abortion is illegal in Mauritius under the Penal Code Ordinance, which states that any person procuring an abortion or supplying the means to procure an abortion is liable to imprisonment for up to 10 years. A similar punishment is prescribed for a woman who induces her own miscarriage. Physicians, surgeons and pharmacists that assist in performing an abortion are liable to imprisonment. However, abortion is permitted to preserve the life of the pregnant woman by the general principles of the law.

Mauritius has undergone a significant demographic transition over the past 30 years. Fertility has declined by about two thirds and is currently at replacement level, whereas only 30 years ago, the total fertility rate was about 6.0 children per woman. Several factors have contributed to this rapid fertility decline. For one thing, the small size of the country made the issue of overcrowding seem very real. For another, first private family planning agencies and then public agencies conducted widespread campaigns, influencing public opinion through the press and other media.

The Mauritius Family Planning Association (MFPA), which was established in 1957, introduced contraception in 1958. In addition, the private Catholic organization, Action familiale, was established in 1962 to encourage the use of natural family planning methods only.

Mauritius was one of the first countries in Africa to formulate a population policy in the early 1970s. At first, however, in part because of the religious diversity of the population, the Government decided not to become directly involved in family planning activities but rather to encourage private, voluntary organizations to promote family planning. MFPA was given official status through Ordinance No.15 of 1967. In 1969, the Government established nationwide family planning services. In 1972, both MFPA and Action familiale were absorbed by the Government, and the family planning programme was integrated into the maternal and child health programme. A national committee was created to coordinate the activities of the two private family planning bodies and the Government incorporated all but two of the MFPA clinics.

The results of the programme have been significant. Due to the educational campaigns conducted by the Government and the family planning associations, the population of Mauritius has increasingly accepted contraception for spacing and limiting births. A study of contraceptive prevalence conducted in 1991 found that 75 per cent of the women on Mauritius Island and 70 per cent of those on Rodrigues Island were using a contraceptive method. The Government's intensive family planning effort brought about a dramatic decline in the birth rate, from 40.3 per 1,000 in 1963 to 18.8 in 1985.

In spite of efforts made by women's groups in 1977, abortion remains illegal in Mauritius. Nevertheless, it is an important birth control method, especially among older women. Methods vary from dilation and curettage for more affluent women to "backstreet" abortions, and abortion complications are a leading cause of maternal death in Mauritius. A study of maternal mortality conducted in 1977 found that 60 per cent of deaths were probably due to complications from clandestine abortions. It was estimated that, during the 1980s, some 5,000 cases of complications arising from abortions performed outside the government medical services were treated in hospitals annually.

Overall, the number of induced abortions in Mauritius is believed to be high. In 1980, it was estimated that there were about 20,000 illegally induced abortions per annum. One estimate indicated that the total number of abortions might be as high as the number of live births, while women's groups claimed that the average number of abortions was three or four per woman.

INCIDENCE OF ABORTION

Place	Year	Measurement	Coverage
National	1966	8.0 abortions/100 live births	HR
National	1971	8.3 abortions/100 live births	HR
National	1976	11.3 abortions/100 live births	HR
National	1981	13.1 abortions/100 live births	HR

Note: PR = provider registration; SP = survey provider; SW = survey of women; HR = hospital admission records. For a detailed description of these abbreviations and information on sources of the data, see technical notes in the annex.

Source: The Population Policy Data Bank maintained by the Population Division of the Department for Economic and Social Information and Policy Analysis of the United Nations Secretariat. For additional sources, see list of references.

Mexico

Grounds on which abortion is permitted:

To save the life of the woman	Yes
To preserve physical health	No*
To preserve mental health	No*
Rape or incest	Yes
Foetal impairment	No*
Economic or social reasons	No
Available on request	No

Additional requirements:

Under most state provisions on abortion, legal abortions must generally be performed during the first 12 weeks (or 90 days) of gestation. Except in emergency cases, all induced abortions must be performed by a physician whose opinion on the necessity of the abortion is corroborated by another physician. Consent of the woman, or in certain instances (minors etc.), that of her husband, parents or guardians, is required before the abortion is performed.

---

* Some state provisions permit abortion on these grounds. Liberal interpretation of the medical indications for abortion may allow abortion to be performed to preserve the physical health of the woman.

FERTILITY AND MORTALITY CONTEXT

Government's view of fertility level:	Too high
Government's intervention concerning fertility level:	To lower
Government's policy on contraceptive use:	Direct support provided
Percentage of currently married women using modern contraception (aged 15-49, 1987):	5
Total fertility rate (1990-1995):	3.2
Age-specific fertility rate (per 1,000 women aged 15-19, 1990-1995):	88
Government has expressed particular concern about:	
Morbidity and mortality resulting from induced abortion	Yes
Complications of child-bearing and childbirth	Yes
Maternal mortality rate (per 100,000 live births):	
National (1986)	200
Central America (around 1988)	160
Female life expectancy at birth (1990-1995):	73.6

BACKGROUND

Although efforts were made during the 1980s to liberalize abortion, the Mexican Criminal Code for the Federal District and Territories (Decree of 2 January 1931, which was last amended on 16 February 1971) remains in force. It applies in the Federal District of Mexico and throughout Mexico to all offences that fall within the jurisdiction of the federal Courts. The law declares abortion to be generally illegal except when it is performed on medical or juridical grounds. According to articles 333-334 of the Code, an abortion can be exempted from punishment if it results from failure of the woman to take proper care of the foetus, if the continuation of the pregnancy will endanger the life of the woman or if the pregnancy is a result of rape. In all instances except emergency cases, a legal abortion must be performed by a physician whose opinion concerning the necessity of the abortion is corroborated by another physician. In 1976, the Federal Ministry of Public Health issued regulations that expressly prohibit qualified lay birth attendants from inducing an abortion. Therapeutic abortion requires the consent of the woman and, in certain instances (minors etc.), that of her spouse, parents or guardians.

Articles 320-332 of the Code set out varying degrees of punishment for the practice of abortion. They provide that any person performing an abortion with the consent of the woman is subject to imprisonment for from one to three years, and without consent, from three to six years. If the abortion is brought about by physical or moral violence, the imprisonment is increased to from six to eight years. A woman wilfully inducing her own miscarriage may be imprisoned for from six months to five years, a considerably harsher punishment than that for the non-medical abortionist. However, the prison term for the woman is reduced to from six months to a year if the interruption of a concealed pregnancy resulting from illegitimate relations was performed by a woman of "good reputation". Punishment is more severe if the person performing the abortion is a physician, surgeon or midwife; these persons can be suspended from the practice of their profession for a period of from two to five years.

Many of the abortion provisions of the state criminal codes are nearly identical to those of the Federal District. However, abortion laws vary by state, with some being relatively more liberal and others more restrictive. Since the mid 1970s, in line with the Government's shift from a pronatalist population policy to an active commitment to reducing fertility and promoting family planning, there have been a number of challenges in the direction of liberalization of abortion laws at the state level.

For example, in addition to the cases enumerated in the Criminal Code of the Federal District, certain states also made provisions in the 1980s for immunity from prosecution for an abortion in cases where the pregnancy resulted from artificial insemination neither requested or assented to by the woman, provided the abortion was carried out within the first 90 days of pregnancy (article 219 of the Criminal Code of Chihuahua, 18 February 1987); or if there was good reason to believe that the unborn child would suffer from severe physical or mental disabilities of genetic or congenital origin (article 293 of the Criminal Code of Coahuila, 19 September 1982). Some other state provisions indicate that an abortion was legal if it was performed on a woman whose health would be seriously jeopardized by continuation of the pregnancy (e.g., article 229 of the Criminal Code of Jalisco, 2 August 1982); or if an abortion was performed for serious and substantial economic reasons in cases where the woman had at least three children (article 391 of the Social Welfare Code of Yucatan, 27 November 1987).

In contrast, other state provisions allow abortion only on narrowly defined grounds. Article 228 of the Criminal Code of Guanajuato (27 February 1987) and article 342 of the Criminal Code of Querétaro (18 July 1987), for instance, authorize abortion only when the pregnancy is a result of rape. In certain states, authorized abortions in the case of rape must be performed within the first 90 days of pregnancy.

Mexico

Despite the restrictive nature of the law in Mexico, abortion is widely practised, due in part to the liberal interpretation of the medical indications for abortion. According to estimates from several studies conducted in the early 1980s, each year approximately 800,000 illegal abortions were induced, and each year about 24 per cent of the women of reproductive age were estimated to have undergone an abortion. Although more legal abortions occurred in urban areas among middle-class women, a higher proportion of poor, illiterate women and women from rural areas obtained illegal abortions. Another study found that, at about the same period, about 6.5 out of 10,000 annual maternal deaths were due to illegally induced abortions performed in unsanitary conditions and by unqualified personnel.

The Mexican Government has expressed serious concern about unplanned pregnancies, particularly among adolescents, and about the relatively high maternal mortality and morbidity associated with illegally induced abortion. The Decree of 25 April 1987 revised and amended the General Law on Health, underlining the Government's efforts to encourage greater contraceptive use, particularly among adolescents. Pressure to reform abortion laws has also been increasing along with the growth of the women's movement in Mexico.

The beginning of the 1990s witnessed some of the most radical changes in abortion legislation in Mexico. A law passed in October 1990 in the state of Chiapas broadened the indications for the performance of legal abortion during the first 12 weeks of pregnancy. In addition to medical and juridical grounds, it allowed abortion on eugenic grounds or for family planning purposes agreed upon by a couple and permitted an abortion when the pregnant woman was single. The new law was, however, regarded as "revolutionary" because in effect, it allowed abortion on request early in pregnancy, a situation found nowhere else in Mexico. For that reason, it was denounced by both the Catholic church and by conservative political groups. In December 1991, the Chiapas legislature voted to suspend temporarily this first experiment at liberalizing abortion law in Mexico. Since then, the abortion debate in Mexico has intensified.

INCIDENCE OF ABORTION

Place	Year	Measurement	Coverage
National	1972	13.5 abortions/100 live births	HR

Note: PR = provider registration; SP = survey provider; SW = survey of women; HR = hospital admission records. For a detailed description of these abbreviations and information on sources of the data, see technical notes in the annex.

Source: The Population Policy Data Bank maintained by the Population Division of the Department for Economic and Social Information and Policy Analysis of the United Nations Secretariat. For additional sources, see list of references.

ABORTION POLICY

Grounds on which abortion is permitted:

To save the life of the woman
To preserve physical health
To preserve mental health
Rape or incest
Foetal impairment
Economic or social reasons
Available on request

Information is not
readily available.

Additional requirements:

Information is not readily available.

FERTILITY AND MORTALITY CONTEXT

Government's view on fertility level: Too high

Government's intervention concerning fertility level: To lower

Government's policy on contraceptive use: Direct support provided

Percentage of currently married women using
    modern contraception (aged 15-49):   ..

Total fertility rate (1990-1995):   ..

Age-specific fertility rate (per 1,000 women aged 15-19, 1990-1995):   ..

Government has expressed particular concern about:
    Morbidity and mortality resulting from induced abortion   ..
    Complications of child-bearing and childbirth   ..

Maternal mortality rate (per 100,000 live births):
    National   ..
    Oceania (around 1988)   600

Female life expectancy at birth (1990-1995):   ..

Micronesia (Federated States of)

The Federated States of Micronesia, formerly known as the Caroline Islands, has passed through several colonial administrations. A German colony beginning in 1899, the Caroline Islands were under Japanese administration for 30 years, between 1914 and 1945, and subsequently under that of the United States of America as a United Nations Trusteeship until 1990. However, there has been an effective Constitution in the Federated States of Micronesia since 1979. Before independence, the Code stated that a person unlawfully performing an abortion was liable for imprisonment for up to five years. Because the new Code of 1982, issued during the transitional status of the Federation before the end of the Trusteeship, contains no provision on abortion, the situation is unclear. It is possible that some local customary law is applied by local courts.

Traditional methods of abortion, such as the use of local herbs, the insertion of foreign bodies into the womb, ritual massages and bathing, are common in the Pacific region. However, it is difficult to quantify the incidence of such practices, as cases are reported only when complications have arisen and hospitalization is required.

The population policy of the Federated States of Micronesia is intended to reduce fertility by ensuring comprehensive family planning services even to remote areas, increasing the number of acceptors in a culturally acceptable manner and intensifying educational programmes. The high population growth rate is due to a combination of high fertility and low mortality. Family planning programmes have had relatively little impact because they have encountered strong resistance, especially among the native population. As a rule, couples do not consider using family planning because of a lack of knowledge and because it is considered to be in contradiction to traditional beliefs. Attitudes towards family planning in the Pacific islands present some very specific features. On the one hand, the Christian religion is dominant and has influenced attitudes towards abortion and family planning. On the other hand, men are frequently opposed to contraception. Sexual activity was traditionally under severe social control in the Pacific island cultures, and pregnancy was the main means of detecting socially unacceptable behaviour, such as infidelity or interruption of post-partum abstinence.

Place	Year	Measurement	Coverage

Information not readily available.

Source: Population Policy Data Bank maintained by the Population Division of the Department for Economic and Social Information and Policy Analysis of the United Nations Secretariat. For additional sources, see list of references.

ABORTION POLICY

Grounds on which abortion is permitted:

To save the life of the woman	Yes
To preserve physical health	No
To preserve mental health	No
Rape or incest	No
Foetal impairment	No
Economic or social reasons	No
Available on request	No

Additional requirements:

Information is not readily available.

FERTILITY AND MORTALITY CONTEXT

Government's view on fertility level:	Too low
Government's intervention concerning fertility level:	To raise
Government's policy on contraceptive use:	Direct support provided
Percentage of currently married women using modern contraception (aged 15-49):	..
Total fertility rate (1990-1995):	..
Age-specific fertility rate (per 1,000 women aged 15-19, 1990-1995):	..

Government has expressed particular concern about:

Morbidity and mortality resulting from induced abortion	No
Complications of child-bearing and childbirth	No

Maternal mortality rate (per 100,000 live births):

National	-
Developed countries (around 1988)	26

Female life expectancy at birth (1990-1995):	..

Monaco

Monaco has one of the strictest abortion laws among the European countries. The Criminal Code (Law No. 829 of 28 September 1967) declares abortion to be illegal on any grounds except when it is necessary to save the life of the pregnant woman. Any person performing an abortion is subject to imprisonment for from one to five years and a fine. A woman who induces her own abortion or consents to have her pregnancy terminated may be imprisoned for from six months to three years and is liable to a fine. Physicians, surgeons, hospital officials and pharmacists that perform abortions are liable to harsher penalties.

The Government of Monaco considers the current fertility level to be too low. Since the early 1950s, Monaco has adopted a number of social policies, including social welfare support, family allowances, assistance to young married couples and maternity leave, to encourage child-bearing and to cope with the negative consequences of low fertility. For example, Ministerial Order No. 85-248 of 2 May 1985 allows female civil servants to benefit from a 16-week maternity leave and raises the leave for women that have multiple births to 18 weeks. If the mother has already given birth to two living children or has two children in her care, the maternity leave is increased to 26 weeks and, in the case of multiple births, to 28 weeks.

INCIDENCE OF ABORTION

Place	Year	Measurement	Coverage

Information not readily available.

Source: The Population Policy Data Bank maintained by the Population Division of the Department for Economic and Social Information and Policy Analysis of the United Nations Secretariat. For additional sources, see list of references.

ABORTION POLICY

Grounds on which abortion is permitted:

To save the life of the woman	Yes
To preserve physical health	Yes
To preserve mental health	Yes
Rape or incest	Yes
Foetal impairment	Yes
Economic or social reasons	Yes
Available on request	Yes

Additional requirements:

An abortion can be performed during the first three months of pregnancy and later if the pregnant woman suffers from an illness seriously threatening her health. Approval of the family or of the spouse is required.

FERTILITY AND MORTALITY CONTEXT

Government's view on fertility level:	Satisfactory
Government's intervention concerning fertility level:	To maintain
Government's policy on contraceptive use:	Direct support provided
Percentage of currently married women using modern contraception (aged 15-49):	..
Total fertility rate (1990-1995):	4.6
Age-specific fertility rate (per 1,000 women aged 15-19, 1990-1995):	44
Government has expressed particular concern about:	
Morbidity and mortality resulting from induced abortion	No
Complications of child-bearing and childbirth	Yes
Maternal mortality rate (per 100,000 live births):	
National (1992)	204
Eastern Asia (around 1988)	120
Female life expectancy at birth (1990-1995):	65.0

Mongolia

Although the Criminal Code of 6 July 1960 provided that abortion was illegal in Mongolia, the general principles of the law permitted abortion when it was necessary to save the life or health of the pregnant woman. Under the Criminal Code, if an abortion was performed by a physician, it was punishable by imprisonment for up to two years. If it was performed by a person lacking the highest medical qualifications, or if performed under unsanitary conditions, the punishment was imprisonment for up to five years. The provision of the Criminal Code seemed to imply that the pregnant woman did not commit an offence by inducing her own abortion or by consenting to it. The modified Criminal Code, as amended in 1986, provides that illegal abortion is a serious offence, except in special circumstances specified by the medical authorities.

Prior to the late 1980s, the abortion laws in Mongolia echoed the pronatalist population policy of the Government. The Government subsequently expressed serious concern over the high fertility and mortality levels, and particularly over short birth intervals, which resulted in poor maternal health and high infant and maternal mortality. The Government's population policy has shifted emphasis to focus more on family planning in order to reduce infant and maternal mortality without reducing population growth too dramatically. In accordance, the Government has acted to liberalize the abortion law. It has amended the public-health law to permit women to decide the number of children they wish to have and when they wish to have them. Abortions can now be performed on demand during the first three months of pregnancy and later if the pregnant woman suffers from an illness seriously threatening her health. The Ministry of Health has drawn up a list of such illnesses, which include various malignant tumours, serious cardiovascular disease and mental disorders. In 1989, some amendments were made to the health law, making abortions and contraceptives available at government expense.

The Government has attributed the relatively high abortion rate, 44.0 per 100 births in 1991, to shortages of modern contraceptives, as well as to lack of knowledge concerning contraceptive use. The Government, however, has reported being hampered in its attempt to improve the situation with regard to family planning, both by the deteriorating economic conditions and by the shift to a market-oriented economy.

Place	Year	Measurement	Coverage
National	1988	23.0 abortions/100 live births	PR
National	1990	40.0 abortions/100 live births	PR
National	1991	44.0 abortions/100 live births	PR

Note: PR= provider registration; SP = survey provider; SW = survey of women; HR = hospital admission records. For a detailed description of these abbreviations and information on sources of the data, see technical notes in the annex.

Source: The Population Policy Data Bank maintained by the Population Division of the Department for Economic and Social Information and Policy Analysis of the United Nations Secretariat. For additional sources, see list of references.

ABORTION POLICY

Grounds on which abortion is permitted:

To save the life of the woman	Yes
To preserve physical health	Yes
To preserve mental health	No
Rape or incest	No
Foetal impairment	No
Economic or social reasons	No
Available on request	No

Additional requirements:

The intervention must be "openly performed" within six weeks of pregnancy by a physician with the consent of the spouse. If the husband refuses or cannot give his consent, the physician is required to obtain the authorization of the chief medical officer of the province or prefecture, by presenting written notification to the effect that the intervention is the only means of safeguarding the health of the woman. If the woman's life is in jeopardy, the only requirement is notification of the chief medical officer of the province or prefecture by the physician.

FERTILITY AND MORTALITY CONTEXT

Government's view on fertility level:	Too high
Government's intervention concerning fertility level:	To lower
Government's policy on contraceptive use:	Direct support provided
Percentage of currently married women using modern contraception (aged 15-49, 1987):	29
Total fertility rate (1990-1995):	4.4
Age-specific fertility rate (per 1,000 women aged 15-19, 1990-1995):	46
Government has expressed particular concern about:	
Morbidity and mortality resulting from induced abortion	No
Complications of child-bearing and childbirth	Yes
Maternal mortality rate (per 100,000 live births):	
National (1974)	200-300
Northern Africa (around 1988)	360
Female life expectancy at birth (1990-1995):	65.0

Morocco

The Royal Decree of 1 July 1967 modified article 453 of the Moroccan Penal Code to provide that abortion is not illegal when it is necessary to safeguard the health of the mother, if it is openly performed by a physician or a surgeon with the consent of the spouse. If the husband refuses or cannot give his consent, the physician is required to obtain the authorization of the chief medical officer of the province or prefecture, by presenting written notification to the effect that the intervention is the only means of safeguarding the health of the woman. If the woman's life is in jeopardy, the only requirement is notification of the chief medical officer of the province or prefecture by the physician.

In all other cases, abortion is illegal under the Criminal Code although there is some evidence that foetal impairment may be taken into account under medical indications. Any person performing an abortion is subject to imprisonment for from one to five years and a fine of 120-500 Moroccan dirhams (DH). These punishments are doubled for persons that habitually perform abortions. In addition, persons that perform an abortion may be subject to exile (*interdiction de séjour*) or be deprived of other rights. Medical and paramedical professionals may be forbidden to practise their profession either temporarily or permanently. A woman who induces her own abortion is subject to imprisonment for from six months to two years and a fine of DH 120-500.

Family planning in Morocco has encountered strong religious and political opposition. Consequently, moves to strengthen family planning efforts have been quite cautious. In the case of abortion, the issue has been complicated by the views of religious scholars concerning the beginnings of life. Some believe that abortion should be allowed only in exceptional circumstances and that the abortion law of Morocco should not be liberalized.

The Government of Morocco has supported family planning since independence in 1956 and has recognized the influence of demographic factors on national development. Royal Decree No. 188-66 of 26 August 1966 established the High Commission for Population at the national level, assisted by other commissions at the provincial and prefectural levels, with the aim of formulating and coordinating the Government's population policy. Also in 1966, the Plan of Action of the Public Health Ministry initiated the establishment of family planning centres.

Royal Decree No. 181-66 of 1 July 1967, which modified the abortion law, also repealed the French law of 10 July 1939, which prohibited the advertisement and sale of contraceptives. Since then, contraceptives have been distributed free of charge in government family planning centres. Beginning with the development plan of 1968-1972, population issues, including family planning, have been accorded high priority in the planning process in Morocco. In 1971, the Association Marocaine de planification familiale, a private body, was established. Its activities have evolved over the years from informational and educational activities to include clinical services.

Family planning activities in Morocco have been fully integrated into the overall health-care facilities, which has resulted in some financial difficulties and has actually hampered access to contraception by subsuming it under medical services. For these reasons, in the early 1980s, the Government assigned to the Ministry of Public Health the responsibility for undertaking a policy of "demedicalization" of family planning services in order to increase access to contraception. In addition, two innovative programmes were introduced, one involving mobile clinics providing maternal and child health and family planning services in remote rural areas and the other involving systematic home visits to encourage the use of contraception and to provide family planning and primary health-care services.

Illegal abortion appears to be quite widespread in Morocco, with many women resorting to abortion as a contraceptive method. In addition, it appears that the incidence of illegal abortion is underestimated, given the fact that many women obtaining an illegal abortion appear to be married women from the urban upper and middle classes, who undergo an abortion in a private clinic. Surveys of public hospitals suggest that a significant number of admissions are of women from lower socio-economic groups suffering from complications due to septic abortion.

INCIDENCE OF ABORTION

Place	Year	Measurement	Coverage

Information not readily available.

Source: The Population Policy Data Bank maintained by the Population Division of the Department for Economic and Social Information and Policy Analysis of the United Nations Secretariat. For additional sources, see list of references.

Mozambique

Grounds on which abortion is permitted:

To save the life of the woman	Yes
To preserve physical health	No*
To preserve mental health	No*
Rape or incest	No*
Foetal impairment	No*
Economic or social reasons	No*
Available on request	No*

Additional requirements:

Information is not readily available.

---

* Official interpretation generally permits abortion on these grounds.

FERTILITY AND MORTALITY CONTEXT

Government's view on fertility level:	Too high
Government's intervention concerning fertility level:	To lower
Government's policy on contraceptive use:	Direct support provided
Percentage of currently married women using modern contraception (aged 15-49):	..
Total fertility rate (1990-1995):	6.5
Age-specific fertility rate (per 1,000 women aged 15-19, 1990-1995):	131

Government has expressed particular concern about:	
Morbidity and mortality resulting from induced abortion	Yes
Complications of child-bearing and childbirth	Yes

Maternal mortality rate (per 100,000 live births):	
National (1981)	300
Eastern Africa (around 1988)	680
Female life expectancy at birth (1990-1995):	48.4

BACKGROUND

Mozambique gained its independence from Portugal in 1975. The pre-independence laws were those of Portugal, where abortion was generally illegal under the Criminal Code Decree of 16 September 1886. According to this law, induced abortion is illegal except to save the life of the pregnant woman. Any person performing an abortion, including the pregnant woman, can be imprisoned for from two to eight years.

The existing (colonial) law, however, is not strictly enforced. In general, the courts do not prosecute if the abortion is performed in a hospital, if a physician must complete an abortion after it has been induced non-medically or if the abortion involves a married woman. Although the Organization of Mozambican Women has recognized induced abortion as a serious problem in regard to reproductive health, the issue has not yet received a great deal of official attention. However, the Government is concerned about the increase in maternal mortality related to induced abortion.

The Government of Mozambique considers levels and trends of fertility to be unsatisfactory in relation to family well-being. Infant mortality and child mortality are extremely high. Therefore, the main objective of the Government's family planning programme is to reduce fertility as well as maternal and infant mortality and morbidity. Family planning services emphasize the provision of intra-uterine devices, the pill and sterilization for women over age 35 that obtain the husband's consent. However, because family planning methods are not widely available in Mozambique, induced abortion, performed largely by traditional practitioners, is often used as a birth control method.

INCIDENCE OF ABORTION

Place	Year	Measurement	Coverage

Information not readily available.

Source: The Population Policy Data Bank maintained by the Population Division of the Department for Economic and Social Information and Policy Analysis of the United Nations Secretariat. For additional sources, see list of references.

Myanmar

Grounds on which abortion is permitted:

To save the life of the woman	Yes
To preserve physical health	No
To preserve mental health	No
Rape or incest	No
Foetal impairment	No
Economic or social reasons	No
Available on request	No

Additional requirements:

Information is not readily available.

FERTILITY AND MORTALITY CONTEXT

Government's view on fertility level:	Satisfactory
Government's intervention concerning fertility level:	No intervention
Government's policy on contraceptive use:	Indirect support provided
Percentage of currently married women using modern contraception (aged 15-49):	..
Total fertility rate (1990-1995):	4.2
Age-specific fertility rate (per 1,000 women aged 15-19, 1990-1995):	32

Government has expressed particular concern about:

Morbidity and mortality resulting from induced abortion	Yes
Complications of child-bearing and childbirth	Yes

Maternal mortality rate (per 100,000 live births):

National (1982)	150
South-eastern Asia (around 1988)	340

Female life expectancy at birth (1990-1995):	59.3

BACKGROUND

According to the Penal Code of Myanmar, abortion is generally illegal and any person performing an abortion is subject to imprisonment for up to three years and/or a fine. A woman who induces her own miscarriage is subject to the same penalties. However, a pregnancy may be legally terminated to save the life of the mother.

A family planning association was established in Myanmar in 1960, but its activities virtually ceased as of 1963. The Government has maintained strict controls over the importation of contraceptives, and modern contraceptive methods are difficult to obtain. Family planning services exist on a limited basis.

Notwithstanding the major political changes that took place in Myanmar in 1988, the Government's position on population issues has remained more or less unchanged. Overpopulation has not been a concern, mainly because the Government is convinced that Myanmar's large unexploited natural resources not only permit additional population growth but also make it necessary to sustain agricultural development. For these reasons, population activities have been directed mainly towards the improvement of health conditions. Family planning services have been established essentially to improve maternal and child health through the spacing of births.

Despite the illegality of abortion in Myanmar, a significant number of abortions apparently have been performed. During the early 1990s, it is believed that the country experienced rising abortion rates. Spurred by the high maternal mortality rates related to illegal abortions, health officials have attempted to persuade the Government to introduce a more liberal policy with regard to contraception. Estimates indicate that Myanmar has an abortion rate of about 80 per 1,000 live births. The available data, which are believed to underreport maternal mortality, yield a maternal mortality rate of 123 per 100,000 live births. Illegal abortion is reported to be the cause of approximately 40 per cent of all maternal deaths.

These data have contributed to the onset of a change in the Government's attitude towards family planning and contraception, although the official policy remains the same. The Government regards the promotion of birth-spacing and the establishment of family planning information services as primarily a means of improving overall health. The Government has decided to improve women's access to family planning information and clinical services as a preventive measure, as it is aware that the problem of excessive population growth could occur in the future. The Government stresses, however, that such measures are currently unnecessary, given the large unexploited natural resources in Myanmar.

INCIDENCE OF ABORTION

Place	Year	Measurement	Coverage

Information not readily available.

Source: Population Policy Data Bank maintained by the Population Division of the Department for Economic and Social Information and Policy Analysis of the United Nations Secretariat. For additional sources, see list of references.

Namibia

ABORTION POLICY

Grounds on which abortion is permitted:

To save the life of the woman	Yes
To preserve physical health	Yes
To preserve mental health	Yes
Rape or incest	Yes
Foetal impairment	Yes
Economic or social reasons	No
Available on request	No

Additional requirements:

Two other physicians in addition to the woman's physician are required to certify to the existence of grounds for an abortion. An abortion must be performed in a government hospital or in an approved medical facility.

FERTILITY AND MORTALITY CONTEXT

Government's view on fertility level:	Too high
Government's intervention concerning fertility level:	No intervention
Government's policy on contraceptive use:	Direct support provided
Percentage of currently married women using modern contraception (aged 15-49, 1989):	26
Total fertility rate (1990-1995):	6.0
Age-specific fertility rate (per 1,000 women aged 15-19, 1990-1995):	163
Government has expressed particular concern about:	
Morbidity and mortality resulting from induced abortion	No
Complications of child-bearing and childbirth	Yes
Maternal mortality rate (per 100,000 live births):	
National	..
Southern Africa (around 1988)	270
Female life expectancy at birth (1990-1995):	60.0

BACKGROUND

Under the Abortion and Sterilization Act of South Africa (1975), which Namibia inherited at the time of independence in March 1990, abortion is allowed only when continuance of the pregnancy would endanger the woman's life or constitute a serious threat to her physical or mental health, when the pregnancy is likely to result in the birth of a child suffering from a physical or mental defect or when the pregnancy results from unlawful intercourse, such as rape or incest, or from intercourse with a woman who is severely mentally retarded. In addition to the woman's physician, two other physicians are required to certify the existence of grounds for an abortion. An abortion must be performed in a government hospital or an approved medical facility. Any person performing an abortion in violation of these provisions is subject to imprisonment for up to five years and/or a fine.

Although few data are available, abortion does not appear to be widely practised in Namibia. Even among adolescents, most unwanted pregnancies are apparently carried to term and child abandonment is rare.

Prior to independence, the South West Africa People's Organization (SWAPO) operated health-care centres and introduced health and sex education curricula into schools located in its refugee camps outside Namibia. Since independence, SWAPO has been addressing a number of the major challenges in Namibia, such as high infant and maternal mortality, high rates of adolescent and overall fertility, large numbers of unplanned births and an extremely low level of family planning awareness and practice. It has decided to promote family planning in Namibia as part of a broader maternal and child health (MCH) programme, with an emphasis on birth-spacing. However, the fragmented administrative structure that exists in the health-care field has hampered the Government's actions. Access to prenatal, obstetric and post-natal care, as well as family planning services, is generally limited. Major constraints contributing to the poor access and quality of MCH and family planning include shortages of trained staff, lack of essential equipment and supplies, lack of information, education and communication material, inadequate transport and communication facilities and the vast distances separating communities and health facilities.

In pre-independence Namibia, the migrant labour system was an important factor in limiting fertility, because of spousal separation, often for periods of longer than one year. This situation is likely to change rapidly. In fact, a law has been passed to reduce the duration of such labour contracts, removing a check to population growth. The fact that breast-feeding and post-partum abstinence during breast-feeding are still prevalent is not expected to constitute a sufficient dampening effect on fertility, particularly because traditional birth-spacing practices are already beginning to be abandoned.

Teenage pregnancy is a matter of serious concern. A high proportion of teenage pregnancies are unwanted; a family health survey, for example, indicated that 35 per cent of adolescents reported their pregnancy to be unwanted.

INCIDENCE OF ABORTION

Place	Year	Measurement	Coverage

Information not readily available.

Source: Population Policy Data Bank maintained by the Population Division of the Department for Economic and Social Information and Policy Analysis of the United Nations Secretariat. For additional sources, see list of references.

Nauru

ABORTION POLICY

Grounds on which abortion is permitted:

To save the life of the woman	Yes
To preserve physical health	No
To preserve mental health	No
Rape or incest	No
Foetal impairment	No
Economic or social reasons	No
Available on request	No

Additional requirements:

An abortion requires the approval of two physicians and the written consent of the spouse or that of the parents if the woman is a minor.

FERTILITY AND MORTALITY CONTEXT

Government's view on fertility level:	Satisfactory
Government's intervention concerning fertility level:	To maintain
Government's policy on contraceptive use:	Direct support provided
Percentage of currently married women using modern contraception (aged 15-49):	..
Total fertility rate (1990-1995):	..
Age-specific fertility rate (per 1,000 women aged 15-19, 1990-1995):	..
Government has expressed particular concern about:	
Morbidity and mortality resulting from induced abortion	..
Complications of child-bearing and childbirth	..
Maternal mortality rate (per 100,000 live births):	
National	..
Oceania (around 1988)	600
Female life expectancy at birth (1990-1995):	..

BACKGROUND

The abortion law of Nauru, a small island nation in the Pacific Ocean, is based on the abortion law of neighbouring Queensland, Australia. Under the First Schedule Criminal Code Act of 1899 (sections 224-226 and 282), abortion is illegal except when the pregnant woman's life is in danger. To obtain an abortion, a woman must have the approval of two physicians and the written consent of her husband, or that of her parents if she is a minor.

Nauru has refrained from introducing an official family planning programme. However, as a welfare state, Nauru provides free health care to all its citizens, as well as support for family planning services. As there are no pharmacies on the island, contraceptives are available only by prescription in government hospitals and clinics.

INCIDENCE OF ABORTION

Place	Year	Measurement	Coverage

Information not readily available.

Source: Population Policy Data Bank maintained by the Population Division of the Department for Economic and Social Information and Policy Analysis of the United Nations Secretariat. For additional sources, see list of references.

Nepal

ABORTION POLICY

Grounds on which abortion is permitted:

To save the life of the woman	No*
To preserve physical health	No*
To preserve mental health	No*
Rape or incest	No*
Foetal impairment	No*
Economic or social reasons	No
Available on request	No

Additional requirements:

Additional information is not readily available.

---

* The Medical Council Rules of 1976 permit abortion to preserve the physical or mental health of the pregnant woman or if there is a possibility that the child would suffer from a physical deformity. A pregnancy due to rape or incest may be terminated under medical indications.

FERTILITY AND MORTALITY CONTEXT

Government's view on fertility level:	Too high
Government's intervention concerning fertility level:	To lower
Government's policy on contraceptive use:	Direct support provided
Percentage of currently married women using modern contraception (aged 15-49, 1986):	14
Total fertility rate (1990-1995):	5.5
Age-specific fertility rate (per 1,000 women aged 15-19, 1990-1995):	86
Government has expressed particular concern about:	
Morbidity and mortality resulting from induced abortion	Yes
Complications of child-bearing and childbirth	Yes
Maternal mortality rate (per 100,000 live births):	
National (1986)	850
Southern Asia (around 1988)	570
Female life expectancy at birth (1990-1995):	53.0

BACKGROUND

The Penal Code of Nepal, as amended up to 1976 (part 4, sections 10 and 28-33), forbids abortion except when performed during an act of "benevolent" nature. However, the law does not clarify or stipulate what constitutes an act of benevolent nature.

The abortion law of Nepal punishes the person performing the abortion, the pregnant woman and any person assisting in the termination of a pregnancy. The severity of the punishment depends upon whether the person performing the intervention knew that the woman was pregnant, whether the abortion was performed with the consent of the pregnant woman, the duration of the gestation period and whether the pregnancy resulted from an act of violence.

A person inducing an abortion without the consent of the pregnant woman may be punished by imprisonment for a period of two years if the duration of the pregnancy is less than six months and for three years if the gestation period exceeds six months. If the abortion is induced with the woman's consent, both the woman and the person performing it are subject to imprisonment for one year if the term of the pregnancy is less than six months and one and one half years if the woman is more than six months pregnant. Any person that knowingly commits an act of violence on a pregnant woman which results in an abortion may be imprisoned for three months if the woman is less than six months pregnant and for six months if the gestation period is over six months. Any person that unintentionally causes an abortion while committing an act of violence on a pregnant woman, but without the knowledge that she is pregnant, is subject to a fine of 25 Nepalese rupees (NRs) if the woman is less than six months pregnant and NRs 50 if the gestation period exceeds six months.

Recent studies indicate that the abortion law is strictly enforced in Nepal. A three-year study conducted in the early 1980s revealed that two thirds of all female inmates in Nepal were imprisoned on charges related to abortion and infanticide.

Abortion is also referred to in a provision of the Medical Council Rules of Nepal (1976) that defines the responsibilities of physicians. Rule 22 (J) of the Medical Council Rules states that a pregnancy can be terminated if its continuation poses a threat to the health of the pregnant woman or if there is a "possibility of physical deformity in the child or mental imbalance in the woman". This provision, however, also states that this "exception does not imply a sanction to do anything against the law". The provision has been interpreted in different ways; some believe that it justifies abortion on specific medical grounds, while others argue that it explicitly states that the exception should not be used to violate the law. Regardless of the interpretation of the law, hospital records show that abortions are performed in hospitals. Although hospitals are not allowed to carry out requests for abortion, they are obliged to admit patients for incomplete, threatened or spontaneous abortions.

Despite the strong social, religious and legal sanctions against abortion in Nepal, hospital-based and sample studies show that abortions are being performed in the country. Given the high fertility rate and a low rate of modern contraceptive use, as many as 11,000 induced abortions are estimated to be performed each year. The majority of the abortions are performed by traditional birth attendants using unsafe folk remedies. More than half of the maternal deaths in five major hospitals at Kathmandu resulted from abortion-related complications. One of the major causes of those deaths was the length of time that elapsed between the attempted abortion and hospitalization. A hospital survey conducted in the Kathmandu valley in the early 1980s found that 9 per cent of all hospital admissions for pregnancy or complications of delivery were due to induced abortion. A study carried out in rural Nepal in 1985 estimated an abortion rate of 3.58 per 1,000 women aged 15-49, which may, however, underestimate the true rate because wealthier Nepalese women tend to travel to neighbouring India to obtain an abortion. Among the chief reasons for seeking an abortion are completed family size, poor health, being economically disadvantaged, an out-of-wedlock pregnancy and contraceptive failure.

Nepal

Due to the unclear situation with regard to the legal status of abortion and its incidence, researchers and policy makers have suggested that the law be liberalized to permit abortion on demand within the first trimester, provided that the procedure is performed by a registered physician. The proposed change would also eliminate the discrepancy between the Nepal Medical Council Act and the Penal Code of Nepal. Efforts to amend the law have not been successful because abortion is prohibited in Nepal because both religion and established customs condemn the practice.

The Government has acknowledged that the high population growth rate and unbalanced population distribution seriously inhibit development. Based on the recommendation of the National Commission on Population, the Government accepted a long-term, comprehensive and multisectoral population strategy in 1983. The target of the strategy is to reduce the total fertility rate from 6.3 children per woman in 1980 to 4.0 by 1990 and to 2.5 by 2000. This goal implies a reduction of the population growth rate from 2.2 per cent in 1985 to 1.9 by 1990 and to 1.2 by 2000. This goal was reiterated in the Eighth Five-Year Plan for 1990-1995. In order to achieve the goal, the Government has placed a high priority on the provision of various family planning methods. Pills and condoms are provided free of charge at all health centres. Menstrual regulation is currently used by some women to terminate unwanted pregnancies. In order to receive this service, however, the couple must agree that the wife will have an intra-uterine device inserted afterward, or that either the husband or wife will undergo sterilization. Sterilization is one of the main methods of family planning in Nepal. The Government encourages couples with two or more children to adopt this method. In July 1983, the Government began to provide NR 100 to sterilization acceptors for lost wages or work time lost while undergoing and recuperating from sterilization.

INCIDENCE OF ABORTION

Place	Year	Measurement	Coverage

Information not readily available.

Source: Population Policy Data Bank maintained by the Population Division of the Department for Economic and Social Information and Policy Analysis of the United Nations Secretariat. For additional sources, see list of references.

ABORTION POLICY

Grounds on which abortion is permitted:

To save the life of the woman	Yes
To preserve physical health	Yes
To preserve mental health	Yes
Rape or incest	Yes
Foetal impairment	Yes
Economic or social reasons	Yes
Available on request	Yes

Additional requirements:

A five-day waiting period is required between the initial consultation and the performance of an induced abortion. An abortion must be performed in a licensed hospital or clinic. The cost of an induced abortion is subsidized by the Government.

FERTILITY AND MORTALITY CONTEXT

Government's view on fertility level:	Satisfactory
Government's intervention concerning fertility level:	No intervention
Government's policy on contraceptive use:	Indirect support provided
Percentage of currently married women using modern contraception (aged 18-37, 1988):	71
Total fertility rate (1990-1995):	1.7
Age-specific fertility rate (per 1,000 women aged 15-19, 1990-1995):	6

Government has expressed particular concern about:
Morbidity and mortality resulting from induced abortion	No
Complications of child-bearing and childbirth	No

Maternal mortality rate (per 100,000 live births):
National (1989)	5
Developed countries (around 1988)	26

Female life expectancy at birth (1990-1995):	80.5

Netherlands

Under the Penal Code of the Netherlands (1886), induced abortion was classified as a capital offence. However, proof that the foetus was alive at the time of the induced abortion was a requirement for conviction under the law. Because such proof was difficult to obtain, it was nearly impossible to convict anyone performing an induced abortion of having committed a capital offence under the existing law. In 1911, the abortion law in the Netherlands was amended to make induced abortion a crime against life and public morality. In practice, induced abortion was illegal in all circumstances except when performed to save the life of the mother. During the 1970s, several attempts were made to liberalize the abortion law, but they were not successful because of strong opposition. However, the existing law was not strictly enforced and induced abortion services were readily available.

On 1 May 1981, a far-reaching abortion law was adopted in the Netherlands. The law repealed the nineteenth-century statutes that severely restricted abortion. Currently, abortion is permitted virtually on request up to 13 weeks of gestation. If the pregnant woman attests to a state of distress, abortion is now allowed after 13 weeks. The law provides for abortions to be performed only in a licensed clinic or hospital. A five-day waiting period between the initial consultation and the procedure is required. During the waiting period, the woman must be counselled on alternative means of coping with her pregnancy; and if she decides to proceed with the abortion, she must be provided with after-care services that include methods of preventing unwanted pregnancy. The five-day waiting period may be waived if the woman's life is threatened. A second-trimester abortion can only be performed in a hospital or in an approved clinic.

Under article 2 of the law, clinics and hospitals that do not wish to perform abortions, on grounds of conscience, can apply for an exemption. Article 20 of the law exempts individuals from being forced to perform an induced abortion if it is against their belief. Religious associations have formulated directives for hospital and medical personnel seeking exemptions from performing abortions.

A physician that performs an induced abortion in an unlicensed clinic may be imprisoned for up to one year. Penalties exist for performing an induced abortion prior to the end of the five-day waiting period and also for failure of the physician to inform the woman of his decision concerning whether to assist with the abortion within the stipulated time period.

Although abortion was legalized in 1981, the regulation governing its practice was not formally adopted until 1984. Prior to the liberalization of the abortion law, abortion was widely available through private non-profit clinics and in some hospitals, due mainly to the widespread acceptance of family planning within the society.

In the Netherlands, family planning was traditionally discouraged because it was regarded as being contrary to the objectives of marriage and as promoting promiscuity. As a result, the practice did not receive the backing and support of the Government or a majority of the population, including health professionals. Contraceptives were not readily available and could not be advertised in the Netherlands until 1969. Moreover, physicians were reluctant to provide family planning services for fear of having to share in the responsibility for an unwanted pregnancy which might occur from contraceptive failure and which might in turn necessitate an induced abortion. This situation contributed to keeping the crude birth rate at the relatively high level of 20.7 per 1,000 during the mid-1960s.

The introduction of the pill in 1964 and its proven high reliability led to the widespread acceptance and practice of family planning. Since about 1965, family planning services have routinely been offered as part of general health-care services.

Even though family planning services had become fully accepted, abortion remained an unresolved problem in the Netherlands throughout much of the 1960s and 1970s. The main issue centred around the specificity and interpretation of the legal provision for allowing abortion on medical grounds. In 1966, an opinion by a highly regarded professor of law argued that the medical grounds for performing an induced abortion went beyond saving the mother's life to include any other grounds acceptable to the medical profession. This interpretation was affirmed by the Netherlands Ministry of Justice as being compatible with the general philosophical thrust of the legal system of the Netherlands. Furthermore, the Dutch Psychiatric Association expressed the opinion that it was the woman alone who could best determine if an abortion was necessary. The latter opinion relieved the physician of the burden of the decision and at the same time reduced the role of the physician to that of ensuring that the abortion procedure did not pose any risk to the woman's health. This situation virtually assured the availability of abortion on demand, even before the law legalizing abortion was passed in 1981.

Since November 1984, Netherlands women may obtain abortions free of charge under the Government-sponsored national health insurance system. The Exceptional Medical Expenses Fund covers the cost of abortions performed in clinics. Payment by this fund has not resulted in a rise in abortions, but rather has caused a shift in the balance of providers from hospitals to clinics. Although foreigners are not prohibited from having an abortion in the Netherlands, they are required to pay for it.

Abortion service providers are obligated under the law to keep systematic records of all abortion procedures, while maintaining the woman's anonymity. Prior to the enactment of the new law on induced abortion, providers routinely maintained records of abortion procedures but were under no obligation to provide such records to the health authorities.

A sizeable proportion of women undergoing induced abortion in the Netherlands are foreign-born. In 1984, out of a total of 43,200 induced abortions performed in the Netherlands, 18,700 were for residents in the Netherlands, and the balance were for women from neighbouring countries. In 1990, the abortion rate for Netherlands nationals was 5.2 per 1,000 women aged 15-44, and the abortion rate per 100 live births was 9.6, an incidence that is one of the lowest in the world. The incidence of induced abortion has been relatively stable in the Netherlands, mainly due to the high contraceptive prevalence rate (over 75 per cent). However, the population most at risk for an unwanted pregnancy are women in the age group 20-30. More than one third are typically married and have mainly used condoms, rhythm or withdrawal as their preferred contraceptive methods. Following an induced abortion, most women choose the pill, intra-uterine device or sterilization.

Netherlands

		INCIDENCE OF ABORTION	

Place	Year	Measurement	Coverage
National	1977	5.5 abortions/1,000 women aged 15-44	PR
National	1978	5.2 abortions/1,000 women aged 15-44	PR
National	1979	5.6 abortions/1,000 women aged 15-44	PR
National	1980	6.2 abortions/1,000 women aged 15-44	PR
National	1981	6.5 abortions/1,000 women aged 15-44	PR
National	1982	6.3 abortions/1,000 women aged 15-44	PR
National	1983	5.9 abortions/1,000 women aged 15-44	PR
National	1984	5.6 abortions/1,000 women aged 15-44	PR
National	1985	5.1 abortions/1,000 women aged 15-44	PR
National	1986	5.3 abortions/1,000 women aged 15-44	PR
National	1987	5.1 abortions/1,000 women aged 15-44	PR
National	1988	5.1 abortions/1,000 women aged 15-44	PR
National	1989	5.1 abortions/1,000 women aged 15-44	PR
National	1990	5.2 abortions/1,000 women aged 15-44	PR
National	1970	6.9 abortions/100 live births	PR
National	1975	8.4 abortions/100 live births	PR
National	1980	10.9 abortions/100 live births	PR
National	1985	9.7 abortions/100 live births	PR
National	1986	9.8 abortions/100 live births	PR
National	1987	9.5 abortions/100 live births	PR
National	1988	9.7 abortions/100 live births	PR
National	1989	9.7 abortions/100 live births	PR

Note: PR = provider registration; SP = survey provider; SW = survey of women; HR = hospital admission records. For a detailed description of these abbreviations and information on sources of the data, see technical notes in the annex.

Source: Population Policy Data Bank maintained by the Population Division of the Department for Economic and Social Information and Policy Analysis of the United Nations Secretariat. For additional sources, see list of references.

ABORTION POLICY

Grounds on which abortion is permitted:

To save the life of the woman	Yes
To preserve physical health	Yes
To preserve mental health	Yes
Rape or incest	Yes*
Foetal impairment	Yes
Economic or social reasons	No
Available on request	No

Additional requirements:

The fact that the pregnant woman is mentally subnormal or that she is near the beginning or the end of the usual child-bearing age, while not being a ground "in itself", can also be taken into account under medical indications. In general, an abortion must be performed by a registered physician in a licensed institution. Termination of pregnancy beyond 12 weeks of gestation may only be performed in an institution with a "full licence". The woman must obtain the approval of two certifying consultants, one of which must be an obstetrician/gynaecologist.

---

* Rape in itself is not a ground for abortion but may be taken into account under medical indications. A pregnancy occurring as a result of incest can be terminated on juridical grounds, while a pregnancy resulting from rape may be terminated under medical indications.

FERTILITY AND MORTALITY CONTEXT

Government's view on fertility level:	Satisfactory
Government's intervention concerning fertility level:	No intervention
Government's policy on contraceptive use:	Indirect support provided
Percentage of currently married women using modern contraception (aged 15 or over and at risk of pregnancy, 1976):	62
Total fertility rate (1990-1995):	2.1
Age-specific fertility rate (per 1,000 women aged 15-19, 1990-1995):	36
Government has expressed particular concern about:	
Morbidity and mortality resulting from induced abortion	No
Complications of child-bearing and childbirth	No
Maternal mortality rate (per 100,000 live births):	
National (1988)	17
Developed countries (around 1988)	26
Female life expectancy at birth (1990-1995):	78.7

New Zealand

Prior to 1977, abortion legislation in New Zealand was largely based on nineteenth-century laws of England and Wales, which had remained virtually unchanged in various criminal law revisions. Abortion was generally illegal except when performed "in good faith" for the preservation of the life of the pregnant woman or her physical or mental health. Because of the lack of clarity as to what constituted physical or mental health, there were variations in interpretation and application. This situation fuelled the arguments for reform of abortion law in New Zealand, particularly after the liberalization of abortion laws in the United Kingdom and in South Australia in the late 1960s.

Further legislation on abortion was enacted in the 1970s. The Crimes Act of 1961 was amended in 1977 and 1978 in order to provide a clearer definition of the grounds for legal abortion. According to sections 182-187A of the Crimes Act, an abortion is permitted during the first 20 weeks of gestation on medical grounds if the pregnancy imposes serious danger (not that normally attendant upon childbirth) to the life or to the physical or mental health of the woman; if there is substantial risk that the child, if born, would be seriously handicapped mentally or physically; if the pregnancy is the result of incest or of sexual intercourse with a girl under care or protection; or if the pregnant woman or girl is mentally "subnormal". In addition, the fact that the woman is near the beginning or the end of the usual child-bearing years or that there exists reasonable grounds for believing that the pregnancy is the result of rape, while not in themselves grounds, may be taken into account in determining whether the continuance of the pregnancy would result in serious danger to the woman's life or to her physical or mental health. After 20 weeks of gestation, an abortion is permitted only when it is necessary to save the life of the woman or to prevent serious permanent injury to her physical or mental health.

At about the same time, the Contraception, Sterilization, and Abortion Act of 1977 (No. 112) was enacted to establish the procedures under which a woman could obtain an abortion. Under sections 10-46 of this Act, a statutory body, the Abortion Supervisory Committee, was established to oversee the operation of abortion laws. The Committee consists of three members, two of whom must be registered physicians. A medical practitioner may apply to the Abortion Supervisory Committee to become a certifying consultant and thereby be empowered to declare that a woman has legal grounds for obtaining an abortion. A woman seeking an abortion must receive a letter of referral from her physician to a certifying consultant. She must then obtain a certificate stating that she has legal grounds signed by two certifying consultants, one of whom must be an obstetrician or a gynaecologist. If one consultant refuses, then the approval of a third may be sought. The agreement of the operating surgeon, who may be one of the two certifying consultants, must also be obtained.

In general an abortion can only be performed in an institution licensed under the Contraception, Sterilization, and Abortion Act. If gestation is more than 12 weeks, an abortion can only be performed in an institution with a "full licence". A woman must also receive counselling from a trained counsellor before the abortion is performed.

Some critics have argued that the procedure described above is so cumbersome that the new legislation has in effect made abortion laws in New Zealand more restrictive than before.

According to the Crimes Act, a person performing an unlawful abortion is subject to imprisonment for up to 14 years. The woman upon whom the abortion is performed is not considered to be a party to this offence. Under the Contraception, Sterilization, and Abortion Act of 1977, however, if she administers her own abortion, she is subject to payment of a fine not to exceed 200 New Zealand dollars ($NZ).

Abortion does not appear to be a major method of fertility regulation in New Zealand and seems to have played a minor role in the fertility decline over the past several decades. Although the incidence of induced abortion in New Zealand is comparatively low, it has risen significantly, increasing from 9.3 abortions per 1,000 women aged 15-44 in 1985 to 14.4 abortions per 1,000 women in 1991.

New Zealand

According to one estimate, about 90 per cent of abortions occurring in 1982 were performed for mental health reasons. The majority of these abortions were performed during the first trimester of pregnancy by vacuum aspiration. Most of the women that sought abortions during the early 1980s were under age 25, single, or had had a live birth or a previous induced abortion. One study conducted in 1991 found that during the period 1981-1989, even though most women obtaining abortions were of European descent, Maori women and women of Pacific island descent were overrepresented in the sample population when compared with their proportions in the total population. Other studies have shown that for the low-fertility population of European origin, induced abortion appears to be used primarily for timing purposes by young (under age 30) nulliparous women to delay their first birth; for the higher fertility minority populations, induced abortion is a backup method in cases of contraceptive failure for women that have achieved their desired family size.

In addition, teenage pregnancy has increasingly become a public issue in New Zealand. A significant proportion of teenage pregnancies are terminated by abortion.

Abortions performed in New Zealand at a public hospital are normally free of charge. Inequality of access to abortion services due to geographical distribution is a concern to policy makers. An issue warranting attention is that most of the women seeking an abortion in New Zealand have experienced contraceptive failure. In fact, more than one third of all women do not use any contraceptive method.

INCIDENCE OF ABORTION

Place	Year	Measurement	Coverage
National	1976	7.1 abortions/1,000 women aged 15-44	PR
National	1977	8.1 abortions/1,000 women aged 15-44	PR
National	1978	3.1 abortions/1,000 women aged 15-44	PR
National	1979	5.3 abortions/1,000 women aged 15-44	PR
National	1980	8.5 abortions/1,000 women aged 15-44	PR
National	1981	9.6 abortions/1,000 women aged 15-44	PR
National	1982	9.6 abortions/1,000 women aged 15-44	PR
National	1983	9.7 abortions/1,000 women aged 15-44	PR
National	1984	9.6 abortions/1,000 women aged 15-44	PR
National	1985	9.3 abortions/1,000 women aged 15-44	PR
National	1986	10.5 abortions/1,000 women aged 15-44	PR
National	1987	11.3 abortions/1,000 women aged 15-44	PR
National	1988	12.8 abortions/1,000 women aged 15-44	PR
National	1989	12.9 abortions/1,000 women aged 15-44	PR
National	1990	14.0 abortions/1,000 women aged 15-44	PR
National	1991	14.4 abortions/1,000 women aged 15-44	PR

Note: PR = provider registration; SP = survey provider; SW = survey of women; HR = hospital admission records. For a detailed description of these abbreviations and information on sources of the data, see technical notes in the annex.

Source: Population Policy Data Bank maintained by the Population Division of the Department for Economic and Social Information and Policy Analysis of the United Nations Secretariat. For additional sources, see list of references.

Nicaragua

ABORTION POLICY

Grounds on which abortion is permitted:

To save the life of the woman	Yes
To preserve physical health	No
To preserve mental health	No
Rape or incest	No
Foetal impairment	No
Economic or social reasons	No
Available on request	No

Additional requirements:

Consultation with a professional or group of professionals is prerequisite to obtaining a legal abortion. The woman's consent, as well as that of three physicians, is also required.

FERTILITY AND MORTALITY CONTEXT

Government's view on fertility level:	Too high
Government's intervention concerning fertility level:	To lower
Government's policy on contraceptive use:	Direct support provided
Percentage of currently married women using modern contraception (aged 15-49, 1981):	3
Total fertility rate (1990-1995):	5.0
Age-specific fertility rate (per 1,000 women aged 15-19, 1990-1995):	153
Government has expressed particular concern about:	
Morbidity and mortality resulting from induced abortion	Yes
Complications of child-bearing and childbirth	Yes
Maternal mortality rate (per 100,000 live births):	
National (88 per cent of national population, 1987)	300
Central America (around 1988)	160
Female life expectancy at birth (1990-1995):	68.5

BACKGROUND

Under the Criminal Code of Nicaragua, abortion is permitted only to save the life of the mother. Family planning services, which had been initiated in 1967, were limited in scope. Under the Sandinista Government, family planning activities were indirectly promoted through the support of non-governmental organizations.

Under the abortion law, a woman having an illegal abortion is subject to from two to four years of imprisonment, whereas the person performing the abortion faces a penalty of from one to two years. The penalty may be reduced if the pregnant woman's sole and principal motive was to conceal her "weakness". Abortion for contraceptive purposes is considered to be illegal.

In the mid-1980s, 45 per cent of all admissions to the largest maternity hospital at Managua were the result of illegal abortion. Media attention generated discussion over the possible liberalization of the abortion law, which medical experts largely favoured on health grounds. It was noted that whereas the number of abortions had remained more or less constant, the number of abortion-related deaths had actually increased, mainly because poorer women were unable to afford the fees charged by private clinics and therefore resorted to traditional midwives.

Since 1988, the major women's groups in Nicaragua have campaigned publicly on issues of women's legal rights, family planning and sex education. Leaders of these movements believe awareness of such matters is prerequisite to changing the abortion law. Since 1989, the Government has supported family planning activities directly through public-health facilities.

INCIDENCE OF ABORTION

Place	Year	Measurement	Coverage
National	1972	12.8 abortions/100 live births	HR

Note: PR = provider registration; SP = survey provider; SW = survey of women; HR = hospital admission records. For a detailed description of these abbreviations and information on sources of the data, see technical notes in the annex.

Source: Population Policy Data Bank maintained by the Population Division of the Department for Economic and Social Information and Policy Analysis of the United Nations Secretariat. For additional sources, see list of references.

Niger

ABORTION POLICY

Grounds on which abortion is permitted:

To save the life of the woman	Yes
To preserve physical health	No
To preserve mental health	No
Rape or incest	No
Foetal impairment	No
Economic or social reasons	No
Available on request	No

Additional requirements:

The attending physician must consult with two additional physicians, one of whom must be taken from a list of experts provided by the court. The physician must attest to the fact that the life of the woman cannot be saved by any other means than the intervention contemplated.

FERTILITY AND MORTALITY CONTEXT

Government's view on fertility level:	Too high
Government's intervention concerning fertility level:	To lower
Government's policy on contraceptive use:	Direct support provided
Percentage of currently married women using modern contraception (aged 15-49):	..
Total fertility rate (1990-1995):	7.1
Age-specific fertility rate (per 1,000 women aged 15-19, 1990-1995):	239

Government has expressed particular concern about:
Morbidity and mortality resulting from induced abortion	Yes
Complications of child-bearing and childbirth	Yes

Maternal mortality rate (per 100,000 live births):
National (1988)	700
Western Africa (around 1988)	760

Female life expectancy at birth (1990-1995):	48.1

174

Abortion legislation in the Niger is based on the Napoleonic Code of 1810, as amended by a French decree of 1939. Under the Penal Code of 15 July 1961 (No. 61-27, article 295), abortion is prohibited except when necessary to save the life of a pregnant woman who is seriously endangered. The penalty for anyone performing or attempting to perform an abortion is imprisonment for a term ranging from one to five years and a fine of 50,000-500,000 CFA francs (CFAF). For persons that routinely perform abortions, the penalty is increased to 5-10 years of imprisonment and/or *interdiction de séjour* (exile). Medical or paramedical personnel performing an abortion can, in addition, be temporarily suspended or completely prohibited from practising. A woman who induces or attempts to induce her own miscarriage may be imprisoned for a term of from six months to two years and fined CFAF 20,000-200,000.

Up to the early 1980s, the Government of the Niger pursued a pronatalist policy, and access to contraception was limited by the Government's adherence to the French law of 31 July 1920, which prohibited the importation, sale and advertisement of contraceptives.

At the first national family planning conference, held in the Niger in the early 1980s, the participants noted that the Koran did not prohibit contraception or abortion if the health of either the mother or child was in jeopardy. This was the first time that this issue was discussed in public, and the agreement of the participants on the issue was very important.

The National Conference on Family Health and Development, held at Niamey in January 1985, provided the impetus to repeal the French anticontraception law of 1920. Although the Government began providing direct support for the provision of contraceptives in 1986, it was only in 1988 that the anticontraception law was actually repealed (Ordinance No. 88-19 Authorizing the Practice of Contraception, 7 April 1988). In 1987, the Government approved an Economic and Social Development Plan (Ordinance No. 87-015) which contained family planning provisions. In 1989, the Family Planning Directorate, which was established within the Ministry of Social Affairs and Women's Promotion, was made responsible for the integration of family planning into all maternal and child health activities. In addition, the Government approved a family health action programme. In 1991, a series of recommendations was approved to facilitate access to contraception in the national family planning programme of the Niger.

Various attempts have been made to legalize abortion but, as of 1992, it remains illegal except to save the life of the woman. Despite a general government policy of promoting family planning, there is still widespread resistance to the concept of abortion among the political and traditional leadership in the Niger.

INCIDENCE OF ABORTION

Place	Year	Measurement	Coverage

Information not readily available.

Source: Population Policy Data Bank maintained by the Population Division of the Department for Economic and Social Information and Policy Analysis of the United Nations Secretariat. For additional sources, see list of references.

Nigeria

Grounds on which abortion is permitted:

To save the life of the woman	Yes
To preserve physical health	No
To preserve mental health	No
Rape or incest	No
Foetal impairment	No
Economic or social reasons	No
Available on request	No

Additional requirements:

Two physicians are required to certify that the pregnancy poses a serious threat to the life of the woman.

FERTILITY AND MORTALITY CONTEXT

Government's view on fertility level:	Too high
Government's intervention concerning fertility level:	To lower
Government's policy on contraceptive use:	Direct support provided
Percentage of currently married women using modern contraception (aged 15-49, 1990):	4
Total fertility rate (1990-1995):	6.4
Age-specific fertility rate (per 1,000 women aged 15-19, 1990-1995):	176
Government has expressed particular concern about:	
Morbidity and mortality resulting from induced abortion	Yes
Complications of child-bearing and childbirth	Yes
Maternal mortality rate (per 100,000 live births):	
National (1988)	800
Western Africa (around 1988)	760
Female life expectancy at birth (1990-1995):	54.3

BACKGROUND

An appreciation of the multiplicity of legal systems coexisting in Nigeria is essential for an understanding of the legal context of abortion in the country. The most common types of laws are: legislative laws; customary/traditional laws; Islamic laws; and English laws. The various systems of laws often treat different legal topics in different ways. In practice, the determination of which system of law will apply for any given case is made on the basis of such factors as the ethnic background and place of residence of the parties, their religious affiliation, the consent of the parties, the legal subject matter and the opinion of traditional elders and/or rulers. In the predominantly Muslim northern states of Nigeria, which contain about half the population of the country, the Penal Code, with heavy Islamic legal influence, is generally applied rather than the Criminal Code. In the southern states, abortion is governed by the Criminal Code.

Abortion law is relatively restrictive in Nigeria. A prison sentence of up to 14 years is provided for anyone convicted of performing an illegal abortion. As specified in sections 228 and 229 of the Criminal Code, any person that, with intent to cause the miscarriage of a woman, regardless of whether she is pregnant, "unlawfully administers to her or causes her to take any poison or other noxious thing, or uses force of any kind, or uses any other means whatsoever" is guilty of a felony and is subject to imprisonment for 14 years. Furthermore, these provisions apply also to any woman, whether or not "with child", that in attempting to cause her miscarriage, uses these means or other means herself, or permits them to be used or administered to her. In this case, she is subject to imprisonment for seven years." Section 230 of the Criminal Code states that persons convicted of knowingly supplying means "intended to be unlawfully used to procure the miscarriage of a woman" are subject to imprisonment for three years.

Under the Criminal Code, abortion is permitted only to save the life of the woman. Section 297 provides that "a person is not criminally responsible for performing in good faith and with reasonable care and skill a surgical operation...upon an unborn child for the preservation of the mother's life if the performance of the operation is reasonable, having regard to the patient's state at the time and all the circumstances of the case".

The Criminal Code law is modelled after the British Offences against the Person Act of 1861. It does not make a distinction between abortion performed by a qualified physician and that performed by an unqualified practitioner.

Section 232 of the Penal Code of northern Nigeria states that any person voluntarily causing a pregnant woman to miscarry, if such an intervention was not done to save the life of the woman, is subject to imprisonment for 14 years. A woman who causes her own miscarriage is considered to be within the meaning of this section. As provided in section 233 of the Penal Code, any person that, with intent to cause the miscarriage of a woman, regardless of whether she is pregnant, does any act that causes her death is subject to imprisonment for 14 years. However, the law does not seem to be strictly enforced, and very few cases of prosecution are reported.

In 1982, an attempt to liberalize abortion law in Nigeria was unsuccessful. A Termination of Pregnancy Bill, sponsored by the Nigerian Society for Gynaecologists and Obstetricians, was presented to the National Assembly. The Bill would have permitted abortion if two physicians certified that the continuation of a pregnancy would involve risk to the life of a pregnant woman, or of injury to her physical and mental health or to any existing children in her family greater than if the pregnancy were terminated. The Bill would also have allowed abortion if "there was a substantial risk that the child, if born, would suffer such physical and mental abnormalities as to be seriously handicapped". If the Bill had been passed, it would have permitted abortion only in the first 12 weeks of pregnancy, except to save the life of the woman. The Bill also would have permitted physicians to refuse to perform an abortion on grounds of conscience. The Bill was strongly opposed by religious leaders and by the Nigerian National Council of Women's Societies, who feared that

Nigeria

its passage would promote sexual promiscuity. A new attempt to liberalize the Nigerian abortion law was being considered in 1992.

Induced abortion is increasing and is considered to be a major cause of maternal mortality, which is quite high in Nigeria. Reports from several surveys, principally from university teaching hospitals, indicate that the highest risk group is young girls between 15 and 19 years old. The fear of interruptions in education, the risk of unemployment and the social stigma of raising a child born out of wedlock are the principal reasons for seeking an abortion. A significant number of incomplete abortions are regularly treated in hospitals in Nigeria, indicating a high incidence of illegal and poorly performed abortions. Moreover, abortion is reported to be widely available in the private sector.

National data on the incidence of abortion are not readily available, mainly because of the social stigma attached to having an abortion and the potentially severe consequences for the patient, as well as for the physician performing an abortion. Although abortion is generally illegal, there appears to be a large discrepancy between the law and the practice of abortion in Nigeria. A survey of hospitals in Nigeria conducted in 1984 indicates that a majority (55 per cent) of abortion cases involved young girls under age 20, for whom illegal abortion is currently the leading cause of death; some 85 per cent of those having an abortion were unmarried and 60 per cent of the women had at least a secondary-school education. In 1980, a Ministerial Committee of Inquiry estimated that there were 500,000 illegal abortions performed during that year.

Concerned about the unsatisfactory state of its population dynamics, the Government of Nigeria adopted a national population policy in 1988. Since then, the Government has actively supported and promoted the availability and distribution of family planning services through government facilities, as well as private and social marketing channels. However, the availability of family planning services is still felt to be limited and the use of modern methods of contraception is very low. Abortion laws have yet to receive any substantial reforms.

INCIDENCE OF ABORTION

Place	Year	Measurement	Coverage

Information not readily available.

Source: Population Policy Data Bank maintained by the Population Division of the Department for Economic and Social Information and Policy Analysis of the United Nations Secretariat. For additional sources, see list of references.

ABORTION POLICY

Grounds on which abortion is permitted:

To save the life of the woman	Yes
To preserve physical health	Yes
To preserve mental health	Yes
Rape or incest	Yes
Foetal impairment	Yes
Economic or social reasons	Yes
Available on request	Yes

Additional requirements:

The application for an abortion must be submitted by the pregnant woman. If the woman is mentally retarded or is suffering from a severe mental illness, the application may be submitted by the guardian. If the woman is under 16 years of age or is mentally retarded, the opinion of a parent or guardian concerning the abortion is also considered. Abortion is available on request during the first 12 weeks of gestation. Thereafter, a legal abortion requires the authorization of a committee composed of two physicians. An abortion must be performed by a physician. If the duration of the pregnancy exceeds 12 weeks, the abortion must be performed in a hospital; otherwise, it can be performed in any approved institution.

FERTILITY AND MORTALITY CONTEXT

Government's view on fertility level:	Satisfactory
Government's intervention concerning fertility level:	No intervention
Government's policy on contraceptive use:	No support provided
Percentage of currently married women using modern contraception (aged 15-49, 1988):	73
Total fertility rate (1990-1995):	2.0
Age-specific fertility rate (per 1,000 women aged 15-19, 1990-1995):	20
Government has expressed particular concern about:	
Morbidity and mortality resulting from induced abortion	No
Complications of child-bearing and childbirth	No
Maternal mortality rate (per 100,000 live births):	
National (1989)	8
Developed countries (around 1988)	26
Female life expectancy at birth (1990-1995):	80.5

Norway

In Norway, the abortion law was first liberalized in 1964 to permit abortion on medical, eugenic and humanitarian grounds. Socio-economic grounds were not considered sufficient reason for abortion, although the woman's overall situation had to be taken into consideration. The next abortion law (Law No. 50 of 13 June 1975) was less restrictive. It established an additional ground for legal abortion—one based exclusively on socio-economic grounds. The laws of 1964 and 1975 both provided that, regardless of the gestation period, the authorization of a committee composed of two physicians, was required before an abortion could be performed.

The third and current abortion law (Law No. 66 of 16 June 1978) is more liberal than those preceding it. This law entitles a woman to obtain abortion on request during the first 12 weeks of pregnancy. Between 12 and 18 weeks of pregnancy, a woman desiring to have an abortion must obtain authorization from a committee composed of two physicians. The committee may authorize the abortion if the pregnancy, childbirth or care of the child would result in unreasonable strain on the physical or mental health of the woman or place her in "difficult circumstances", if foetal impairment is suspected, if the pregnancy resulted from a criminal act or if the woman is suffering from severe mental illness or mental retardation. Under this law, if a woman requests an abortion on medical, eugenic or socio-economic grounds, the committee must consider her overall situation, including the extent to which she can provide satisfactory care for the child. The woman's assessment of her situation should also be taken into consideration. An abortion may not be performed after 18 weeks of gestation unless there are particularly important grounds for doing so. Authorization to terminate a pregnancy may not be granted if it is believed that the foetus is viable.

The woman must submit an application for abortion to a physician. If the duration of pregnancy exceeds 12 weeks, the woman must also submit her application to a committee of physicians. If the pregnant woman is under the age of 16, or is mentally retarded or suffering from severe mental illness, her parent or guardian is given an opportunity to express a view with regard to the abortion, unless there are particular reasons to the contrary. If the woman is mentally retarded or severely mentally ill, the application must be submitted by a parent or guardian.

Prior to the abortion, the physician is required to provide the pregnant woman (or, where appropriate, her parent or guardian) with information on the medical nature and effects of the procedure. A woman can also be provided information concerning other assistance that can be made available to her, if she so chooses. An abortion performed after 12 weeks of pregnancy must be performed in a hospital; before that limit, an abortion can be performed in other approved institutions. A legal abortion must be performed by a physician.

Under the Norwegian abortion law, health-care personnel that, on grounds of conscience, do not wish to assist with an abortion, must express this fact in writing, along with substantiating details, to the administrative director of the institution. The right to refuse in assisting in an abortion is only granted to personnel that perform or assist in the actual procedure and not to those providing services, care and treatment to the woman before or after the procedure. The right of health-care personnel to refuse to assist in an abortion has not been a major problem in Norway.

Any person that deliberately terminates a pregnancy or collaborates in such a termination in the absence of legal conditions for the operation or of a decision authorizing an abortion shall be sentenced to three years of imprisonment. Any person that deliberately gives false information in an application for an abortion or that illegally violates professional secrecy shall be subject to a fine or up to three months of imprisonment. The penal provisions do not apply to a woman who terminates her own pregnancy or assists in such a termination.

The liberalization of abortion legislation in Norway is closely tied to the development of the women's liberation movement. During the period 1921-1968, women's organizations played a minor role in abortion politics, with the medical profession and the Labour Party being the two major participants in the abortion debate. During the 1970s, the women's liberation movement made a significant contribution to abortion law by making it a political and ideological issue. Mainly because of the efforts of the women's groups, abortion was ultimately defined as part of the overall women's emancipation policy.

The Norwegian Fertility Survey conducted in 1977 found that the proportion of all pregnancies that were terminated by induced abortion increased from 2 to 11 per cent between 1950 and 1970. The incidence of abortion did not increase after liberalization of the abortion law. Beginning in 1975, the number of abortions and the abortion rates declined substantially.

Abortions in Norway are often used to time births. For example, studies show that the rate of induced abortion is high among women pursuing an education. Young women are also more likely to have an abortion than older women. In 1966, 30 per cent of women having an abortion were under age 25. The figure increased to 40 per cent in 1971 and to 50 per cent in 1979 and subsequent years. In addition, half of all pregnancies occurring to women under age 20 end in abortion.

INCIDENCE OF ABORTION

Place	Year	Measurement	Coverage
National	1968	7.3 abortions/1,000 women aged 15-44	PR
National	1969	8.9 abortions/1,000 women aged 15-44	PR
National	1970	10.9 abortions/1,000 women aged 15-44	PR
National	1971	14.1 abortions/1,000 women aged 15-44	PR
National	1972	16.4 abortions/1,000 women aged 15-44	PR
National	1973	18.2 abortions/1,000 women aged 15-44	PR
National	1974	20.0 abortions/1,000 women aged 15-44	PR
National	1975	19.7 abortions/1,000 women aged 15-44	PR
National	1976	18.9 abortions/1,000 women aged 15-44	PR
National	1977	19.6 abortions/1,000 women aged 15-44	PR
National	1978	18.4 abortions/1,000 women aged 15-44	PR
National	1979	17.7 abortions/1,000 women aged 15-44	PR
National	1980	16.3 abortions/1,000 women aged 15-44	PR
National	1981	16.4 abortions/1,000 women aged 15-44	PR
National	1982	15.8 abortions/1,000 women aged 15-44	PR
National	1983	15.7 abortions/1,000 women aged 15-44	PR
National	1984	15.9 abortions/1,000 women aged 15-44	PR
National	1985	16.3 abortions/1,000 women aged 15-44	PR
National	1986	17.1 abortions/1,000 women aged 15-44	PR
National	1987	16.8 abortions/1,000 women aged 15-44	PR
National	1988	17.1 abortions/1,000 women aged 15-44	PR
National	1989	17.9 abortions/1,000 women aged 15-44	PR
National	1990	16.7 abortions/1,000 women aged 15-44	PR

Note: PR = provider registration; SP = survey provider; SW = survey of women; HR = hospital admission records. For a detailed description of these abbreviations and information on sources of the data, see technical notes in the annex.

Source: Population Policy Data Bank maintained by the Population Division of the Department for Economic and Social Information and Policy Analysis of the United Nations Secretariat. For additional sources, see list of references.

V. ADDITIONAL AND REVISED COUNTRY PROFILES

ABORTION POLICY

Grounds on which abortion is permitted:

To save the life of the woman	Yes
To preserve physical health	Yes
To preserve mental health	Yes
Rape or incest	Yes
Foetal impairment	Yes
Economic or social reasons	Yes
Available on request	Yes

Additional requirements:

An abortion requires the consent of the pregnant woman; it is authorized if performed by a licensed physician in a hospital or other recognized medical institution. Abortion is available on request during the first 12 weeks of gestation. Thereafter, induced abortion is available within 28 weeks from conception on judicial, genetic, vital, broad medical and social grounds, as well as for personal reasons if authorized by a commission of local physicians.

FERTILITY AND MORTALITY CONTEXT

Government's view on fertility level:	Satisfactory
Government's intervention concerning fertility level:	To maintain
Government's policy on contraceptive use:	Direct support provided
Percentage of currently married women using modern contraception (aged 15-49, 1990):	12
Total fertility rate (1985-1990):	2.6
Age-specific fertility rate (per 1,000 women aged 15-19, 1985-1990):	62
Government has expressed particular concern about:	
Morbidity and mortality resulting from induced abortion	Yes
Complications of child-bearing and childbirth	Yes
Maternal mortality rate (per 100,000 live births):	
National (1990)	40.1
Developed countries (around 1988)	26
Female life expectancy at birth (1985-1990):	72.8

Armenia

As was the case with all of the former Soviet republics, Armenia, known prior to 1992 as the Armenian Soviet Socialist Republic, was subject to the abortion legislation and regulations of the former Union of Soviet Socialist Republics. As a result, abortion practices in Armenia were similar to those throughout the former USSR.

The description given below pertains to the situation in Armenia prior to independence.

The Soviet law of 27 June 1936 prohibited induced abortion in most circumstances, permitting it only for eugenic reasons. Physicians and non-medical personnel that performed abortions in hospitals or as part of an out-patient service were subject to a maximum of three years in prison. A husband, relative or physician who pressured a woman into having an abortion could be sentenced to a maximum of two years in prison. The pregnant woman could be prosecuted by public trial and/or be required to pay a large fine.

In a decree of 23 November 1955, the Soviet Government repealed the prohibition of abortion. Regulations issued in 1956 and subsequently in 1982 specified that abortions could be performed during the first 12 weeks of gestation, although not less than six months after a woman's previous abortion. An abortion was considered illegal if not performed in a hospital or if the person performing the abortion did not have an advanced medical education. The maximum penalty for an illegal abortion was set at eight years in a labour camp.

In 1974, the Ministry of Public Health of the USSR published a document entitled "On the side-effects and complications of oral contraceptives", in which the mass use of oral contraception was de facto prohibited. On 5 June 1987, in Order No. 757, the Ministry of Public Health legalized and officially permitted the provision of early vacuum aspirations in any clinic regardless of the place of residence of the woman. Vacuum aspiration had been the method of induced abortion provided during the first 20 days of pregnancy with the obligatory diagnosis of pregnancy.

In the 1980s, the Ministry of Public Health continued its efforts to decrease the number of illegal abortions by formally broadening the grounds on which abortions were legal and increasing their availability. Most of the later changes were not followed by a simultaneous increase in actual de facto accessibility of abortion services. On 31 December 1987, the Ministry of Public Health published Order No. 1342, which permits induced abortion during the first 28 weeks of gestation on judicial, genetic, broad medical and social grounds (for example, more than five children in the family), as well as on demand with the special authorization of a commission of local physicians.

The high incidence of abortion has been attributed to a number of factors, including shortages of high-quality modern contraceptives and reliance upon less reliable traditional methods, a lack of knowledge among couples of contraception and of the detrimental health consequences of frequent abortions and the absence of adequate training for physicians, nurses, teachers and other specialists. In 1989, the availability of condoms in the entire former Soviet Union amounted to only 11 per cent of demand; intra-uterine devices (IUDs), 30 per cent; and pills, 2 per cent. Data from the All-Union sample survey of contraceptive use conducted in 1990 indicate that, in Armenia, 12 per cent of all women aged 15-49 years regularly used contraception, 10 per cent sometimes used contraception, 60 per cent did not use any contraceptive method and 18 per cent knew nothing about contraception. Sample survey data show that in 1988 at Erevan, the capital of Armenia, of every 100 contraceptive users, 43 per cent used condoms, 12 per cent used the vaginal douche method, 11 per cent practised coitus interruptus, 10 per cent used an IUD and the remaining 24 per cent used other methods.

In 1989, a total of 26,141 induced abortions were registered in Armenia, giving an abortion rate of 31.2 per 1,000 women aged 15-49 years, one of the lowest rates in the former Soviet Union. The actual figure is much higher, because this total does not include most abortions performed in departmental health services and commercial clinics, early vacuum aspirations and self-induced abortions. Over 70 per cent of all induced abortions at Erevan were performed on women over age 25 or after the second or third delivery, and they were used to prevent subsequent births. In 1988, 4 per cent of all induced abortions were performed on primigravidae. No early vacuum aspirations were recorded in 1988. In 1989, illegal abortions calculated on the basis of their registered complications accounted for 22 per cent of all abortions and 75 per cent of all abortions among primigravidae. Among women under age 17, they accounted for 71 per cent of all induced abortions.

Maternal mortality rates in Armenia were 27.0 and 29.4 per 100,000 births in 1980 and 1988, respectively, one of the lowest rates in the former Soviet Union; in 1988, 10 per cent of all maternal deaths were due to criminal abortion.

INCIDENCE OF ABORTION

Place	Year	Measurement	Coverage
National	1970	71.3 abortions/1,000 women aged 15-49	PR
National	1975	60.5 abortions/1,000 women aged 15-49	PR
National	1980	38.8 abortions/1,000 women aged 15-49	PR
National	1985	38.4 abortions/1,000 women aged 15-49	PR
National	1988	33.0 abortions/1,000 women aged 15-49	PR
National	1989	31.2 abortions/1,000 women aged 15-49	PR
National	1990	30.1 abortions/1,000 women aged 15-49	PR

Note: PR = provider registration; SP = survey provider; SW = survey of women; HR = hospital admission records. For a detailed description of these abbreviations and information on sources of the data, see technical notes in the annex.

Source: Population Policy Data Bank maintained by the Population Division of the Department for Economic and Social Information and Policy Analysis of the United Nations Secretariat. For additional sources, see list of references.

Azerbaijan

Grounds on which abortion is permitted:

To save the life of the woman	Yes
To preserve physical health	Yes
To preserve mental health	Yes
Rape or incest	Yes
Foetal impairment	Yes
Economic or social reasons	Yes
Available on request	Yes

Additional requirements:

An abortion requires the consent of the pregnant woman; it is authorized if performed by a licensed physician in a hospital or other recognized medical institution. Abortion is available on request during the first 12 weeks of gestation. Thereafter, induced abortion is available within 28 weeks from conception on judicial, genetic, vital, broad medical and social grounds, as well as for personal reasons if authorized by a commission of local physicians.

FERTILITY AND MORTALITY CONTEXT

Government's view on fertility level:	Satisfactory
Government's intervention concerning fertility level:	To maintain
Government's policy on contraceptive use:	Direct support provided
Percentage of currently married women using modern contraception (aged 15-49, 1990):	7
Total fertility rate (1985-1990):	2.8
Age-specific fertility rate (per 1,000 women aged 15-19, 1985-1990):	24

Government has expressed particular concern about:
Morbidity and mortality resulting from induced abortion	Yes
Complications of child-bearing and childbirth	Yes

Maternal mortality rate (per 100,000 live births):
National (1990)	9.3
Developed countries (around 1988)	26

Female life expectancy at birth (1985-1990):	73.8

188

BACKGROUND

As was the case with all of the former Soviet republics, Azerbaijan, known prior to 1992 as the Azerbaijan Soviet Socialist Republic, was subject to the abortion legislation and regulations of the former Union of Soviet Socialist Republics. As a result, abortion practices in Azerbaijan were similar to those throughout the former USSR.

The description given below pertains to the situation in Azerbaijan prior to independence.

The Soviet law of 27 June 1936 prohibited induced abortion in most circumstances, permitting it only for eugenic reasons. Physicians and non-medical personnel that performed abortions in hospitals or as part of an out-patient service were subjected to a maximum of three years in prison. A husband, relative or physician who pressured a woman into having an abortion could be sentenced to a maximum of two years in prison. The pregnant woman could be prosecuted by public trial and/or be required to pay a large fine.

In a decree of 23 November 1955, the Soviet Government repealed the prohibition of abortion. Regulations issued in 1956 and subsequently in 1982 specified that abortions could be performed during the first 12 weeks of gestation, although not less than six months after a woman's previous abortion. An abortion was considered illegal if not performed in a hospital or if the person performing the abortion did not have an advanced medical education. The maximum penalty for an illegal abortion was set at eight years in a labour camp.

In 1974, the Ministry of Public Health of the USSR published a document entitled "On the side-effects and complications of oral contraceptives", in which the mass use of oral contraception was de facto prohibited. On 5 June 1987, in Order No. 757, the Ministry of Public Health legalized and officially permitted the provision of early vacuum aspirations in any clinic regardless of the place of residence of the woman. Vacuum aspiration had been the method of induced abortion provided during the first 20 days of pregnancy with the obligatory diagnosis of pregnancy.

During the 1980s, the Ministry of Public Health continued its efforts to decrease the number of illegal abortions by formally broadening the grounds on which abortions were legal and increasing their availability. Most of the later changes were not followed by a simultaneous increase in actual de facto accessibility of abortion services. On 31 December 1987, the Ministry of Public Health published Order No. 1342, which permits induced abortion during the first 28 weeks of gestation on judicial, genetic, broad medical and social grounds (for example, more than five children in the family), as well as on demand with the special authorization of a commission of local physicians.

The high incidence of abortion has been attributed to a number of factors, including shortages of high-quality modern contraceptives and reliance upon less reliable traditional methods, a lack of knowledge among couples of contraception and of the detrimental health consequences of frequent abortions and the absence of adequate training for physicians, nurses, teachers and other specialists. In 1989, the availability of condoms in the entire former Soviet Union amounted to only 11 per cent of demand; intra-uterine devices (IUDs), 30 per cent; and pills, 2 per cent. Data from the 1990 All-Union sample survey of contraceptive use indicate that, in Azerbaijan, 6.5 per cent of all women aged 15-49 years regularly used contraception, 10.1 per cent sometimes used contraception, 41.9 per cent did not use any contraceptive method and 35.3 per cent knew nothing about contraception.

In 1989, a total of 42,134 induced abortions were registered in Azerbaijan, giving an abortion rate of 23.9 per 1,000 women aged 15-49 years, the lowest rate in the former Soviet Union. The actual figure is much higher, because this total does not include most abortions performed in departmental health services and commercial clinics, early vacuum aspirations and self-induced abortions. In 1988, 2.9 per cent of all induced abortions were performed on primigravidae, and 10 per cent of all induced abortions were vacuum

Azerbaijan

aspirations. In 1989, illegal abortions, calculated on the basis of their registered complications, accounted for 23.8 per cent of all abortions and 75.1 per cent of all abortions among primigravidae. Among women under age 17, they accounted for 100 per cent of all induced abortions.

Maternal mortality rates in Azerbaijan were 38.7 and 21.7 per 100,000 births in 1980 and 1988, respectively, one of the lowest rates in the former Soviet Union; in 1988, 7.5 per cent of all maternal deaths were due to criminal abortion.

INCIDENCE OF ABORTION

Place	Year	Measurement	Coverage
National	1970	56.6 abortions/1,000 women aged 15-49	PR
National	1975	43.3 abortions/1,000 women aged 15-49	PR
National	1980	39.0 abortions/1,000 women aged 15-49	PR
National	1985	30.8 abortions/1,000 women aged 15-49	PR
National	1988	26.6 abortions/1,000 women aged 15-49	PR
National	1989	23.9 abortions/1,000 women aged 15-49	PR
National	1990	14.1 abortions/1,000 women aged 15-49	PR

Note: PR = provider registration; SP = survey provider; SW = survey of women; HR = hospital admission records. For a detailed description of these abbreviations and information on sources of the data, see technical notes in the annex.

Source: Population Policy Data Bank maintained by the Population Division of the Department for Economic and Social Information and Policy Analysis of the United Nations Secretariat. For additional sources, see list of references.

ABORTION POLICY

Grounds on which abortion is permitted

To save the life of the woman	Yes
To preserve physical health	Yes
To preserve mental health	Yes
Rape or incest	Yes
Foetal impairment	Yes
Economic or social reasons	Yes
Available on request	Yes

Additional requirements

Medical consultation is required if gestation is greater than 12 weeks. The abortion must be performed by a licensed physician in a hospital or other approved establishment, with the consent of the woman.

FERTILITY AND MORTALITY CONTEXT

Government's view on fertility level:	Satisfactory
Government's intervention concerning fertility level:	To maintain
Government's policy on contraceptive use:	Direct support provided
Percentage of currently married women using modern contraception (aged 15-49, 1990):	13
Total fertility rate (1985-1990):	2.0
Age-specific fertility rate (per 1,000 women aged 15-19, 1985-1990):	36
Government has expressed particular concern about:	
Morbidity and mortality resulting from induced abortion	Yes
Complications of child-bearing and childbirth	Yes
Maternal mortality rate (per 100,000 live births):	
National (1990)	22
Developed countries (around 1988)	26
Female life expectancy at birth (1985-1990):	75.9

Belarus

As was the case with all of the former Soviet republics, Belarus, known prior to 1991 as the Byelorussian Soviet Socialist Republic, was subject to the abortion legislation and regulations of the former Union of Soviet Socialist Republics. As a result, abortion practices in Belarus were similar to those throughout the former USSR.

The description given below pertains to the situation in Belarus prior to independence.

The Soviet law of 27 June 1936 prohibited induced abortion in most circumstances, permitting it only for eugenic reasons. Physicians and non-medical personnel that performed abortions in hospitals or as part of an out-patient service were subject to a maximum of three years in prison. A husband, relative or physician who pressured a woman into having an abortion could be sentenced to a maximum of two years in prison. The pregnant woman could be prosecuted by public trial and/or be required to pay a large fine.

In a decree of 23 November 1955, the Soviet Government repealed the prohibition of abortion. Regulations issued in 1956 and subsequently in 1982 specified that abortions could be performed during the first 12 weeks of gestation, although not less than six months after a woman's previous abortion. An abortion was considered illegal if not performed in a hospital or if the person performing the abortion did not have an advanced medical education. The maximum penalty for an illegal abortion was set at eight years in a labour camp.

In 1974, the Ministry of Public Health of the USSR published a document entitled "On the side-effects and complications of oral contraceptives", in which the mass use of oral contraception was de facto prohibited. On 5 June 1987, in Order No. 757, the Ministry of Public Health legalized and officially permitted the provision of early vacuum aspirations in any clinic regardless of the place of residence of the woman. Vacuum aspiration had been the method of induced abortion provided during the first 20 days of pregnancy with the obligatory diagnosis of pregnancy.

During the 1980s, the Ministry of Public Health continued its efforts to decrease the number of illegal abortions by formally broadening the grounds on which abortions were legal and increasing their availability. Most of the later changes were not followed by a simultaneous increase in actual de facto accessibility of abortion services. On 31 December 1987, the Ministry of Public Health published Order No. 1342, which permits induced abortion during the first 28 weeks of the gestation period on judicial, genetic, broad medical and social grounds (for example, more than five children in the family), as well as on demand with the special authorization of a commission of local physicians.

The high incidence of abortion has been attributed to a number of factors, including shortages of high-quality modern contraceptives and reliance upon less reliable traditional methods, a lack of knowledge among couples of contraception and of the detrimental health consequences of frequent abortions and the absence of adequate training for physicians, nurses, teachers and other specialists. In 1989, the availability of condoms in the entire former Soviet Union amounted to only 11 per cent of demand; intra-uterine devices (IUDs), 30 per cent; and pills, 2 per cent. Data from the 1990 All-Union sample survey of contraceptive use indicate that, in Belarus, 13 per cent of all women aged 15-49 years regularly used contraception, 9.8 per cent sometimes used contraception, 60.4 per cent did not use any contraceptive method and 11.8 per cent knew nothing about contraception.

In 1989, a total of 250,905 induced abortions were registered in Belarus, giving an abortion rate of 114.7 per 1,000 women aged 15-44 years, one of the highest rates in the former Soviet Union. The actual figure is much higher, because this total does not include most abortions performed in departmental health services and commercial clinics, early vacuum aspirations and self-induced abortions. In 1988, 6.9 per cent of all induced abortions were performed on primigravidae, and 2.6 per cent of all abortions were early vacuum aspirations. In 1989, illegal abortions, calculated on the basis of their registered complications, accounted for 15.6 per cent of all abortions and 24 per cent of all abortions among primigravidae. Among women under age 17, they accounted for 23 per cent of all induced abortions.

Maternal mortality rates in Belarus were 29.1 and 24.5 per 100,000 births in 1980 and 1988, respectively, one of the lowest rates in the former Soviet Union; in 1988, 25 per cent of all maternal deaths were due to criminal abortion.

INCIDENCE OF ABORTION

Place	Year	Measurement	Coverage
National	1970	91.3 abortions/1,000 women aged 15-49	PR
National	1975	93.0 abortions/1,000 women aged 15-49	PR
National	1980	94.1 abortions/1,000 women aged 15-49	PR
National	1985	94.3 abortions/1,000 women aged 15-49	PR
National	1988	62.3 abortions/1,000 women aged 15-49	PR
National	1989	114.7 abortions/1,000 women aged 15-49	PR
National	1990	114.3 abortions/1,000 women aged 15-49	PR

Note: PR = provider registration; SP = survey provider; SW = survey of women; HR = hospital admission records. For a detailed description of these abbreviations and information on sources of the data, see technical notes in the annex.

Source: Population Policy Data Bank maintained by the Population Division of the Department for Economic and Social Information and Policy analysis of the United Nations Secretariat. For additional sources, see list of references.

Bosnia and Herzegovina

ABORTION POLICY

Grounds on which abortion is permitted:

To save the life of the woman	Yes
To preserve physical health	Yes
To preserve mental health	Yes
Rape or incest	Yes
Foetal impairment	Yes
Economic or social reasons	Yes
Available on request	Yes

Additional requirements:

An abortion must be performed in a hospital or other authorized health-care facility. If the woman is a minor, approval of her parents or guardian is required, unless she is aged 16 or over and earns her own living. After the first 10 weeks of pregnancy, special authorization by a commission, composed of a gynaecologist-obstetrician, a general physician or a specialist in internal medicine and a social worker or a psychologist, is required.

FERTILITY AND MORTALITY CONTEXT

Government's view on fertility level:	Satisfactory
Government's intervention concerning fertility level:	To maintain
Government's policy on contraceptive use:	Direct support provided
Percentage of currently married women using modern contraception (aged 15-49, 1976):	47
Total fertility rate (1985-1990):	1.8
Age-specific fertility rate (per 1,000 women aged 15-19, 1985-1990):	38
Government has expressed particular concern about:	
Morbidity and mortality resulting from induced abortion	No
Complications of child-bearing and childbirth	No
Maternal mortality rate (per 100,000 live births):	
National (1990)	10.5
Developed countries (around 1988)	26
Female life expectancy at birth (1985-1990):	74.4

BACKGROUND

Bosnia and Herzegovina achieved independence from the former State of Yugoslavia in 1991 and adopted a new Constitution. However, abortion is still regulated by the Law of 7 October 1977 passed by the former republic to implement article 191 of the Federal Constitution of Yugoslavia of 21 February 1974, which proclaims that "it is a human right to decide on the birth of children". According to the law of Bosnia and Herzegovina, abortion is allowed on request during the first 10 weeks of pregnancy. The intervention must be performed in a hospital or other authorized health-care facility. If the woman is a minor, approval of her parents or guardian is required, unless she is aged 16 or over and earns her own living. After the first 10 weeks of pregnancy, special authorization by a commission, composed of a gynaecologist-obstetrician, a general physician or a specialist in internal medicine and a social worker or a psychologist, is required. The Commission may consent to an abortion when it is medically established that it would be impossible to save the woman's life or prevent damage to her health, whether it be during pregnancy, delivery or post-partum condition; when it is medically established that it is probable that the child would be born with a serious congenital physical or mental defect; or when the conception is a consequence of a criminal act of rape, criminal act of sexual intercourse with an incompetent person, criminal act of sexual intercourse in consequence of abuse of authority, criminal act of sexual intercourse with a child or criminal act of incest. The woman can appeal to the Commission of Second Instance if the Commission of First Instance rejects her request. After 20 weeks of gestation, abortion may be allowed only to save the life or health of a woman who is seriously endangered.

Penal provisions are imposed on medical organizations that violate provisions of the law. The Criminal Code provides sanctions for the performance of illegal abortions; a woman, however, is never held criminally responsible for inducing her own abortion or for cooperating in such a procedure.

Beginning in 1952, abortion legislation in Yugoslavia went through a process of liberalization in response to the significant increase in illegal abortions associated with high levels of morbidity and mortality. The subsequent changes in the abortion laws—general principles were adopted at the federal level and laws were implemented at the local level—were expressly directed to facilitating access to legal abortion in order to discourage illegal practices. For instance, a significant decline in the number of illegal abortions is attributed to the decision in 1969 to eliminate the requirement of a commission's approval for termination of pregnancies of less than 10 weeks' duration, a requirement which had been a practical and psychological obstacle to abortion. The policy of liberalizing legal regulations with regard to abortion, which was pursued by the former Government of Yugoslavia, was furthered by increased numbers of medical institutions, better access to information on abortion services and higher levels of education. Although abortion rates continued to be very high, the former Government essentially achieved its objective: illegal abortions were practically eliminated and the country experienced a significant decline in maternal morbidity and mortality related to abortion. For example, mortality associated with abortion declined from 180 per 100,000 abortions in 1960 to 11 per 100,000 in 1976.

High rates of abortion, as well as a high rate of repeat abortions, an increase in second-trimester abortions, and an increase in abortions among adolescents, are problems experienced throughout the country. They demonstrate that women rely upon abortion as a contraceptive method, with consequent increased health risks. A major area of concern for Bosnia and Herzegovina is the high rate of abortion among adolescents, compared with the relatively low overall incidence of abortion, particularly in comparison with the other republics.

Family planning services have been a part of the regular medical services in Yugoslavia since the mid-1950s. A family planning institution was established in 1963 at the national and local levels, and the Family Planning Association, affiliated with the International Planned Parenthood Federation, has existed since 1966. However, sex education in the schools and family planning counselling have not been systematically developed, and family planning has encountered continuing resistance throughout the country. As a result,

Bosnia and Herzegovina

insufficient knowledge and fear of modern methods of contraception is widespread. According to official data, the percentage of married women using any method of contraception in Bosnia and Herzegovina decreased slightly between 1970 and 1976—from 48.8 to 46.6. However, withdrawal accounted for 73.6 per cent of the total. It is estimated that contraceptive practices were similar in the 1980s.

In the late 1980s, the former Government indicated deep concern about the high abortion rates and low rates of usage of modern contraceptive methods. In the Resolution on Population Development and Family Planning of 1989, which set out general principles and directions with regard to population matters, special emphasis was given to fertility and family planning. The resolution, while reconfirming the right of each person to decide freely on the number and spacing of children, as established in the Constitution of 1974, was directed to attaining replacement-level fertility in all areas of the country. In part to reduce the incidence of abortion and in part to reduce fertility in some republics, specific measures to disseminate contraceptive information and supplies more widely were adopted at the federal level. Social welfare measures, such as prolonged maternity leave, child allowances and child-care facilities, were also strengthened in areas of the country where fertility was below replacement level. In the former State of Yugoslavia, the republics and autonomous provinces were responsible for implementing within their borders the general principles of population policy adopted by the Federal Assembly. However, the republics and autonomous provinces often abstained from executing federally adopted policies. Implementation of population policies in particular was often hampered by the sensitivity of demographic issues in maintaining the fragile equilibrium between individual republics and the national minorities.

INCIDENCE OF ABORTION

Place	Year	Measurement	Coverage
National	1983	44.2 abortions/1,000 women aged 15-49	PR
National	1984	47.4 abortions/1,000 women aged 15-49	PR
National	1985	51.0 abortions/1,000 women aged 15-49	PR
National	1986	52.7 abortions/1,000 women aged 15-49	PR
National	1987	55.0 abortions/1,000 women aged 15-49	PR
National	1988	57.5 abortions/1,000 women aged 15-49	PR

Note: PR = provider registration; SP = survey provider; SW = survey of women; HR = hospital admission records. For a detailed description of these abbreviations and information on sources of the data, see technical notes in the annex.

Source: Population Policy Data Bank maintained by the Population Division of the Department for Economic and Social Information and Policy Analysis of the United Nations Secretariat. For additional sources, see list of references.

ABORTION POLICY

Grounds on which abortion is permitted:

To save the life of the woman	Yes
To preserve physical health	Yes
To preserve mental health	Yes
Rape or incest	Yes
Foetal impairment	Yes
Economic or social reasons	Yes
Available on request	Yes

Additional requirements:

An abortion can be performed on request within the first six months of gestation, with the consent of the spouse. Second-trimester abortions must be performed in a hospital or clinic.

FERTILITY AND MORTALITY CONTEXT

Government's view on fertility level:	Too high
Government's intervention concerning fertility level:	To lower
Government's policy on contraceptive use:	Direct support provided
Percentage of currently married women using modern contraception (aged 15-49, 1988):	71
Total fertility rate (1990-1995):	2.2
Age-specific fertility rate (per 1,000 women aged 15-19, 1990-1995):	17
Government has expressed particular concern about:	
Morbidity and mortality resulting from induced abortion	Yes
Complications of child-bearing and childbirth	Yes
Maternal mortality rate (per 100,000 live births):	
National (1982)	50
Eastern Asia (around 1988)	120
Female life expectancy at birth (1990-1995):	72.6

China

BACKGROUND

The Criminal Code of China (enacted by the National People's Congress on 1 July 1979) does not contain any provisions under which abortion, performed with the consent of the pregnant woman, constitutes an offence. Early abortions are performed in a clinic by medical personnel using the vacuum aspiration technique; second-trimester abortions are performed in a hospital by a physician. Abortion services are provided by the Chinese Government as a public service. A woman receives 14 days of paid sick leave for a first-trimester abortion or 30 days if the pregnancy is terminated after the first trimester. In some parts of the country, paid sick leave is extended if a woman who has an abortion has an intra-uterine device (IUD) inserted or is sterilized after the abortion is performed. Although most abortions are performed in the early months of pregnancy, the Government permits abortions to be performed up to six months of gestation.

In the early 1950s, an abortion was permitted only under certain conditions. At that time, official statements of the central Government indicated that abortion was allowed when continuation of the pregnancy was medically undesirable, when the spacing of children was too close or when a mother with a child that is four months or less in age had again become pregnant and experienced difficulties in breast-feeding. In such cases, a joint application of the couple and certification of a physician were required before the abortion could be performed. Under certain circumstances, special work or work (or study) that was too heavy could also be used as a legitimate reason for an abortion, but any request for the operation had to first be certified by the key personnel of the responsible organization and also approved by a medical organization. Abortions were to be performed as early as possible, preferably within the first month of pregnancy and at the latest not beyond the second month.

The results of data from the 1953 census contributed to the Government's decision to introduce and support the use of contraception and abortion to reduce the rate of population growth. On 12 April 1957, the Public Health Ministry announced that, from that date, all applications for abortion or sterilization would be free of restrictions concerning age, number of children and approval procedures. However, abortion could only be performed once a year and was permitted only within the first 10 weeks of the gestation period. The Government stressed the necessity for promoting contraception as a preventive measure, with abortion being used mainly as a backup measure in cases of contraceptive failure.

In the early 1970s, the Chinese Government began to incorporate population activities into the planning of its national economy. The planned birth model was introduced, national goals were set and an education model of communication was developed. The "Later-Longer-Fewer" (Wan-Xi-Shao) campaign was followed in 1979 by the one-child per couple policy. An article of the Chinese constitution provided that individual couples were required to practise and the Government to support family planning. Family planning policy has been implemented primarily through a nationwide family planning programme that includes a strong information and education component, free contraceptive services and a system of economic and social incentives and disincentives, which vary by province and between rural and urban areas.

In 1990, contraceptive use by women of reproductive age was reportedly above 85 per cent, a rate that is close to the level in most developed countries and well above the rates in other Asian countries. A majority of contraceptive users in China rely upon one of three methods—IUD, female sterilization or male sterilization, although many other methods, such as the pill and condoms, are also available and widely used. However, the contraceptive failure rate is relatively high in China.

Studies have shown that, in many cases following an IUD expulsion, no other method was substituted to prevent pregnancy. Therefore, due to contraceptive non-use and to contraceptive failure, abortion has assumed a greater role in controlling fertility. Government officials have estimated that 70 per cent of the abortions in China are due to contraceptive failure. The number of abortions was in the range of from 4 million to 5 million per annum between 1971 and 1978. In 1979, when the one-child policy went into effect, the incidence of abortion was about 7.9 million. The number reached an all-time high around 1983, with a recorded 14.4 million, and then gradually declined to about 10.6 million in 1989.

According to statistics released by the National Family Planning Commission at the end of 1990, the incidence of abortion was not uniform across the country. In general, there were lower ratios of abortions to births in the inland provinces than in the coastal provinces. The populations of some inland provinces include large numbers of minorities that have been exempt from some of the population policy measures. With a few exceptions, abortion ratios were higher in cities and towns than in rural areas. Part of these rural/urban differentials has been attributed to behavioural factors and part to the possibility that many rural women seeking a late-trimester abortion have had the procedure performed in a large hospital in a city.

According to some studies undertaken in the late 1980s, abortion rates, in general, increase sharply the higher the order of pregnancy. A clinical study on abortion conducted in 1990, covering certain regions and cities in provinces—such as Jiangsu, Shanghai and Sichuan municipality—reported an average of 1.08 children for the urban respondents versus 1.60 children for the rural respondents.

INCIDENCE OF ABORTION

Place	Year	Measurement	Coverage
National	1971	23.0 abortions/1,000 women aged 15-44	PR
National	1972	27.6 abortions/1,000 women aged 15-44	PR
National	1973	28.7 abortions/1,000 women aged 15-44	PR
National	1974	27.3 abortions/1,000 women aged 15-44	PR
National	1975	27.2 abortions/1,000 women aged 15-44	PR
National	1976	24.7 abortions/1,000 women aged 15-44	PR
National	1977	26.6 abortions/1,000 women aged 15-44	PR
National	1978	26.6 abortions/1,000 women aged 15-44	PR
National	1979	37.7 abortions/1,000 women aged 15-44	PR
National	1980	44.3 abortions/1,000 women aged 15-44	PR
National	1981	39.1 abortions/1,000 women aged 15-44	PR
National	1982	54.0 abortions/1,000 women aged 15-44	PR
National	1983	60.4 abortions/1,000 women aged 15-44	PR
National	1984	36.2 abortions/1,000 women aged 15-44	PR
National	1985	43.0 abortions/1,000 women aged 15-44	PR
National	1986	44.3 abortions/1,000 women aged 15-44	PR
National	1987	38.6 abortions/1,000 women aged 15-44	PR
National	1988	45.9 abortions/1,000 women aged 15-44	PR
National	1989	37.5 abortions/1,000 women aged 15-44	PR

Note: PR = provider registration; SP = survey provider; SW = survey of women; HR = hospital admission records. For a detailed description of these abbreviations and information on sources of the data, see technical notes in the annex.

Source: Population Policy Data Bank maintained by the Population Division of the Department for Economic and Social Information and Policy Analysis of the United Nations Secretariat. For additional sources, see list of references.

Croatia

Grounds on which abortion is permitted:

To save the life of the woman	Yes
To preserve physical health	Yes
To preserve mental health	Yes
Rape or incest	Yes
Foetal impairment	Yes
Economic or social reasons	Yes
Available on request	Yes

Additional requirements:

An abortion must be performed in a hospital or other authorized health-care facility. If the pregnant woman is under age 16, the consent of her parents or guardian is required. After the first 10 weeks of pregnancy, special authorization by a commission, composed of a gynaecologist-obstetrician, a general physician or a specialist in internal medicine and a social worker or a psychologist, is required.

FERTILITY AND MORTALITY CONTEXT

Government's view on fertility level:	Satisfactory
Government's intervention concerning fertility level:	To maintain
Government's policy on contraceptive use:	Direct support provided
Percentage of currently married women using modern contraception (aged 15-49, 1976):	70
Total fertility rate (1985-1990):	1.7
Age-specific fertility rate (per 1,000 women aged 15-19, 1985-1990):	34
Government has expressed particular concern about:	
Morbidity and mortality resulting from induced abortion	No
Complications of child-bearing and childbirth	No
Maternal mortality rate (per 100,000 live births):	
National (1990)	10.4
Developed countries (around 1988)	26
Female life expectancy at birth (1985-1990):	75.4

BACKGROUND

When Croatia achieved independence from the former Federal Republic of Yugoslavia in 1991 and adopted a new Constitution, the law regulating abortion was not modified. To implement article 191 of the Federal Constitution of Yugoslavia of 21 February 1974, which proclaims that "it is a human right to decide on the birth of children", the former republic passed a comprehensive law on 21 April 1978 concerning all aspects of fertility regulation (e.g., contraception, sterilization, abortion and the treatment of infertility). It also modified the Criminal Code, with respect to sanctions for unlawful abortion. According to the Croatian law, abortion is allowed on request during the first 10 weeks of pregnancy. The intervention must be performed in a hospital or other authorized health-care facility. If the woman is under age 16, the authorization of her parents or guardian is required. After the first 10 weeks of pregnancy, the intervention must be approved by a commission of experts, composed of a specialist in gynaecology and obstetrics, a general physician or a specialist in internal medicine and a social worker or a psychologist. The Commission may consent to an abortion when it is medically established that it would be impossible to save the woman's life or prevent damage to her health, whether it be during pregnancy, delivery, or post-partum condition; when it is medically established that it is probable that the child would be born with a serious congenital physical or mental defect; or when the conception is a consequence of a criminal act of rape, criminal act of sexual intercourse with an incompetent person, criminal act of sexual intercourse in consequence of abuse of authority, criminal act of sexual intercourse with a child or criminal act of incest. The woman can appeal to a Commission of Second Instance if the Commission of First Instance rejects her request. An abortion can always be performed if the life or health of the pregnant woman is seriously endangered or if an abortion has already been initiated.

A fine of 2,000-10,000 dinars is imposed upon medical organizations that violate provisions of the law in performing an intervention. A fine of 1,000-5,000 dinars is imposed upon an organization that does not notify the competent authority after performing an intervention. Minor fines are imposed upon persons responsible for the violation. According to the Criminal Code, any persons performing an abortion in violation of the provisions of the law may be punished by imprisonment for from three months to three years. The penalty is increased to imprisonment for from six months to five years if the person performing the abortion earns his living by such an activity or if the intervention results in serious injury to the pregnant woman. If the pregnancy termination was performed without the consent of the pregnant woman, the penalty is imprisonment for from one to eight years.

Beginning in 1952, abortion legislation in Yugoslavia went through a process of liberalization in response to the significant increase in illegal abortions associated with high levels of morbidity and mortality. The subsequent changes in the abortion laws—general principles were adopted at the federal level and laws were implemented at the local level—were expressly directed at facilitating access to legal abortion in order to discourage illegal practices. For instance, a significant decline in the number of illegal abortions is attributed to the decision in 1969 to eliminate the requirement of a commission's approval for termination of pregnancies of less than 10 weeks, a requirement which had served as a practical and psychological obstacle to abortion. The policy of liberalizing legal regulations with regard to abortion, which was pursued by the former Government of Yugoslavia, was furthered by increased numbers of medical institutions, better access to information on abortion services and higher levels of education. Although abortion rates continued to be very high, the former Government essentially achieved its objective: illegal abortions were practically eliminated and the country experienced a significant decline in maternal morbidity and mortality related to abortion. For example, in Croatia, mortality associated with abortion declined from 18 deaths per 10,000 abortions in 1960 to 0.4 deaths per 10,000 abortions in 1977.

High rates of abortion, as well as the high rate of repeat abortion, an increase in second-trimester abortions and an increase in abortions among adolescents, are problems experienced throughout the country. They demonstrate that women rely upon abortion as a contraceptive method, with consequent increased health risks. With regard to its overall abortion rates, Croatia is situated in the middle range among the former Yugoslav republics.

Croatia

Family planning services had been a part of the regular medical services in Yugoslavia since the mid-1950s. A family planning institution was established in 1963 at the national and local levels, and the Family Planning Association (affiliated with the International Planned Parenthood Federation) has existed since 1966. However, sex education in the schools and family planning counselling have not been systematically developed, and family planning has encountered continuing resistance throughout the country. As a result, insufficient knowledge and fear of modern methods of contraception is widespread. Although Croatia has a higher contraceptive prevalence rate than the other former Yugoslav republics and is one of the few republics where contraceptive use has increased since the 1970s, use of modern contraceptive methods is still very limited and abortion remains a basic means of birth control. According to official data, the percentage of married women using any method of contraception in Croatia increased slightly between 1970 and 1976 from 68.3 to 69.5. However, withdrawal accounted for 76.2 per cent of the total. It is estimated that contraceptive practices were similar in the 1980s.

In the late 1980s, the federal Government indicated deep concern about the high abortion rates and low rates of usage of modern contraceptive methods. In the Resolution on Population Development and Family Planning of 1989, which set out general principles and directions with regard to population matters, special emphasis was given to fertility and family planning. The resolution, while reconfirming the right of each person to decide freely on the number and spacing of children as established in the Constitution of 1974, was directed to attaining replacement-level fertility in all areas of the country. In part to reduce the incidence of abortion and in part to reduce fertility, in some republics specific measures to disseminate contraceptive information and supplies more widely were taken at the federal level. Social welfare measures, such as prolonged maternity leave, child allowances and child-care facilities, were also strengthened in areas of the country where fertility was below replacement level. In the former State of Yugoslavia, the Republics and autonomous provinces were responsible for implementing within their borders the general principles of population policy adopted by the Federal Assembly. However, the republics and provinces often abstained from executing federally adopted policies. Implementation of population policies, in particular, was often hampered by the sensitivity of demographic issues in maintaining the fragile equilibrium between individual republics and the national minorities.

Croatia was one of the more economically advanced republics in Yugoslavia. Before independence, Croatia was experiencing fertility rates below replacement level (1.7 children per woman in the 1980s). The republic has long implemented policy measures to promote higher fertility. For instance, in 1973, Croatia became the first republic to extend maternity leave until the child reached one year of age.

INCIDENCE OF ABORTION

Place	Year	Measurement	Coverage
National	1983	47.4 abortions/1,000 women aged 15-49	PR
National	1984	48.5 abortions/1,000 women aged 15-49	PR
National	1985	48.8 abortions/1,000 women aged 15-49	PR
National	1986	48.0 abortions/1,000 women aged 15-49	PR
National	1987	50.2 abortions/1,000 women aged 15-49	PR
National	1988	44.3 abortions/1,000 women aged 15-49	PR

Note: PR = provider registration; SP = survey provider; SW = survey of women; HR = hospital admission records. For a detailed description of these abbreviations and information on sources of the data, see technical notes in the annex.

Source: Population Policy Data Bank maintained by the Population Division of the Department for Economic and Social Information and Policy Analysis of the United Nations Secretariat. For additional sources, see list of references.

ABORTION POLICY

Grounds on which abortion is permitted:

To save the life of the woman	Yes
To preserve physical health	Yes
To preserve mental health	Yes
Rape or incest	Yes
Foetal impairment	Yes
Economic or social reasons	Yes
Available on request	Yes

Additional requirements:

Abortion can be legally performed until the seventh month of pregnancy. Abortions are performed at provincial hospitals free of charge.

FERTILITY AND MORTALITY CONTEXT

Government's view on fertility level:	Satisfactory
Government's intervention concerning fertility level:	To maintain
Government's policy on contraceptive use:	Direct support provided
Percentage of currently married women using modern contraception (aged 15-49):	..
Total fertility rate (1990-1995):	2.4
Age-specific fertility rate (per 1,000 women aged 15-19, 1990-1995):	26
Government has expressed particular concern about: Morbidity and mortality resulting from induced abortion	..
Complications of child-bearing and childbirth	..
Maternal mortality rate (per 100,000 live births): National	..
Eastern Asia (around 1988)	120
Female life expectancy at birth (1990-1995):	73.9

Democratic People's Republic of Korea

The Criminal Code of March 1950 states that abortion is allowed in the Democratic People's Republic of Korea "for important reasons". The particulars of these reasons are not specified in the law. If an abortion is induced in the absence of an "important reason", the person performing the abortion is subject to penalties, including imprisonment for up to three years. However, neither a woman having an abortion nor one inducing her own abortion are held criminally liable.

Although information on the abortion law of the Democratic People's Republic of Korea is difficult to obtain, reports suggest that abortion is permitted on request, up to the seventh month of pregnancy, as women do not usually resort to abortion unless they have a strong justification which can easily qualify as "an important reason". It has been reported that abortion is performed at provincial maternity hospitals free of charge.

Family planning programmes have been operative in the Democratic People's Republic of Korea since the early 1970s. Such programmes are integrated into maternal and child health services and are administered by the Ministry of Public Health. Information, education and communication activities are important elements of the programme. The Ministry of Public Health provides contraceptives and consultations in the obstetrics-gynaecology departments of all hospitals and clinics. These services are also provided through the "section doctor system", whereby one physician is responsible for the health of a group of neighbourhood families. Because the country's family planning programme relied heavily upon locally produced intra-uterine devices (IUDs) (the method used by 80-90 per cent of all contraceptive users), which had high failure rates and caused serious side-effects, international assistance was provided for the importation of IUDs.

INCIDENCE OF ABORTION

Place	Year	Measurement	Coverage

Information not readily available.

Source: Population Policy Data Bank maintained by the Population Division of the Department for Economic and Social Information and Policy Analysis of the United Nations Secretariat. For additional sources, see reference section.

ANNEX

Technical notes

The most commonly employed sources of abortion statistics include provider registration (PR), surveys of providers (SP), surveys of women (SW) and hospital admission records (HR). A detailed description of each source of data and its deficiencies is included in the main text in the section concerning statistics on induced abortion. These notes describe, for each country[a] for which abortion data were obtained, the source of data and the type of data obtained.

ARMENIA

The estimates are based on numbers of abortions and female age distributions obtained from *Naselenie SSSR, 1987* and *1988*; and *Demografichesky Ezhegodnik SSSR, 1990* (USSR, State Committee on Statistics, 1988, 1989, 1990); and from the Statistical Committee of the Commonwealth of Independent States. The rates include officially registered abortions and exclude illegal abortions. After 1988, the data include early-stage abortions performed by vacuum aspiration.

AZERBAIJAN

The estimates are based on numbers of abortions and female age distributions obtained from *Naselenie SSSR, 1987* and *1988*; and *Demografichesky Ezhegodnik SSSR, 1990* (USSR, State Committee on Statistics, 1988, 1989, 1990); and from the Statistical Committee of the Commonwealth of Independent States. The rates include officially registered abortions and exclude illegal abortions. After 1988, the data include early-stage abortions performed by vacuum aspiration.

BELARUS

The estimates are based on numbers of abortions and female age distributions obtained from *Naselenie SSSR, 1987* and *1988*; and *Demografichesky Ezhegodnik SSSR, 1990* (USSR, State Committee on Statistics, 1988, 1989, 1990); and from the Statistical Committee of the Commonwealth of Independent States. The rates include officially registered abortions and exclude illegal abortions. After 1988, the data include early-stage abortions performed by vacuum aspiration.

BOSNIA AND HERZEGOVINA

Abortion rates were obtained from the Federal Statistical Office and the Federal Institute for Health Care of the former State of Yugoslavia.

CHINA

Chinese data on abortion are considered to be fairly reliable. If anything, they may be overestimating true abortion rates, as abortion records are the basis on which the health department is reimbursed for procedures performed by the planned births office. However, given scarce resources, the planned births office was careful

---

[a] Countries covered in chapters IV and V are listed alphabetically in these notes.

CROATIA

The data were obtained from the Federal Statistical Office and the Federal Institute for Health Care of the former State of Yugoslavia.

GEORGIA

The estimates are based on numbers of abortions and female age distributions obtained from *Naselenie SSSR, 1987* and *1988*; and *Demografichesky Ezhegodnik SSSR, 1990* (USSR, State Committee on Statistics, 1988, 1989, 1990); and from the Statistical Committee of the USSR and the Committee on Socio-economic Information of the Republic of Georgia. Rates include officially registered abortions and exclude illegal abortions. After 1988, the data include early-stage abortions performed by vacuum aspiration.

GERMANY

Figures for the former Federal Republic of Germany and the former German Democratic Republic were obtained from Höhn, Memmey and Wendt (1990) and from Henshaw and Morrow (1990). Estimates for 1990 and 1991 are based on numbers of abortions derived from German Information Centre (1992) and female age distributions reported by national statistical offices. For calculation of rates for combined Germany, age distributions of women from the United Nations assessment in 1992 were also used.

GREECE

The estimates are based on numbers of abortions, births and female age distribution reported by the national statistical office.

GUATEMALA

The data were obtained from Viel (1988). The abortion ratio represents the number of hospitalized abortions per number of births among the beneficiaries of the social services in Guatemala. The figure includes both induced and spontaneous abortions.

GUYANA

The figures were obtained from a World Health Organization report on the frequency and mortality of unsafe abortion (WHO, 1990). The data are based on hospital admission records for admissions for complications from abortion (including spontaneous induced, illegal, septic, complete and incomplete).

HONDURAS

The data were obtained from Viel (1988). The abortion ratio represents the number of hospitalized abortions per number of births among the beneficiaries of the social services in Honduras. The figure includes both induced and spontaneous abortions.

HUNGARY

The estimated rates are based on numbers of abortions obtained from the Council of Europe (1991) and on age distributions of women derived from the United Nations assessment in 1992 and various issues of the United Nations *Demographic Yearbook*.

ICELAND

The estimated rates are based on numbers of abortions obtained from the Council of Europe (1991) and on age distributions of women derived from the United Nations assessment in 1992 and various issues of the United Nations *Demographic Yearbook*.

INDIA

The estimated rates are based on numbers of abortions reported by the country and on female age distributions derived from various issues of the United Nations *Demographic Yearbook*.

INDONESIA

The figures were obtained from a World Health Organization report on the frequency and mortality of unsafe abortion (WHO, 1990). The data are based on abortions, excluding legal abortions, performed in hospitals at Jakarta.

IRELAND

The data up to 1987 were derived from Henshaw and Morrow (1990) and for 1988-1990 from the Alan Guttmacher Institute. The rates are based only on numbers of abortions obtained in England and Wales by residents of Ireland. They exclude an unknown number of residents of Ireland that gave an address in England.

ISRAEL

The estimated rates are based on numbers of abortions derived from *Statistical Abstract of Israel, 1991* and from various issues of the United Nations *Demographic Yearbook* and on female age distributions reported by country.

ITALY

The estimated rates are based on numbers of abortions obtained from the Council of Europe (1991) and on age distributions of women derived from the United Nations assessment in 1992 and various issues of the United Nations *Demographic Yearbook*.

JAPAN

Up to 1987, the rates were obtained from Henshaw and Morrow (1990). For the years 1988-1990, rates are estimated on the basis of numbers of abortions and age distributions of women reported by the national statistical office. For 1990, the age distribution was taken from the United Nations assessment in 1992.

KAZAKHSTAN

The estimates are based on numbers of abortions and female age distributions obtained from *Naselenie SSSR, 1987* and *1988*; and *Demografichesky Ezhegodnik SSSR, 1990* (USSR, State Committee on Statistics, 1988, 1989, 1990); and from the Statistical Committee of the Commonwealth of Independent States. The rates include officially registered abortions and exclude illegal abortions. After 1988, the data include early-stage abortions performed by vacuum aspiration.

KUWAIT

The figures were obtained from a World Health Organization report on the frequency and mortality of unsafe abortion (WHO, 1990). The data are based on hospital admissions for complications from abortion (including spontaneous induced, illegal, septic, complete and incomplete).

KYRGYZSTAN

The estimates are based on numbers of abortions and female age distributions obtained from *Naselenie SSSR, 1987* and *1988*; and *Demografichesky Ezhegodnik SSSR, 1990* (USSR, State Committee on Statistics, 1988, 1989, 1990); and from the Statistical Committee of the Commonwealth of Independent States. The rates include officially registered abortions and exclude illegal abortions. After 1988, the data include early-stage abortions performed by vacuum aspiration.

LATVIA

The estimates are based on numbers of abortions and female age distributions derived from *Estestvennoe dvizhenie i migratsiya naseleniya v Latviisko Respublike v 1991* (Latvia, 1992); and from *Naselenie SSSR, 1987* and *1988*; and *Demografichesky Ezhegodnik SSSR, 1990* (USSR, State Committee on Statistics, 1988, 1989, 1990); and the Statistical Committee of the USSR. The rates include officially registered abortions and exclude illegal abortions. After 1988, the data include early-stage abortions performed by vacuum aspiration.

LITHUANIA

The estimates are based on numbers of abortions and female age distributions obtained from *Women and Family in Lithuania* (Lithuania, 1992); and from *Naselenie SSSR, 1987* and *1988*; and *Demografichesky Ezhegodnik SSSR, 1990* (USSR, State Committee on Statistics, 1988, 1989, 1990); and the Statistical Committee of the USSR. The rates include officially registered abortions and exclude illegal abortions. After 1988, the data include early-stage abortions performed by vacuum aspiration.

MAURITIUS

The figures were obtained from a World Health Organization report on the frequency and mortality of unsafe abortion (WHO, 1990). The data are based on hospital admission records for admissions for complications from abortion (including spontaneous induced, illegal, septic, complete and incomplete).

MEXICO

The data were obtained from Viel (1988). The abortion ratio represents the number of hospitalized abortions per number of births among the beneficiaries of the social services in Mexico. The figure includes both induced and spontaneous abortions.

MONGOLIA

Abortion rates were obtained from Dashzeveg (1992).

NETHERLANDS

The estimated rates up to 1988 are based on numbers of abortions derived from the Council of Europe (1991), and on age distributions of women derived from the United Nations assessment in 1992 and various issues of the United Nations *Demographic Yearbook.* For 1989-1990, the data were obtained from the Alan Guttmacher Institute.

NEW ZEALAND

The figures are derived from *Demographic Trends, 1992* (New Zealand, 1993).

NICARAGUA

The data were obtained from Viel (1988). The abortion ratio represents the number of hospitalized abortions per number of births among the beneficiaries of the social services in Nicaragua. The figure includes both induced and spontaneous abortions.

NORWAY

The estimated rates are based on numbers of abortions obtained from the Council of Europe (1991) and various issues of *Statistical Yearbook of Norway*, and on female age distributions from the United Nations assessment in 1992 and various issues of the United Nations *Demographic Yearbook.*

REFERENCES

The references for this volume are divided into two sections: the first contains the general references used for the introductory chapters as well as for background information throughout the volume; the second contains the references used in the individual country profiles. The latter references are presented by country. Unless otherwise indicated, data used in the country profiles were taken from replies to the Sixth and Seventh United Nations Population Inquiry among Governments and from other materials in the Population Policy Data Bank maintained by the Population Division of the Department for Economic and Social Information and Policy Analysis of the United Nations Secretariat.

A. FOR THE INTRODUCTION AND BACKGROUND TEXT

Boland, Reed (1992). Selected legal developments in reproductive health in 1991. *Family Planning Perspectives* (New York), vol. 24, No. 4 (July/August), pp. 178-185.

Cairns, Gail (1984). Law and the status of women in Latin America: a survey. Development Law and Policy Program Working Paper, No. 13. New York: Columbia University, Center for Population and Family Health.

Cook, Rebecca J. (1989). Abortion laws and policies: challenges and opportunities. In "Women's health in the third world: the impact of unwanted pregnancy", A. Rosenfield and others, eds. *International Journal of Gynecology and Obstetrics* (Limerick, Ireland), Supplement No. 3, pp. 61-87.

_____, and Bernard M. Dickens (1979). Abortion laws in Commonwealth countries. In "Women's health in the third world: the impact of unwanted pregnancy", A. Rosenfield and others, eds. *International Digest of Health Legislation* (Geneva), vol. 30, pp. 395-502.

_____ (1982). *Emerging Issues in Commonwealth Abortion Laws, 1982.* London: Commonwealth Secretariat.

_____ (1986). *Issues in Reproductive Health Law in the Commonwealth.* London: Commonwealth Secretariat.

David, Henry P. (1983). Abortion: its prevalence, correlates, and costs. In *Determinants of Fertility in Developing Countries*, Rodolfo A. Bulatao and Ronald D. Lee, eds., with Paula E. Hollerbach and John Bongaarts, vol. 2. New York: Academic Press.

David, René, and John E. C. Brierley (1978). *Major Legal Systems in the World Today.* London: Stevens & Sons.

El-Kammash, Magdi M. (1971). Islamic countries. In *Population and Law*, Luke T. Lee and Arthur Larson, eds. Leiden, Netherlands: A. W. Sijthoff; and Durham, North Carolina: Rule of Law Press.

El-Moiz Nigm, Abd (1986). Human rights and health care. Cairo, Egypt: Assuit University Faculty of Law.

Francome, Colin (1988). United Kingdom. In *International Handbook on Abortion*, Paul Sachdev, ed. New York; Westport, Connecticut; and London: Greenwood Press.

Glendon, Mary Ann (1987). *Abortion and Divorce in Western Law.* Cambridge, Massachusetts: Harvard University Press.

Hecht, Jacqueline (1987). La législation de l'avortement en Europe de l'Est et en Union Soviétique. *Politiques de population: études et documents* (Louvain-la-Neuve, Belgium), vol. III, No. 1 (juin), pp. 89-105.

Henshaw, Stanley K., and Evelyn Morrow (1990). *Induced Abortion: A World Review, 1990 Supplement.* New York: The Alan Guttmacher Institute.

International Planned Parenthood Federation (1986). *Family Planning in Five Continents,* London.

Kloss, Diana M., and Bertram L. Raisbeck (1973). *Law and Population Growth in the United Kingdom.* Law and Population Monograph Series, No. 11. Medford, Massachusetts: Tufts University, The Fletcher School of Law and Diplomacy.

Knoppers, Bartha Maria, and Isabel Brault (1989). *La loi et l'avortement dans les pays francophones.* Montreal, Canada: Les Editions Thémis.

Lee, Luke T., and Arthur Larson, eds. (1971). *Population and Law.* Leiden, Netherlands: A. W. Sijthoff; and Durham, North Carolina: Rule of Law Press.

Liskin, Laurie S. (1980). *Complications of Abortion in Developing Countries.* Population Reports, Series F, No. 7. Baltimore, Maryland: The Johns Hopkins University, Population Information Program.

Moore-Čavar, Emily Campbell (1974). *International Inventory on Information on Induced Abortion.* New York: Columbia University, International Institute for the Study of Human Reproduction.

Pan American Health Organization (1990). *Health Conditions in the Americas: 1990 Edition,* vol. I. Scientific Publication, No. 524, Washington, D.C.

Royston, Erica, and Sue Armstrong, eds. (1989). *Preventing Maternal Deaths.* Geneva: World Health Organization.

Sachdev, Paul, ed. (1988). *International Handbook on Abortion.* New York; Westport, Connecticut; and London: Greenwood Press.

Tietze, Christopher, and Stanley K. Henshaw (1986). *Induced Abortion: A World Review, 1986.* New York: The Alan Guttmacher Institute.

United Nations (1987). *World Population Policies,* vol. I, *Afghanistan to France.* Population Studies, No. 102. Sales No. E.87.XIII.4.

_____ (1989a). *Adolescent Reproductive Behaviour,* vol. II, *Evidence from Developing Countries.* Population Studies, No. 109A. Sales No. E.89.XIII.10.

_____ (1989b). *World Population Policies,* vol. II, *Gabon to Norway.* Population Studies, No. 102/Add.1. Sales No. E.90.XIII.3.

_____ (1990). *World Population Policies,* vol. III, *Oman to Zimbabwe.* Population Studies, No. 102/Add.2. Sales No. E.90.XIII.2.

_____ (1992). *World Population Monitoring, 1991: With Special Emphasis on Age Structure.* Population Studies, No. 126. Sales No. E .92.XIII.2.

_____ (1993). *World Population Prospects: the 1992 Revision.* Sales No. E.93.XIII.7.

United Nations Children's Fund (1991). *The State of the World's Children, 1991.* Oxford, United Kingdom: Oxford University Press.

United Nations Fund for Population Activities (1979). *Survey of Laws on Fertility Control.* New York.

_____ (various years). Country reports of the Mission on Needs Assessment for Population Assistance. New York.

_____ (various years). *Annual Review of Population Law.* New York.

World Health Organization (1975). *International Classification of Diseases,* vol. 1, 9th rev. Geneva.

_____ (1989a). *Maternal Mortality: A Global Factbook.* Compiled by Carla Abou Zahr and Erica Royston. Geneva.

_____ (1991b). *Tabulation of Available Information on Maternal Mortality Rates.* Geneva.

_____ (various years). *International Digest of Health Legislation.* Geneva.

B. FOR COUNTRY PROFILES [a]

Armenia

Borisov, V.A., compiler (1989). *Naselenie Mira: Demographychesky Spravochnik* (World population: demographic reference book). Moscow: Mysl'.

David, Henry P., and Robert I. McIntyre (1981). *Reproductive Behavior: Central and Eastern European Experience.* New York: Springer Publishing Company.

---

[a] All countries covered in chapter IV and V are listed alphabetically in the reference list.

Markarian, L. P., and others (1988), Sotsial'no-psikhologicheskie aspeckty iskusstvennogo preryvaniia nezhelatel'noi beremennosti (Social and psychological aspects of artificial interruption of unwanted pregnancy). In *Tezisy dokladov Vsesoiuznoi Naucho-prakticheskoi Konferentsii Planirovanie Sem'i i Natsinal'nye Traditsii* (Abstracts of reports of the Scientific-practical Conference on Family Planning and National Traditions).

Popov, Andrej A. (1991). Family planning and induced abortion in the USSR: basic health and demographic characteristics. *Studies in Family Planning* (New York), vol. 22, No. 6 (November/December), pp. 368-377.

Union of Soviet Socialist Republics, Ministry of Public Health (1974). *O Pobochnom Deistvii i Oslozhneniyakh Pri Primenenii Oral'nykh Kontratseptivov: Informatsionnoe Pis'mo* (On complications and side-effects of oral contraceptives: information letter).

_____ (1982). *O Poryadke Provedeniya Operatsii Iskusstvennogo Preryvaniya Beremennosti* (On the artificial interruption of pregnancies). Decree No. 234, 16 March.

_____ (1987). *O Poryadke Provedeniya Operatsii Iskusstvennogo Preryvaniya Beremennosti Rannikh Srokov Metodom Vacuum-aspiratsii* (On the artificial interruption of early-stage pregnancies by vacuum aspiration). Decree No. 757, 5 June.

_____ (1987). *O Poryadke Provedeniya Operatsii Iskusstvennogo Preryvaniya Beremennosti Po Nemeditsinskim Pokazaniyam* (On the artificial interruption of pregnancies for non-medical reasons). Decree No. 1342, 31 December.

_____ (1989). *Zdorov'e Naseleniya SSSR i Deyatelnost' Uchrezhdenii Zdravookhraneniya v 1988* (Health of the population of the USSR and activities of public-health services in 1988). Moscow.

_____ (1990). *Zdravookhraneniye v SSSR v 1989: Statisticheskie Materialy* (Public health in the USSR in 1989: statistical data). Moscow.

_____, Moscow State University (1985). *Demografichesky Entsiclopedichesky Slovar'* (Demographic encyclopedic dictionary). Moscow: Sovetskaya entsiclopediya.

_____, Presidium of the Supreme Soviet (1958). Ob otmene zapreshcheniya abortov (On the repeal of the prohibition of abortions). Decree of 23 November 1955. In *Postanovleniya KPSS i Sovetskogo Pravitel'stva ob Okhrane Zdorov'ya Naroda* (Decrees of CPSU and the Soviet Government on public-health care). Moscow: Medgiz.

_____, State Committee on Statistics (1988, 1989). *Naselenie SSSR, 1987 and 1988*. Moscow: Finance and Statistics.

_____ (1990). *Demografichesky Ezhegodnik SSSR, 1990* (Demographic yearbook of the USSR,1990). Moscow: Finance and Statistics.

_____ (1991). Problemy sem'i, okhrany materinstva i detstva. (Problems of family, maternal and child care). *Vestnik Statistiki* (Moscow), No. 8, pp. 55-64.

United Nations Children's Fund/World Health Organization (1992). The looming crisis in health and the need for international support: overview of the reports on the Commonwealth of Independent States and the Baltic countries. Prepared by the UNICEF/WHO Collaborative Missions with the participation of UNFPA, WFP AND UNDP, 17 February - 2 March 1992. Unpublished.

Azerbaijan

Borisov, V., A., Compiler (1989). *Naselenie Mira: Demographychesky Spravochnik* (World population: demographic reference book). Moscow: Mysl'.

David, Henry P., and Robert I. McIntyre (1981). *Reproductive Behavior: Central and Eastern European Experience*. New York: Springer Publishing.

Popov, Andrej A. (1991). Family planning and induced abortion in the USSR: basic health and demographic characteristics. *Studies in Family Planning* (New York), vol. 22, No. 6 (November/December), pp. 368-377.

Union of Soviet Socialist Republics, Ministry of Public Health (1974). *O Pobochnom Deistvii i Oslozhneniyakh Pri Primenenii Oral'nykh Kontratseptivov: Informatsionnoe Pis'mo* (On the side-effects and complications of oral contraceptives: information letter). Compiled by E. A. Babaiian, A. S. Loptain and I. G. Lavretskii. Moscow.

United Nations High Commissioner for Refugees/United Nations Children's Fund (1992). Fact-finding mission to Azerbaijan. Interim report of a joint UNHCR/UNICEF mission to Azerbaijan, 3-13 February. Unpublished.

Belarus

Borisov, V. A., compiler (1989). *Naselenie Mira: Demographychesky Spravochnik* (World population: demographic reference book). Moscow: Mysl'.

Hecht, Jacqueline (1987). La législation de l'avortement en Europe de l'Est et en Union Soviétique. *Politiques de population, études et documents* (Louvain-la-Neuve, Belgium), vol. III, No. 1 (juin), pp. 89-105.

Union of Soviet Socialist Republics, Ministry of Public Health (1974). *O Pobochnom Deistvii i Oslozhneniyakh Pri Primenenii Oral'nykh Konstratseptivov: Informatsionnoe Pis'mo* (On the side-effects and complications of oral contraceptives: information letter). Compiled by E. A. Babaiian, A. S. Lopatin and I. G Lavretskii. Moscow.

_____ (1982). *O Poryadke Provedeniya Operatsii Iskusstvennogo Preryvaniya Beremennosti* (On the artificial interruption of pregnancies). Decree No. 234, 16 March.

_____ (1987). *O Poryadke Provedeniya Operatsii Iskusstvennogo Preryvaniya Beremennosti Rannikh Srokov Metodom Vacuum-aspiratsii* (On the artificial interruption of early-stage pregnancies by vacuum aspiration). Decree No. 757, 5 June.

_____ (1987). *O Poryadke Provedeniya Operatsii Iskusstvennogo Preryvaniya Beremennosti Po Nemeditsinskim Pokazaniyam* (On the artificial interruption of pregnancies for non-medical reasons). Decree No. 1342, 31 December.

_____ (1989). *Zdorov'e Naseleniya SSSR i Deyatelnost' Uchrezhdenii Zdravookhraneniya v 1988* (Health of the population of the USSR and activities of public-health services in 1988). Moscow.

_____ (1990). *Zdravookhraneniye v SSSR v 1989: Statisticheskie Materialy* (Public health in the USSR in 1989: statistical data). Moscow.

_____, Moscow State University (1985). *Demografichesky Entsiclopedichesky Slovar'* (Demographic encyclopedic dictionary). Moscow: Sovetskaya entsiclopediya.

_____, Presidium of the Supreme Soviet (1958). Ob otmene zapreshcheniya abortov (On the repeal of the prohibition of abortions). Decree of 23 November 1955. In *Postanovleniya KPSS i Sovetskogo Pravitel'stva ob Okhrane Zdorov'ya Naroda* (Decrees of CPSU and the Soviet Government on public-health care). Moscow: Medgiz.

State Committee on Statistics (1988, 1989). *Naselenie SSSR, 1987 and 1988*. Moscow: Finance and Statistics.

_____, (1990). *Demografichesky Ezhegodnik SSSR 1990* (Demographic yearbook of the USSR, 1990). Moscow: Finance and Statistics.

_____ (1991). Problemy sem'i, okhrany materinstva i detstva (Problems of family, maternal and child care). *Vestnik Statistiki*, No. 8 (Moscow), pp. 55-64.

United Nations Children's Fund/World Health Organization (1992). The looming crisis in health and the need for international support: overview of the reports on the Commonwealth of Independent States and the Baltic countries. Prepared by the UNICEF/WHO Collaborative Missions with the participation of UNFPA, WFP and UNDP, 17 February - 2 March 1992. Unpublished.

United Nations Fund for Population Activities (1979). *Survey of Laws on Fertility Control*. New York.

World Health Organization, Regional Office for Europe (1990). Family planning in the USSR. *Entre nous: The European Family Planning Magazine* (Copenhagen, Denmark), No. 16 (September), pp. 5-9.

Bosnia and Herzegovina

Andolšek, Lidija (1988). Yugoslavia. In *International Handbook on Abortion*, Paul Sachdev, ed. New York; Westport, Connecticut; and London: Greenwood Press.

Cook, Rebecca J. (1989). Abortion laws and policies: challenges and opportunities. In "Women's health in the third world: the impact of unwanted pregnancy", A. Rosenfield and others, eds. *International Journal of Gynecology and Obstetrics* (Limerick, Ireland), Supplement No. 3, pp. 61-87.

_____, and Bernard M. Dickens (1988). International developments in abortion laws: 1977-88. *American Journal of Public Health* (Washington, D.C.), vol. 78, No. 10 (October), pp. 1305-1311.

David, Henry P. and Robert J. McIntyre (1981). *Reproductive Behavior: Central and Eastern European Experience*. New York: Springer Publishing Company.

Kapor-Stanulovic, Nila (1989). Liberal approach for a patchwork population. *People* (London), vol. 16, No. 3, pp. 16-18.

Malačic, Janez (1989). Family planning, population policy and declining birth rates in Yugoslavia. *Planned Parenthood in Europe* (London), vol. 18, No. 2 (September).

_____ (1990). Political changes in Yugoslavia and family planning. *Planned Parenthood in Europe* (London), vol. 19, No. 2 (September).

_____ Royston, Erica, and Sue Armstrong, eds. (1989). *Preventing Maternal Deaths*. Geneva: World Health Organization.

United Nations Fund for Population Activities (1976). *Survey of Contraceptive Laws: Country Profiles, Checklists and Summaries*. New York.

_____ (1979). *Annual Review of Population Law, 1978*. New York.

_____ (1979). *Survey of Laws on Fertility Control*. New York.

World Health Organization (1970). Comparative health legislation: abortion laws. *International Digest of Health Legislation* (Geneva), vol. 21, No. 3, pp. 437-512.

_____, Regional Office for Europe (1990). Yugoslavia. *Entre nous: The European Family Planning Magazine* (Copenhagen, Denmark), No. 16 (September), pp. 11-12.

China

Chen, Pichao, and Adrienne Kols (1982). *Population and Birth Planning in the People's Republic of China*. Population Report, Series J, No. 25. Baltimore, Maryland: The Johns Hopkins University, Population Information Program.

China (various years). *Public Health Yearbook of China*. Beijing: People's Public Health Publication House.

Henshaw, Stanley K. (1990). Induced abortion: a world review, 1990. In *Induced Abortion: A World Review, 1990 Supplement*, by Stanley K. Henshaw and Evelyn Morrow. New York: The Alan Guttmacher Institute.

Lee, Luke T. (1973). *Brief Survey of Abortion Laws of the Five Largest Countries*. Law and Population Monograph Series, No. 14. Reprinted from Population Report, Series F, No. 10 (published by the George Washington University Medical Center, Washington, D.C.). Medford, Massachusetts: Tufts University, The Fletcher School of Law and Diplomacy.

Lim, V. C., and others (1990). Characteristics of women having abortion in China. *Social Science and Medicine* (Elmsford, New York), vol. 31, No. 4, pp. 445-453.

Peng, Peiyun (1992). Statement made at the Fourth Asian and Pacific Population Conference, Bali, Indonesia, 19-27 August.

Ross, John A., and others (1992). *Family Planning and Child Survival Programs as Assessed in 1991*. New York: The Population Council.

Tien, H. Yuan, and others (1992). *China's Demographic Dilemmas*. Population Bulletin, vol. 47, No. 1. Washington, D.C.: Population Reference Bureau.

Tuan, Chi-Hsien (1988). China. In *International Handbook on Abortion*, Paul Sachdev, ed. New York; Westport, Connecticut; and London: Greenwood Press.

United Nations (1989). *Case Studies in Population Policy: China*. Population Policy Paper, No. 20. Sales No. E.90.XIII.21.

United Nations Fund for Population Activities (1979). *Survey of Laws on Fertility Control*. New York.

_____, (1980). *Annual Review of Population Law, 1979*. New York.

United Nations Population Fund and Harvard Law School Library (1990). *Annual Review of Population Law, 1987*, vol. 14. New York: UNFPA.

Croatia

Andolšek, Lidija (1988). Yugoslavia. In *International Handbook on Abortion*, Paul Sachdev, ed. New York; Westport, Connecticut; and London: Greenwood Press.

Cook, Rebecca J. (1989). Abortion laws and policies: challenges and opportunities. In "Women's health in the third world: the impact of unwanted pregnancy", A. Rosenfield and others, eds. *International Journal of Gynecology and Obstetrics* (Limerick, Ireland), Supplement No. 3, pp. 61-87.

_____, and Bernard M. Dickens (1988). International developments in abortion laws: 1977-88. *American Journal of Public Health* (Washington, D.C.), vol. 78, No. 10 (October), pp. 1305-1311.

David, Henry P., and Robert J. McIntyre (1981). *Reproductive Behavior: Central and Eastern European Experience*. New York: Springer Publishing Company.

Kapor-Stanulovic, Nila (1989). Liberal approach for a patchwork population. *People* (London), vol. 16, No. 3, pp. 16-18.

_____ (1990). Political changes in Yugoslavia and family planning, *Planned Parenthood in Europe* (London), vol. 19, No. 2 (September).

Malačič, Janez (1989). Family planning, population policy and declining birth rates in Yugoslavia. *Planned Parenthood in Europe* (London), vol. 18, No. 2 (September).

Royston, Erica, and Sue Armstrong, eds. (1989). *Preventing Maternal Deaths*. Geneva: World Health Organization.

United Nations Fund for Population Activities (1976). *Survey of Contraceptive Laws: Country Profiles, Checklists, and Summaries*. New York.

_____ (1979). *Annual Review of Population Law, 1978*. New York.

_____ (1979). *Survey of Laws on Fertility Control*. New York.

World Health Organization (1970). Comparative health legislation: abortion laws. In *International Digest of Health Legislation* (Geneva), vol. 21, No. 3, pp. 437-512.

_____, Regional Office for Europe (1990). Yugoslavia. *Entre nous: The European Family Planning Magazine* (Copenhagen, Denmark), No. 16 (September), pp. 11-12.

Democratic People's Republic of Korea

Corsa, Leslie Jr. (1967). Abortion: a world view. In *The Case for Legalized Abortion Now*, Alan F. Guttmacher, ed. Berkeley, California: Diablo Press.

United Nations (1982). *World Population Trends and Policies: 1981 Monitoring Report*, vol. II, *Population Policies*. Population Studies, No. 79/Add.1. Sales No. E.82.XIII.3.

Yunde, Liu (1989). *Trip Report: Visit to Democratic People's Republic of Korea*. New York: United Nations Population Fund.

Gabon

Henshaw, Stanley K. (1990). Induced abortion: a world review, 1990. In *Induced Abortion: A World Review, 1990 Supplement*, by Stanley K. Henshaw and Evelyn Morrow. New York: The Alan Guttmacher Institute.

Knoppers, Bartha Maria, and Isabel Brault (1989). *La loi et l'avortement dans les pays francophones*. Montreal, Canada: Les Editions Thémis.

_____, and Elizabeth Sloss (1990). Abortion law in francophone countries. *American Journal of Comparative Law* (Berkeley, California), vol. 38, No. 4 (Fall), pp. 889-922.

Royston, Erica, and Sue Armstrong, eds. (1989). *Preventing Maternal Deaths*. Geneva: World Health Organization.

Tietze, Christopher, and Stanley K. Henshaw (1986). *Induced Abortion: A World Review, 1986*. New York: The Alan Guttmacher Institute.

United Nations Fund for Population Activities (1976). *Survey of Contraceptive Laws: Country Profiles, Checklists, and Summaries*. New York.

_____ (1979). *Survey of Laws on Fertility Control*. New York.

World Health Organization (1970). Comparative health legislation: abortion laws. *International Digest of Health Legislation* (Geneva), vol. 21, No. 3, pp. 437-512.

Gambia

Gambia (1982). *Five Year Plan for Economic and Social Development, 1981/82-1985/86*. Banjul: Ministry of Economic Planning and Industrial Development.

Gambia Family Planning Association, Family Health International and Pathfinder Fund (1988). *Reproductive Health Survey of Young Adults in Greater Banjul, the Gambia: Final Report*. Kanifing, Gambia: Gambia Family Planning Association.

Gelbart, Alene, and Carla Jones (1984). Demographic Data for Development. *Population Policy Review: The Gambia*. Columbia, Maryland: Westinghouse Social Sciences International.

Graham, Wendy, William Brass and Robert W. Snow (1989). Estimating maternal mortality: the sisterhood method. *Studies in Family Planning* (New York), vol. 20, No. 3 (May/June), pp. 125-135.

Taylor-Thomas, J. T. (1989). The Gambian national population policy and programmes. In *Proceedings of the Colloquium on the Impact of Family Planning Programmes in Sub-Saharan Africa: Current Issues and Prospects*. Legon, Ghana: University of Ghana, Regional Institute for Population Studies.

United Nations Fund for Population Activities (1979). *Survey of Laws on Fertility Control*. New York.

Georgia

Borisov, V. A., compiler (1989). *Naselenie Mira: Demographychesky Spravochnik* (World population: demographic reference book). Moscow: Mysl'.

David, Henry P., and Robert I. McIntyre (1981). *Reproductive Behavior: Central and Eastern European Experience*. New York: Springer Publishing Company.

Imnadze, T. E. (1985). Sovremennoe sostoyanie problemy kontratseptsii. Kratkii obzor (Current state of contraception). In *Materialy 1-i respublikanskoi nauchnoi konferentsii molodykh uchenykh Gruzii po probleme "Besplodnyi brak"* (Report of the First Scientific Conference of Georgian Junior Scientists on the Problem of Infertility in Marriage). Tbilisi.

Nizharadze, T. A., and others (1985). Sotsiologo-demograficheskie aspekty vosproizvodstva naseleniya GSSR (Sociologic and demographic aspects of population reproduction of Georgian SSR). In *Mediko-sotsiologicheskie aspekty rozhdaemosti*. (Medico-sociological aspects of fertility). Tbilisi.

Popov, Andrej A. (1991). Family planning and induced abortion in the USSR: basic health and demographic characteristics. *Studies in Family Planning* (New York), vol. 22, No. 6 (November/December), pp. 368-377.

Union of Soviet Socialist Republics, Ministry of Public Health (1974). *O Pobochnom Deistvii i Oslozhneniyakh Pri Primenenii Oral'nykh Kontratseptivov: Informatsionnoe Pis'mo* (On complications and side-effects of oral contraceptives: information letter). Compiled by E. A. Babaiian, A. S. Lopatin and I. G. Lavretskii. Moscow.

_____ (1982). *O Poryadke Provedeniya Operatsii Iskusstvennogo Preryvaniya Beremennosti* (On the artificial interruption of pregnancies). Decree No. 234, 16 March.

_____ (1987). *O Poryadke Provedeniya Operatsii Iskusstvennogo Preryvaniya Beremennosti Rannikh Srokov Metodom Vacuum-aspiratsii* (On the artificial interruption of early-stage pregnancies by vacuum aspiration). Decree No. 757, 5 June.

_____ (1987). *O Poryadke Provedeniya Operatsii Iskusstvennogo Preryvaniya Beremennosti Po Nemeditsinskim Pokazaniyam* (On the artificial interruption of pregnancies for non-medical reasons). Decree No. 1342, 31 December.

_____ (1989). *Zdorov'e Naseleniya SSSR i Deyatelnost' Uchrezhdenii Zdravookhraneniya v 1988* (Health of the population of the USSR and activities of public-health services in 1988) Moscow.

_____ (1990). *Zdravookhraneniye v SSSR v 1989. Statisticheskie Materialy* (Public health in the USSR in 1989: statistical data). Moscow.

_____, Moscow State University (1985). *Demografichesky Entsiclopedichesky Slovar'* (Demographic encyclopedic dictionary). Moscow: Sovetskaya entsiclopediya.

_____, Presidium of the Supreme Soviet (1958). Ob otmene zapreshcheniya abortov (On repeal of the prohibition of abortions). Decree of 23 November 1955. In *Postanovleniya KPSS i Sovetskogo Pravitel'stva ob Okhrane Zdorov'ya Naroda.* (Decrees if CPSU and the Soviet Government on public-health care). Moscow: Medgiz.

_____ (1990). *Demografichesky Ezhegodnik SSSR 1990* (Demographic yearbook of the USSR, 1990). Moscow: Finance and Statistics.

_____ (1991). Problemy sem'i, okhrany materinstva i detstva (Problems of family, maternal and child care). *Vestnik Statistiki* (Moscow), No. 8, pp. 60-61.

United Nations Children's Fund/World Health Organization (1992). The looming crisis in health and the need for international support: overview of the reports on the Commonwealth of Independent States and the Baltic countries. Prepared by the UNICEF/WHO Collaborative Missions with the participation of UNFPA, WFPA and UNDP, 17 February - 2 March 1992. Unpublished.

Viazov, O. E., R. F. Kalashnikova-Papitashvili and T. A. Nizharadze (1983). Nekotorye demograficheskie problemy abortov: po materialam dvukh rodil'nykh domov goroda Tbilisi za 1981 god (Some demographic problems of abortions: notes based on two maternity wards of the city of Tbilisi in 1981). In *Sotsiologo-demograficheskie i Kliniko-eksperimental'nye Aspekty Reproduktologii* (Sociological-demographic and clinical-experimental aspects of reproduction). Tbilisi: Zhordania Institute of Human Reproduction.

Germany

Cook, Rebecca J., and Bernard M. Dickens (1988). International developments in abortion laws: 1977-88. *American Journal of Public Health* (Washington, D.C.), vol. 78, No. 10 (October), pp. 1305-1311.

German Information Centre (1990). Bundestag struggles with the abortion issue: decision imminent. *The Week in Germany.* 26 June.

Glendon, Mary Ann (1987). *Abortion and Divorce in Western Law.* Cambridge, Massachusetts: Harvard University Press.

Henshaw, Stanley K. (1990). Induced abortion: a world review, 1990. In *Induced Abortion: A World Review, 1990 Supplement*, by Stanley K. Henshaw and Evelyn Morrow. New York: The Alan Guttmacher Institute.

_____, and Evelyn Morrow (1990). *Induced Abortion: A World Review, 1990 Supplement.* New York: The Alan Guttmacher Institute.

Höhn, Charlotte, Ulrich Mammey and Hartmut Wendt (1990). Bericht 1990 zur demographischen Lage (Report on the demographic situation, 1990). *Zeitschrift für Bevolkerungswissenschaft* (Weisbaden, Germany), vol. 16, No. 2, pp. 135-205.

Institut national d'études démographiques (1981). *L'interruption volontaire de grossesse dans l'Europe des Neuf.* Travaux et Documents, Cahier No. 91. Paris, France: Presses universitaires de France.

International Planned Parenthood Federation (1989). Abortion laws in Europe. *Planned Parenthood in Europe* (London), vol. 18, No. 1 (Spring), supplement, pp. 1-10.

Kraiker, Gerhard (1988). Federal Republic of Germany. In *International Handbook on Abortion*, Paul Sachdev, ed. New York; Westport, Connecticut; and London: Greenwood Press.

217

Mehlan, K. H. (1988). German Democratic Republic. In *International Handbook on Abortion*, Paul Sachdev, ed. New York; Westport, Connecticut; and London: Greenwood Press.

Royston, Erica, and Sue Armstrong, eds. (1989). *Preventing Maternal Deaths*. Geneva: World Health Organization.

Tietze, Christopher, and Stanley K. Henshaw (1986). *Induced Abortion: A World Review, 1986*. New York: The Alan Guttmacher Institute.

Thoss, Elke (1991). German reunification brings new challenges. *People* (London), vol. 18, No. 4, pp. 34-35.

Tuffs, Annette (1990). Germany: divided on abortion. *The Lancet* (Baltimore, Maryland; and London), vol. 336, No. 8709 (28 July), p. 43.

_____ (1992). Germany: abortion, the woman's choice. *The Lancet* (Baltimore, Maryland; and London), vol. 340 (4 July).

_____ (1992). Germany: hitch in abortion law. *The Lancet* (Baltimore, Maryland; and London), vol. 340, No. 8816 (15 August), p. 419.

United Nations Fund for Population Activities (1976). *Survey of Contraceptive Laws: Country Profiles, Checklists, and Summaries*. New York.

_____ (1979). *Survey of Laws on Fertility Control*. New York.

von Baross, Joachim (1991). Abortion checks at German-Dutch border. *Planned Parenthood in Europe* (London), vol. 20, No. 1 (May), p. 26.

World Health Organization (1970). Comparative health legislation: abortion laws. *International Digest of Health Legislation* (Geneva), vol. 21, No. 3, pp. 437-512.

_____ (1988). *International Digest of Health Legislation* (Geneva), vol. 39, No. 1, p. 80.

Sadrozinski, R. (1990). *Die ungleiche Praxis des Par. 218* (Unequal practice under paragraph 218). Cologne: Böll Stiftung.

Ghana

Benneh, G., J. S. Nabila and B. Gyepi-Garbrah (1989). *Twenty Years of Population Policy in Ghana*. Legon, Ghana: University of Ghana, Department of Geography, Population Impact Project (PIP/Ghana).

Bleek, Wolf (1987). Lying informants: a fieldwork experience from Ghana. *Population and Development Review* (New York), vol 13, No. 2 (June), pp. 314-322.

Cook, Rebecca J., and Bernard M. Dickens (1986). *Issues in Reproductive Health Law in the Commonwealth*. London: Commonwealth Secretariat.

Gyepi-Garbrah, B. (1987). *Some Implications of Early Childbearing in Ghana*. Legon, Ghana: University of Ghana, Department of Geography, Population Impact Project (PIP/Ghana).

Lamptey, P., and others (1985). Abortion experience among obstetric patients at Korle-Bu Hospital, Accra, Ghana. *Journal of Biosocial Science* (London), vol. 17, No. 2 (April), pp. 195-203.

Oppong, C., and Abu, K. (1987). *Seven Roles of Women: Impact of Education, Migration and Employment on Ghanaian Mothers*. Women, Work and Development, Series No. 13. Geneva: International Labour Organisation.

Ross, John A., and others (1992). *Family Planning and Child Survival Programs As Assessed in 1991*. New York: The Population Council.

Turkson, Richard B. (1975). *Law and Population Growth in Ghana*. Law and Population Monograph Series, No. 33. Medford, Massachussetts: Tufts University, The Fletcher School of Law and Diplomacy.

United Nations Fund for Population Activities (1979). *Survey of Laws on Fertility Control*. New York.

_____, and Harvard Law School Library (1985). *Annual Review of Population Law, 1985*, vol. 12. New York.

Greece

Cominos, Anthony C. (1988). Greece. In *International Handbook on Abortion*, Paul Sachdev, ed. New York; Westport, Connecticut; and London: Greenwood Press.

Despina, Naziri (1990). The triviality of abortion in Greece. *Planned Parenthood in Europe* (London), vol. 20, No. 2.

Glendon, Mary Ann (1987). *Abortion and Divorce in Western Law*. Cambridge, Massachusetts: Harvard University Press.

Tietze, Christopher, and Stanley K. Henshaw (1986). *Induced Abortion: A World Review, 1986*. New York, The Alan Guttmacher Institute.

United Nations (1981). *World Population Trends and Policies: 1981 Monitoring Report*, vol. 2, *Population Policies*. Population Studies, No. 79/Add.1. Sales No. E.82.XIII.3.

Grenada

Cook, Rebecca J. (1989). Abortion laws and policies: challenges and opportunities. In "Women's health in the third world: the impact of unwanted pregnancy", A. Rosenfield and others, eds. *International Journal of Gynecology and Obstetrics* (Limerick, Ireland), Supplement No. 3, pp. 61-87.

_____, and Bernard M. Dickens (1986). *Issues in Reproductive Health Law in the Commonwealth*. London: Commonwealth Secretariat.

_____ (1988). International developments in abortion laws: 1977-88. *American Journal of Public Health* (Washington, D.C.), vol. 78, No. 10 (October), pp. 1305-1311.

International Planned Parenthood Federation (1988). *Family Planning in Latin America and the Carribbean*. Country Fact Sheets. New York.

Menon, P. K. (1976). The law of abortion with special reference to the Commonwealth Carribean. *Anglo-American Law Review* (Chichester, United Kingdom), vol. 5, No. 4 (october-December), pp. 311-345.

Royston, Erica, and Sue Armstrong, eds. (1989). *Preventing Maternal Deaths*. Geneva: World Health Organization.

United Nations Fund for Population Activities (1976). *Survey of Contraceptive Laws: Country Profiles, Checklists, and Summaries*. New York.

_____ (1979) *Survey of Laws on Fertility Control*. New York.

World Health Organization (1970). Comparative health legislation: abortion laws. *International Digest of Health Legislation* (Geneva), vol. 21, No. 3, pp. 437-512.

Pan American Health Organization (1990). *Health Conditions in the Americas, 1990 Edition*, vol. II. Scientific Publication, No. 524. Washington, D.C.

_____ (1986). *Health Conditions in the Americas, 1981-1984*, vol. II. Scientific Publication, No. 500. Washington, D.C.

Guatemala

Pan American Health Organization (1990). *Health Conditions in the Americas, 1990 Edition*, vol. II. Scientific Publication, No. 524. Washington, D.C.

Santiso Galvez, R., and others (1981). *Abortos espontaneos y abortos ilegales inducidos: casos tratados en hospitales de Guatemala: estudio retrospectivo, 1976-1977*. Guatemala City, Guatemala: Asociación Pro-Bienestar de la Familia de Guatemala.

United Nations (1982). *World Population Trends and Policies: 1981 Monitoring Report*, vol. II, *Population Policies*. Population Studies, No. 79/Add.10. Sales No. E.82.XIII.3.

United Nations Children's Fund (1987). Country programme recommendation: Guatemala. E/ICEF/1987/P/L.16.

United Nations Fund for Population Activities (1979). *Survey of Laws on Fertility Control*. New York.

Viel, Benjamin (1988). Latin America. In *International Handbook on Abortion*, Paul Sachdev, ed. New York: Westport, Connecticut; and London: Greenwood Press.

Guinea

Henshaw, Stanley K.(1990). Induced abortion: a world review, 1990. In *Induced Abortion: A World Review, 1990 Supplement*, by Stanley K. Henshaw and Evelyn Morrow. New York: The Alan Guttmacher Institute.

Knoppers, Bactha Maria, and Isabel Brault (1989). *La loi et l'avortement dans les pays francophones*. Montreal, Canada: Les Editions Thémis.

_____, and Elizabeth Sloss (1990). Abortion law in francophone countries. *American Journal of Comparative Law* (Berkeley, California), vol. 38, No. 4 (Fall), pp. 889-922.

Royston, Erica, and Sue Armstrong, eds. (1989). *Preventing Maternal Deaths*. Geneva: World Health Organization.

United Nations Fund for Population Activities (1976). *Survey of Contraceptive Laws*. New York.

_____ (1979). *Guinea: Report of Mission on Needs Assessment for Population Assistance*. Report No. 30. New York.

_____ (1979). *Survey of Laws on Fertility Control*. New York.

Tietze, Christopher, and Stanley K. Henshaw (1986). *Induced Abortion: A World Review, 1986*. New York: The Alan Guttmacher Institute.

World Health Organization (1970). Comparative health legislation: abortion laws. *International Digest of Health Legislation* (Geneva), vol. 21, No. 3, pp. 437-512.

Guinea-Bissau

Royston, Erica, and Sue Armstrong, eds. (1989). *Preventing Maternal Deaths*. Geneva: World Health Organization.

United Nations Fund for Population Activities (1988). *Guinée-Bissau: rapport de mission sur l'évaluation des besoins d'aide en matière de population*. Report No. 94. New York.

Guyana

Cook, Rebecca J., and Bernard M. Dickens (1986). *Issues in Reproductive Health Law in the Commonwealth*. London: Commonwealth Secretariat.

Pan American Health Organization (1990). *Health Conditions in The Americas, 1990 Edition*. Scientific Publication, No. 524. Washington, D.C.

United Nations Fund for Population Activities (1979). *Survey of Laws on Fertility*. New York.

World Health Organization (1990). Safe motherhood: abortion. A tabulation of available data on the frequency and mortality of unsafe abortion. Geneva. Unpublished report.

Haiti

Allman, James, and John May (1979). Fertility, mortality, migration and family planning in Haiti. *Population Studies* (London), vol. 33, No. 3 (November), pp. 505-521.

Ayad, Moh.1amed, Fritz Pierre and Hédi Jemai (1985). *Planificacion familiale, fécondité et santé familiale en Haïti: rapport les résultats de l'Enquéte haitienne sur la prevalence de la contraception*. Port-au-Prince: Département de la santé publique et de la population; and Columbia, Maryland: Westinghouse Public Applied Systems.

Cook, Rebecca J. (1989). Abortion laws and policies: challenges and opportunities. In "Women's health in the third world: the impact of unwanted pregnancy", A. Rosenfield and others, eds. *International Journal of Gynecology and Obstetrics* (Limerick, Ireland), Supplement No. 3, pp. 61-87.

_____, and Bernard M. Dickens (1988). International developments in abortion laws: 1977-88. *American Journal of Public Health* (Washington, D.C.), vol. 78, No. 10 (October), pp. 1305-1311.

International Planned Parenthood Federation (1988). *Family planning in Latin America and the Caribbean*. Country Fact Sheets. New York.

Knoppers, Bertha Maria, and Isabel Brault (1989). *La loi et l'avortement dans les pays francophones*. Montreal, Canada: Les Editions Thémis.

_____, and Elizabeth Sloss (1990). Abortion law in francophone countries. *American Journal of Comparative Law* (Berkeley, California), vol. 38, No. 4 (Fall), pp. 889-922.

Pan American Health Organization (1986). *Health Conditions in the Americas, 1981-1984*, vol. II. Scientific Publication, No. 500. Washington, D.C.

_____ (1990). *Health Conditions in the Americas, 1990 Edition*, vol. II. Scientific Publication, No. 524. Washington, D.C.

Royston, Erica, and Sue Armstrong, eds. (1989). *Preventing Maternal Deaths*. Geneva: World Health Organization.

United Nations (1990). *Monographies sur les politiques de population: Haïti*. Population Policy Paper, No. 25. Sales No. F.90.XIII.24.

United Nations Fund for Population Activities (1976). *Survey of Contraceptive Laws: Country Profiles, Checklists, and Summaries*. New York.

_____ (1979). *Survey of Laws on Fertility Control*. New York.

Weniger, B. (1981). Les plantes utilisées en Haïti pour le contrôle des naissances. *Haïti santé*,(Port-au-Prince), vol. 1, No. 5 (décembre), pp. 11-13.

_____, M. Haag-Berrurier and R. Anton (1980). Plantes d'Haïti et antifécondité. *Planta Medica,* (Stuttgart, Germany), vol. 39, No. 3 (July), p. 260.

World Health Organization (1970). Comparative health legislation: abortion laws. *International Digest of Health Legislation* (Geneva), vol. 21, No. 3, pp. 437-512.

Holy See

John Paul II, Pope (1991). *Letter on Combatting Abortion and Euthanasia*. 21 June.

Ratzinger, Cardinal Joseph (1991). The problem of threats to human life. *L'Osservatore Romano*, No. 14 (8 April), pp. 2-4.

Riding, Alan (1992). New catechism for Catholics defines sins of modern world. *The New York Times* (17 November 1992), pp. A1 and A14.

Schotte, Bishop Jan (1984). Statement presented at the International Conference on Population, Mexico City, 6-13 August 1984.

Honduras

International Planned Parenthood Federation (1969). *Honduras: Family Planning*. IPPF Situation Report.

Pan American Health Organization (1982). *Health Conditions in the Americas, 1981-1984*, vol. II. Scientific Publication, No. 500. Washington, D.C.

United Nations (1982). *World Population Trends and Policies: 1981 Monitoring Report*, vol. II, *Population Policies*. Population Studies, No. 79/Add.1. Sales No. E.82.XIII.3.

United Nations Fund for Population Activities (1979). *Survey on Laws of Fertility Control*. New York.

Viel, Benjamin (1988). Latin America. In *International Handbook on Abortion*, Paul Sachdev, ed. New York: Westport, Connecticut; and London: Greenwood Press.

World Health Organization (1965). *International Digest of Health Legislation* (Geneva), vol. 16, No. 2, pp. 313-329.

Hungary

Council of Europe (1991). *Recent Demographic Developments in Europe, 1991 Edition.* Strasbourg.

David, Henry P. (1970). *Family Planning and Abortion in the Socialist Countries of Central and Eastern Europe.* New York: The Population Council.

Hecht, Jacqueline (1987). La législation de l'avortement en Europe de l'Est et en Union Soviétique. *Politiques de population: études et documents* (Louvain-la-Neuve, Belgium), vol. III, No. 1 (juin), pp. 89-105.

Klinger, András. (1988). Hungary. In *International Handbook on Abortion*, Paul Sachdev, ed. New York; Westport, Connecticut; and London: Greenwood Press.

Tietze, Christopher, and Stanley K. Henshaw (1986). *Induced Abortion: A World Review, 1986.* New York: The Alan Guttmacher Institute.

United Nations (1982). *World Population Trends and Policies: 1981 Monitoring Report*, vol. II, *Population Policies.* Population Studies, No. 79/Add.1. Sales No. E.82.XIII.3.

_____ (various years). *Demographic Yearbook.*

World Health Organization (1989). *International Digest of Health Legislation* (Geneva), vol. 40, No. 3. pp. 595-596.

_____ (1993). New abortion law in Hungary. *Entre nous: The European Family Planning Magazine* (Copenhagen, Denmark), No. 22-23 (June), p. 17.

Iceland

Council of Europe (1991). *Recent Demographic Developments in Europe, 1991 Edition.* Strasbourg.

Glendon, Mary Ann (1987). *Abortion and Divorce in Western Law.* Cambridge, Massachusetts: Harvard University Press.

Tietze, Christopher, and Stanley K. Henshaw (1986). *Induced Abortion: A World Review.* New York: The Alan Guttmacher Institute.

United Nations (1982). *World Population Trends and Policies: 1981 Monitoring Report*, vol. II, *Population Policies.* Population Studies, No. 79/Add.1. Sales No. E.82.XIII.3.

_____ (various years). *Demographic Yearbook.*

World Health Organization (1977). *International Digest of Health Legislation* (Geneva), vol. 28, No. 3, pp. 614-620.

India

Cook, Rebecca J., and Bernard M. Dickens (1979). Abortion laws in Commonwealth countries. *International Digest of Health Legislation* (Geneva), vol. 30, No. 3, pp. 395-502.

Coyagi, B. (1990). Safe Motherhood and RU 486 in the Third World. *People* (London), vol 17, No. 3, pp. 13-15.

Henshaw, Stanley K. (1990). Induced abortion: a world review, 1990. In *Induced Abortion: A World Review, 1990 Supplement*, by Stanley K. Henshaw and Evelyn Morrow. New York: The Alan Guttmacher Institute.

_____, and Evelyn Morrow (1990). *Induced Abortion: A World Review, 1990 Supplement.* New York: The Alan Guttmacher Institute.

Institute for Resource Development, Inc. (1986). *Population Policy Brief: India.* Columbia, Maryland.

International Planned Parenthood Federation (1988). Maharashtra clamps down on pre-natal set tests. *People* (London), vol. 15, No. 3, p. 6.

Lee, Luke T. (1973). *Brief Survey of Abortion Laws of Five Largest Countries.* Law and Population Monograph Series, No. 14. Reprinted from Population Report, Series F, No. 10 (published by the George Washington University Medical Center, Washington, D.C.). Medford, Massachusetts: Tufts University, The Fletcher School of Law and Diplomacy.

Malhotra, S., and A. N. Gupta (1981). Maternal mortality with septic abortions. In *Proceedings of the Third International Seminar on Maternal and Perinatal Mortality, Pregnancy Termination and Sterilization, New Delhi, 3-5 October 1980,* V. Hingorani, R. D. Pandit and V. L. Bhargova, eds. Bombay, India: Federation of Obstetric and Gynaecological Societies of India.

Mukherjee, S. N. (1981). Medical termination of pregnancy in India. In *Proceedings of the Third International Seminar on Maternal and Perinatal Mortality, Pregnancy Termination and Sterilization, New Delhi, 3-5 October 1980,* V. Hingorani, R. D. Pandit and V. L. Bahrgova, eds. Bombay, India: Federation of Obstetric and Gynaecological Societies of India.

Nair, P. S., and K. B. Kurup (1985). Factors influencing low performance of legal abortion in India: a community study. *Journal of Family Welfare* (Bombay), vol. 32, No. 1 (September), pp. 30-40.

Ramachandran, Prema (1988). India. In *International Handbook on Abortion,* Paul Sachdev, ed. New York; Westport, Connecticut; and London: Greenwood Press.

Shiva, M. (1991). Of human rights and women's health. *Health for the Millions* (New Delhi, India), vol. 17, No. 3 (June), pp. 34-36.

_____ (1991). Of human rights and women's health. *Women's Global Network for Reproductive Rights Newsletter* (Amsterdam), No. 36 (July/September), pp. 55-57.

Tietze, Christopher (1983). *Induced Abortion: A World Review, 1983.* New York: The Population Council.

United Nations Fund for Population Activities (1979). *Survey of Laws on Fertility Control.* New York.

Visaria, P., and A. K. Jain (1982). India. In *International Encyclopedia of Population,* vol. 4, J. A. Ross, ed. New York: Free Press.

Weisman, Stephen R. (1988). No more guarantees of a son's birth. *The New York Times* (20 July 1988), pp. 1-10.

Indonesia

Hull, Terence H., Sarsanto W. Sarwono and Ninuk Widyantoro (1993). Induced abortion in Indonesia. *Studies in Family Planning* (New York), vol. 24, No. 4 (July/August), pp. 241-251.

Judono, H. Marsidi, Sundraji Sumapraja and F. A. Moeloek (1988). Indonesia. In *International Handbook on Abortion,* Paul Sachdev, ed. New York; Westport, Connecticut; and London: Greenwood Press.

Samil, R. S. (1989). Commentary on menstrual regulation as a health service: challenges in Indonesia. In "Women's health in the third world: the impact of unwanted pregnancy", A. Rosenfield and others, eds. *International Journal of Gynecology and Obstetrics* (Limerick, Ireland), Supplement No. 3, pp. 29-32.

Sampoerno, D., and S. Sadli (1975). Indonesia. In *Proceedings of the Asian Regional Research Seminar on Psychological Aspects of Abortion,* Kathmandu, Nepal, 26-29 November 1974, Henry P. David and others, eds. Washington, D.C.: American Institute for Research.

Soewondo, N. (1986). Health programme and laws. In *Proceedings of the East and South East Asia and Oceania Region (ESEAOR) Seminar on Women's Rights and Reproductive Health,* part 2, Cheng Yin Mooi, ed. London: International Planned Parenthood Federation.

Suyono, Haryono (1993). Population programmes: the case-study of Indonesia. In *Population Policies and Programmes.* Proceedings of the United Nations Expert Group Meeting, Cairo, Egypt, 12-16 April, 1992. Sales No. E.93.XIII.5.

United Nations Fund for Population Activities (1979). *Survey of Laws on Fertility Control.* New York.

World Health Organization (1990). Safe motherhood: abortion. A tabulation of available data on the frequency and mortality of unsafe abortion. Geneva. Unpublished report.

Iran (Islamic Republic of)

Aghajanian, Akbar (1991). Population change in Iran, 1966-86: a stalled demographic transition. *Population and Development Review* (New York), vol. 17, No. 4 (December), pp. 703-715.

Alavi-Naini, M. (1971). The incidence of induced and spontaneous abortion among high socio-economic classes in Iran. In *Induced Abortion: A Hazard to Public Health*? Isam R. Nazer, ed. Proceedings of the First Conference of the IPPF Middle East and North Africa Region, Beirut, Lebanon, February. Beirut: International Planned Parenthood Federation, Middle and North Africa Region.

Boland, Reed (1992). Legal developments in reproductive health in 1991. *Family Planning Perspectives* (New York), vol. 24, No. 4 (July/August), pp. 178-185.

Henshaw, Stanley K. (1990). Induced abortion: a world review, 1990. In *Induced Abortion: A World Review, 1990 Supplement*, by Stanley K. Henshaw and Evelyn Morrow. New York: The Alan Guttmacher Institute.

Mohit, B. (1971). The abortion situation in Iran. In *Induced Abortion: A Hazard to Public Health*? Isam R. Nazer, ed. Proceedings of the First Conference of the IPPF Middle East and North Africa Region, Beirut, Lebanon, February. Beirut: International Planned Parenthood Federation, Middle and North Africa Region.

World Health Organization (1976). *International Digest of Health Legislation* (Geneva), vol. 27, No. 4, p. 789.

Tietze, Christopher (1983). *Induced Abortion: A World Review, 1983*, 5th edition. New York: The Population Council.

_____, and Stanley K. Henshaw (1986). *Induced Abortion: A World Review, 1986*, 6th edition. New York: The Alan Guttmacher Institute.

Iraq

Ghali, F. H. (1972). Abortion in Iraq: a preliminary report. In *Induced Abortion: A Hazard to Public Health?*, Isam R. Nazer, ed. Proceedings of the First Conference of the IPPF Middle East and North Africa Region, Beirut, Lebanon, February. Beirut: International Planned Parenthood Federation, Middle and North Africa Region.

International Planned Parenthood Federation (1971). *Medical Bulletin* (London), vol. 5, No. 2 (April), pp. 1-2.

_____ (1990). Iraqi population 19 million and growing. IPPF Open File: news digest of the world's largest voluntary family planning organization. (two weeks ending December), p. 13. London. Mimeographed.

_____ (1991). Iraq allows free trading of contraceptives. IPPF Open File: a news digest of the International Planned Parenthood Federation (London) (July), p. 6.

Tyler, Patrick E. (1991). Study says Iraq's child mortality rate has tripled. *The New York Times* (27 October 1991), p. A6. New York.

United Nations (1981). *World Population Trends and Policies: 1981 Monitoring Report*, vol. II, *Population Policies*. Population Studies, No. 79/Add. 1. Sales No. E.82.XIII.3.

Ireland

Brahams, Diana (1987). Advising pregnant women in Ireland to go abroad for abortion is unlawful. *The Lancet* (Baltimore, Maryland; and London), vol. 2, No. 8563 (10 October), p. 868.

_____ (1991). Abortion information, an Irish case. *Lancet* (Baltimore, Maryland; and London), vol. 338, No. 8773 (19 October), p. 1006.

Cook, Rebecca J. (1989). Abortion laws and policies: challenges and opportunities. In "Women's health in the third world: the impact of unwanted pregnancy", A. Rosenfield and others, eds. *International Journal of Gynecology and Obstetrics* (Limerick, Ireland), Supplement No. 3, pp. 61-87.

_____, and Bernard M. Dickens (1988). International developments in abortion laws: 1977-88. *American Journal of Public Health* (Washington, D.C.), vol. 78, No. 10 (October), pp. 1305-1311.

Henshaw, Stanley K. (1990). Induced abortion: a world review, 1990. In *Induced Abortion: A World Review, 1990 Supplement*, by Stanley K. Henshaw and Evelyn Morrow. New York: The Alan Guttmacher Institute.

_____, and Evelyn Morrow (1990). *Induced Abortion: A World Review, 1990 Supplement*. New York: The Alan Guttmacher Institute.

Institut national d'études démographiques (1981). L'interruption volontaire de grossesse dans l'Europe des Neuf. *Travaux et documents*, Cahier No. 91. Paris, France: Presses universitaires de France.

O'Brien, Jon (1991). Access to abortion information denied to Irish women. *Planned Parenthood in Europe* (London), vol. 20, No. 2.

O'Higgins, Kathleen (1986). Family planning services in Ireland with particular reference to minors. In *The Adolescent Dilemma*, Hyman Rodman and Jan Trost, eds. New York: Praeger.

Rynne, A. (1982). *Abortion: the Irish Question*. Dublin, Ireland: Ward River Press.

Tietze, Christopher, and Stanley K. Henshaw (1986). *Induced Abortion: A World Review, 1986*. New York: The Alan Guttmacher Institute.

United Nations Fund for Population Activities (1976). *Survey of Contraceptive Laws: Country Profiles, Checklists, and Summaries*. New York.

_____ (1979). *Survey of Laws on Fertility Control*. New York.

World Health Organization (1970). Comparative health legislation: abortion laws. *International Digest of Health Legislation* (Geneva), vol. 21, No. 3, pp. 437-512.

Israel

Henshaw, Stanley K. (1990). Induced abortion: a world review, 1990. In *Induced Abortion: A World Review, 1990 Supplement*, by Stanley K. Henshaw and Evelyn Morrow. New York: The Alan Guttmacher Institute.

_____, and Evelyn Morrow (1990). *Induced Abortion: A World Review, 1990 Supplement*. New York: The Alan Guttmacher Institute.

Friedlander, Dov, and Calvin Goldscheider (1984). *Israel's Population: The Challenge of Pluralism*. Population Reference Bureau Bulletin, vol. 39, No. 2. Washington, D.C.: Population Reference Bureau.

Israel (1991). *Statistical Abstract of Israel, 1991, No. 42*. Jerusalem: Central Bureau of Statistics.

Lancet, M., (1973). Family planning in Israel. *World Medical Journal* (Cologne, Germany), vol. 20, No. 4, p. 69.

Sabatello, Eitan F. (1992). Estimates of demand for abortion among Soviet immigrants in Israel. *Studies in Family Planning* (New York), vol. 23, No. 4 (July/August), pp. 268-273.

_____, and Nurit Yaffe (1988). Israel. In *International Handbook on Abortion*, Paul Sachdev, ed. New York; Westport, Connecticut: Greenwood Press.

United Nations Fund for Population Activities (1978). *Annual Review of Population Law, 1977*. New York.

_____ (1980). *Annual Review of Population Law, 1979*. New York.

Italy

Blangiardo, Gian Carlo, and Franco Bonarini (1988). *Aboritivitá e contollo dei conceptimenti* (Abortion and birth control). Secondo rapporto sulla situazione demografica italiana. Rome: Instituto di Ricerca sulla Popolazione.

Council of Europe (1991). *Recent Demographic Developments in Europe, 1991 Edition*. Strasbourg.

Figa-Talamanca, Irene (1988). Italy. In *International Handbook on Abortion*, Paul Sachdev, ed. New York; Westport, Connecticut; and London: Greenwood Press.

Filicori, Marco, and Carlo Flamigni (1981). Legal abortion in Italy, 1978-1979. *Family Planning Perspectives* (New York), vol. 13, No. 5, (September/October) pp. 228-232.

Henshaw, Stanley K. (1990). Induced abortion: a world review, 1990. In *Induced Abortion: A World Review, 1990 Supplement*, by Stanley K. Henshaw and Evelyn Morrow. New York: The Alan Guttmacher Institute.

Owen, Margaret (1990). Setbacks in Italy. *People* (London), vol. 17, No. 4, p. 6.

Riphagen, F. E., and P. Lehert (1989). A survey of contraception in five West European countries. *Journal of Biosocial Science* (London), vol. 2, No. 1 (January), pp. 23-46.

Spinelli, Angela, and Michelle E. Grandolfo (1991). Induced abortion and contraception in Italy. *Planned Parenthood in Europe* (London), vol. 20, No. 2.

Swartz, Barbra (1983). *Family Planning Legislation*. EURO Reports and Studies. No. 85. Copenhagen, Denmark: World Health Organization, Regional Office for Europe.

Tietze, Christopher, and Stanley K. Henshaw (1986). *Induced Abortion: A World Review, 1986*. New York: The Alan Guttmacher Institute.

United Nations (various years). *Demographic Yearbook*.

United Nations Fund for Population Activities (1976). *Survey of Contraceptive Laws: Country Profiles, Checklists, and Summaries*. New York.

_____ (1979). *Survey of Laws on Fertility Control*. New York.

Walston, James (1980). Legal abortion in Italy. *Planned Parenthood in Europe* (London), vol. 9, No. 1, (April), pp. 1-2.

World Health Organization (1970). Comparative health legislation: abortion laws. *International Digest of Health Legislation* (Geneva), vol. 21, No. 3, pp. 437-512.

_____ (1978). *International Digest of Health Legislation* (Geneva), vol. 29, No. 3. pp. 589-597.

Jamaica

Cook, Rebecca J., and Bernard M. Dickens (1979). Abortion laws in Commonwealth Countries. *International Digest of Health Legislation* (Geneva), vol. 30, No. 3, pp. 395-502.

International Planned Parenthood Federation (1989). Maternal Deaths in Jamaica twice official rates. IPPF Open file: news digest of the world's largest voluntary family planning organization (two weeks ending 7 December), p. 13. London. Mimeographed.

Rosen, Robert C. (1973). *Law and Population Growth in Jamaica*. Law and Population Monograph Series, No. 10. Medford, Massachusetts: Tufts University, The Fletcher School of Law and Diplomacy.

Walker, G. J., and others (1975). Maternal mortality in Jamaica. *The Lancet* (Baltimore, Maryland; and London), vol. 1, No. 8497 (1 March), pp. 486-488.

Japan

Henshaw, Stanley K. (1990). Induced abortion: a world review, 1990. In *Induced Abortion: A World Review, 1990 Supplement*, by Stanley K. Henshaw and Evelyn Morrow. New York: The Alan Guttmacher Institute.

_____, and Evelyn Morrow (1990). *Induced Abortion: A World Review, 1990 Supplement*. New York: The Alan Guttmacher Institute.

International Advisory Committee on Population and Law (1975). *Annual Review of Population Law, 1974*. Medford, Massachusetts: Tufts University, The Fletcher School of Law and Diplomacy.

Kitamura, Kunio (1991). Every child should be a wanted child. *Integration* (Tokyo), No. 30 (December), pp. 40-44.

Kondo, Yuri (1983). Abortion concern in Japan. *People* (London), vol. 10, No. 2. p. 29.

Kuroda, Toshio (1984). *Population of Japan: Population Policy*. NUPRI Reprint Series, No. 14. Tokyo: Nihon University, Population Research Institute.

Madden C., and others (1990). Japan. In *Country Profiles: Bangladesh, Brazil, China, Egypt, India, Indonesia, Japan, Mexico, Nigeria, Pakistan, Turkey, Union of Soviet Socialist Republics, United Kingdom, United States of America*. Atlanta, Georgia: Emory University, School of Medicine.

Muramatsu, Minoru (1988). Japan. In *International Handbook on Abortion*, Paul Sachdev, ed. New York; Westport, Connecticut; and London: Greenwood Press.

Tietze, Christopher (1983). *Induced Abortion: A World Review, 1983*, 5th edition. New York: The Population Council.

United Nations Fund for Population Activities (1979). *Survey of Laws on Fertility Control*. New York.

Wagatsuma, Takashi (1986). Japan's long wait for modern contraception. *People* (London), vol. 13, No. 4, pp. 17-18.

Weisman, Stephen R. (1992). Japan keeps ban on birth control pills. *The New York Times* (19 March 1992), p. A3.

World Health Organization (1965). Japan. *International Digest of Health Legislation* (Geneva), vol. 16, No. 4, pp. 690-699.

Jordan

Henshaw, Stanley K. (1990). Induced abortion: a world review, 1990. In *Induced Abortion: A World Review, 1990 Supplement*, by Stanley K. Henshaw and Evelyn Morrow. New York: The Alan Guttmacher Institute.

Moore-Čavar, Emily Campbell (1974). *International Inventory of Information on Induced Abortion*. New York: Columbia University, International Institute for the Study of Human Reproduction.

Ross, John A., and others (1992). *Family Planning and Child Survival Programs As Assessed in 1991*. New York: The Population Council.

United Nations (1989). *World Population Policies*, vol. II, *Gabon to Norway* . Population Studies, No. 102/Add.1. Sales No. E.89.XIII.3.

United Nations Fund for Population Activities (1979). *Survey of Laws on Fertility Control*. New York.

Kazakhstan

Borisov, V. A., compiler (1989). *Naselenei Mira: Demographichesky Spravochnik* (World population: demographic reference book). Moscow: Msyl'.

David, Henry P., and Robert I. McIntyre (1981). *Reproductive Behavior: Central and Eastern European Experience*. New York: Springer Publishing.

Popov, Andrej A. (1991). Family planning and induced abortion in the USSR: basic health and demographic characteristics. *Studies in Family Planning* (New York), vol. 22, No. 6 (November/December), pp. 368-377.

Russian Soviet Federative Socialist Republic, People's Commissariat of Public Health, People's Comissariat of Justice (1992). Ob iskusstvennom preyvanii beremennosti (On the artificial interruption of pregnancy). *Postnaovleniia KPSS i Sovetskogo Pravitel'stva ob Okhrane Zdorov'ya* (Decrees of CPSU and the Soviet Government on public health).

_____ Union of Soviet Socialist Republics, Ministry of Public Health (1974). *O Pobochnom Deistvii i Oslozhneniyakh Pri Primenenii Oral'nykh Kontratseptivov: Informatsionnoe Pis'mo* (On the side-effects and complications of oral contraceptives: information letter). Compiled by E. A. Babaiian, A. S. Lopatin and I. G. Lavretskii. Moscow.

_____ (1982). *O Poryadke Provedeniya Operatsii Iskusstvennogo Preryvaniya Beremennosti* (On the artificial interruption of pregnancies). Decree No. 234, 16 March.

_____ (1987). *O Poryadke Provedeniya Operatsii Iskusstvennogo Preryvaniya Beremennosti Rannikh Srokov Metodom Vacuum-aspiratsii* (On the artificial interruption of early-stage pregnancies by vacuum aspiration). Decree No. 757, 5 June.

_____ (1987). *O Poryadke Provedeniya Operatsii Iskusstvennogo Preryvaniya Beremennosti Po Nemeditsinskim Pokazaniyam* (On the artificial interruption of pregnancies for non-medical reasons). Decree No. 1342, 31 December.

_____ (1989). *Zdorov'e Naseleniya SSSR i Deyatelnost' Uchrezhdenii Zdravookhraneniya v 1988* (Health of the population of the USSR and activities of public-health services in 1988) (Moscow).

_____ (1990). *Zdravookhraneniye v SSSR v 1989. Statisticheskie Materialy* (Public health in the USSR in 1989; statistical data) (Moscow).

_____, Moscow State University (1985). *Demografichesky Entsiclopedichesky Slovar'* (Demographic encyclopedic dictionary). Moscow: Sovetskaya entsiclopediya.

_____, Presidium of the Supreme Soviet (1958). Ob otmene zapreshcheniya abortov (On repeal of the prohibition of abortions). Decree of 23 November 1955. In *Postanovleniya KPSS i Sovetskogo Pravitel'stva ob Okhrane Zdorov'ya Naroda* (Decrees of CPSU and the Soviet Government on public-health care). Moscow: Medgiz.

_____, State Committee on Statistics (1988, 1989). *Naselenie SSSR, 1987 and 1988.* Moscow: Finance and Statistics.

_____ (1990). *Demografichesky Ezhegodnik SSSR 1990* (Demographic yearbook of the USSR 1990). Moscow: Finance and Statistics.

_____ (1991). Problemy sem'i, okhrany materinstva i detstva (Problems of family, maternal and child care). *Vestnik Statistiki* (Moscow), No. 8, pp. 60-61.

United Nations (1992). The *1992 Revision* of world population prospects. *Population Newsletter* (New York), No. 54 (December), p. 1.

United Nations Children's Fund/World Health Organization (1992). Independent Republic of Kazakhstan. A social protection strategy for a nation in transition. Report of a joint UNICEF/WHO/UNFPA/UNDP and WFP mission to the Russian Federation, 17-26 February. Unpublished.

_____ (1992). The looming crisis and fresh opportunity: health in Kazakhstan, Kyrgyzstan, Tadjkistan, Turkmenistan and Uzbekistan with emphasis on women and children. Report of a joint UNICEF/WHO/UNFPA/UNDP and WFP mission to the Russian Federation, 17 February - 2 March. Unpublished.

_____ (1992c). The looming crisis in health and the need for international support: overview of the reports on the Commonwealth of Independent States and the Baltic countries. Prepared by the UNICEF/WHO Collaborative Missions with the participation of UNFPA, WFP and UNDP, 17 February - 2 March 1992. Unpublished.

Kenya

Baker, Jean, and Shanyisa Khasiani (1992). Induced abortion in Kenya: case histories. *Studies in Family Planning* (New York), vol. 23, No. 1 (January/February), pp. 34-44.

Cook, Rebecca J., and Benjamin M. Dickens (1979). Abortion laws in Commonwealth countries. *International Digest of Health Legislation* (Geneva), vol. 30, No. 3, pp. 395-502.

Kenya, Ministry of Home Affairs and National Heritage and National Council for Population and Development; and Institute for Resource Development/Macro Systems, Inc. (1989). *Kenya Demographic and Health Survey.* Nairobi, Kenya; and Columbia, Maryland.

Makokha, A. E. (1991). Medico-social and socio-demographic factors associated with maternal mortality at Kenyatta National Hospital, Nairobi, Kenya. *Journal of Obstetrics and Gynaecology of Eastern and Central Africa* (Nairobi, Kenya), vol. 9, No. 1, pp. 3-6.

Rogo, Khama (1990). Induced abortion in Africa. Paper prepared for the Annual Meeting of the Population Association of America, Toronto, Canada, 3-5 May.

Uche, U. U. (1974). *Law and Population Growth in Kenya.* Law and Population Monograph Series, No. 22. Medford, Massachusetts: Tufts University, The Fletcher School of Law and Diplomacy.

United Nations Fund for Population Activities (1979). *Survey of Laws on Fertility Control.* New York.

Kiribati

United Nations (1989). *World Population Policies*, vol. II, *Gabon to Norway*. Population Studies, No. 102/Add.1. Sales No. E.89.XIII.3.

Kuwait

Fahmy-K. (1984). Maternal mortality in Kuwait: a twelve year study. In *Medical Education in the Field of Primary Maternal Child Health Care*, M. M. Fayad, and others, eds. Cairo, Egypt: Cairo University, Faculty of Medicine.

Lapham, Robert J., ed. (1977). Other West Asian and North African countries. In *Family Planning in the Developing World: A Review of Programs*, W. B. Watson, ed. New York: The Population Council.

Mostafa, A. A., and K. I. Marakat (1979). The abortion load in the Kuwait Maternity Hospital: five years' study. *Journal of the Kuwait Medical Association*, vol. 13, No. 2 (June), pp. 93-95.

Shah, Nasra M., and Makhdoom Ali Shah (1987). *The Rapid Mortality Transition in Kuwait: The Role of Health and Development Policies*. Kuwait: Kuwait University.

United Nations (1992). *World Population Monitoring, 1991: With Special Emphasis on Age Structure*. Population Studies, No. 126. Sales No. E.92.XIII.2.

United Nations Fund for Population Activities (1979). *Survey of Laws on Fertility Control*. New York.

_____(1982). *Annual Review of Population Law, 1981*, vol. 8. New York.

_____, and Harvard Law School Library (1987). *Annual Review of Population Law, 1984*, vol. 11. New York.

World Health Organization (1990). Safe motherhood: abortion. A tabulation of available data on the frequency and mortality of unsafe abortion. Geneva. Unpublished report.

Kyrgyzstan

Abdylbaeva, I. A., and K. D. Abdullin (1986). Primenenie protivozachatochnykh sredstv zhenshchinami g. Frunze (Contraception use among women of the city of Frunze). *Sovetskoe Zdravookhranenie* (Moscow), No. 6, pp. 40-42.

Borisov, V. A., compiler (1989). *Naselenei Mira: Demographichesky Spravochnik* (World population: demographic reference book). Moscow: Msyl'.

David, Henry P., and Robert I. McIntyre (1981). *Reproductive Behavior: Central and Eastern European Experience*. New York: Springer Publishing Company.

Popov, Andrej A. (1991). Family planning and induced abortion in the USSR: basic health and demographic characteristics. *Studies in Family Planning* (New York), vol. 22, No. 6 (November/December), pp. 368-377.

Union of Soviet Socialist Republics, Ministry of Public Health (1974). *O Pobochnom Deistvii i Oslozhneniyakh Pri Primenenii Oral'nykh Kontratseptivov: Informatsionnoe Pis'mo* (On side-effects and complications of oral contraceptives: information letter). Compiled by E. A. Babaiian, A. S. Lopatin and I. G. Lavretskii. Moscow.

_____ (1982). *O Poryadke Provedeniya Operatsii Iskusstvennogo Preryvaniya Beremennosti* (On the artificial interruption of pregnancies). Decree No. 234, 16 March.

_____ (1987). *O Poryadke Provedeniya Operatsii Iskusstvennogo Preryvaniya Beremennosti Rannikh Srokov Metodom Vacuum-aspiratsii* (On the artificial interruption of early-stage pregnancies by vacuum aspiration). Decree No. 757, 5 June.

_____ (1987). *O Poryadke Provedeniya Operatsii Iskusstvennogo Preryvaniya Beremennosti Po Nemeditsinskim Pokazaniyam* (On the artificial interruption of pregnancies for non-medical reasons). Decree No. 1342, 31 December.

_____ (1989). *Zdorov'e Naseleniya SSSR i Deyatelnost' Uchrezhdenii Zdravookhraneniya v 1988* (Health of the population of the USSR and activities of public-health services in 1988. Moscow.

_____ (1990). *Zdravookhraneniye v SSSR in 1989. Statisticheskie Materialy* (Public health in the USSR in 1989. statistical data). Moscow.

_____, Moscow State University (1985). *Demografichesky Entsiclopedichesky Slovar'* (Demographic encyclopedic dictionary). Moscow: Sovetskaya entsiclopediya.

_____, Presidium of the Supreme Soviet (1958). Ob otmene zapreshcheniya abortov (On repeal of the prohibition of abortions). Decree of 23 November 1955. In *Postanovleniya KPSS i Sovetskogo Pravitel'stva ob Okhrane Zdorov'ya Naroda*. Moscow.

State Committee on Statistics (1988, 1989). *Naselenie SSSr, 1987 and 1988*. Moscow: Finance and Statistics.

_____ (1990). *Demografichesky Ezhegodnik SSSR 1990* (Demographic yearbook of the USSR, 1990). Moscow: Finance and Statistics..

_____ (1991). Problemy sem'i, okhrany materinstva i detstva (Problems of family, maternal and child care). *Vestnik Statistiki* (Moscow), No. 8, pp. 60-61.

United Nations (1992). The *1992 Revision* of world population prospects. *Population Newsletter* (New York), No. 54 (December), p. 1.

United Nations Children's Fund/ World Health Organization (1992). The looming crisis of children and women in Kyrgizstan. Report of a joint UNICEF/WHO/UNFPA/UNDP and WFP Mission, 21-26 February. Unpublished.

_____ (1992). The looming crisis in health and the need for international support: overview of the reports on the Commonwealth of Independent States and the Baltic countries. Prepared by the UNICEF/WHO Collaborative Missions with the participation of UNFPA, WFP and UNDP, 17 February - 2 March 1992. Unpublished.

Lao People's Democratic Republic

Frisen, Carl M. (1991). Population characteristics in the Lao People's Democratic Republic. *Asia-Pacific Population Journal* (Bangkok), vol. 6, No. 2 (June), pp. 55-66.

United Nations (1989). *Trends in Population Policy, 1976-1986*. Population Studies, No. 114. Sales No. E.89.XIII.13.

United Nations Fund for Population Activities (1979). *Survey of Laws on Fertility Control*. New York.

United Nations Development Programme (1993). UNFPA proposed projects and programmes. Recommendation by the Executive Director. Assistance to the Government of the Lao People's Democratic Republic; support for a comprehensive population programme. DP/FPA/CP/120.

Latvia

Cook, Rebecca J. (1989). Abortion laws and policies: challenges and opportunities. In "Women's health in the third world: the impact of unwanted pregnancy", A. Rosenfield and others, eds. *International Journal of Gynecology and Obstetrics* (Limerick, Ireland), Supplement No. 3, pp. 51-87.

_____, and Bernard M. Dickens (1988). International developments in abortion laws: 1977-88. *American Journal of Public Health* (Washington, D.C.), vol. 78, No. 10 (October), pp. 1305-1311.

Latvia (1992). *Estestvennoe Dvizhenie i Migratsiya Naseleniya v Latviisko Respublike v 1991* (Natural increase and migration of population in the Latvia Republic in 1991). Statistical Bulletin. Riga: Statistical Committee.

Popov, Andrej A. (1991). Family planning and induced abortion in the USSR: basic health and demographic characteristics. *Studies in Family Planning* (New York), vol. 22, No. 6 (November/December).

_____ (1992). Induced abortions in the USSR at the end of the 1980s: the basis for the national model of family planning. Paper presented at the Annual Meeting of the Population Association of America, Denver, Colorado, 30 April - 2 May.

Royston, Erica, and Sue Armstrong, eds. (1989). *Preventing Maternal Deaths*. Geneva: World Health Organization.

Union of Soviet Socialist Republics, State Committee on Statistics (1988, 1989). *Naselenie SSSR, 1987 and 1988*. Moscow: Finance and Statistics.

_____ (1990). *Demografichesky Ezhegodnik SSSR, 1990* (Demographic yearbook of the USSR, 1990). Moscow. Finance and Statistics.

United Nations Children's Fund/World Health Organization (1992). The looming crisis in health and the need for international support: overview of the reports on the Commonwealth of Independent States and the Baltic countries. Prepared by the UNICEF/WHO Collaborative Missions with the participation of UNFPA, WFP and UNDP, 17 February - 2 March 1992. Unpublished.

United Nations Fund for Population Activities (1976). *Survey of Contraceptive Laws: Profiles, Checklists, and Summaries.* New York.

_____ (1979). *Survey of Laws on Fertility Control.* New York.

World Health Organization (1970). Comparative health legislation: abortion laws. *International Digest of Health Legislation* (Geneva), vol. 21, No. 3, pp. 437-512.

_____, Regional Office for Europe (1990). Family Planning in the USSR. *Entre nous: The European Family Planning Magazine* (Copenhagen, Denmark), No. 16 (September), pp. 5-8.

Zvidrinch, Peter (1992). Trends in the population of Estonia, Latvia and Lithuania. Report prepared for the Population Division of the Department of Economic and Social Development of the United Nations Secretariat. Riga, Latvia: University of Latvia, Department of Statistics and Demography.

Lebanon

Dib, George M. (1975). *Law and Population in Lebanon.* Law and Population Monograph Series, No. 29. Medford, Massachusetts: Tufts University, The Fletcher School of Law and Diplomacy.

Bickers, W. (1972). Serious complications of induced abortion in Lebanon. In *Induced Abortion: A Hazard to Public Health?*, Isam R. Nazer, ed. Proceedings of the First Conference of the IPPF Middle East and North Africa Region, Beirut, Lebanon, February. Beirut: International Planned Parenthood Federation, Middle East and North Africa Region.

International Planned Parenthood Federation (1984). Lebanon's National Population Council. IPPF Open File: news digest of the world's largest voluntary family planning organization (two weeks ending 9 March). London. Mimeographed.

_____ (1984). Continuing crisis in Lebanon. IPPF Open File: news digest of the world's largest voluntary family planning organization (two weeks ending 29 June). London. Mimeographed.

United Nations (1982). Population policy digest: indicators, perceptions and policies in the countries of the Economic and Social Commission for Western Asia. ESA/P/WP/78. New York.

United Nations Fund for Population Activities (1979). *Annual Review of Population Law, 1979.* New York.

_____ (1979). *Survey of Laws on Fertility Control.* New York.

_____, and Harvard Law School Library (1985). *Annual Review of Population Law, 1983*, vol. 10. New York.

_____ (1987). *Annual Review of Population Law, 1984*, vol. 11. New York: UNFPA.

United Nations Population Fund, and Harvard Law School Library (1989). *Annual Review of Population Law, 1986*, vol. 13. New York: UNFPA.

Lesotho

Cook, Rebecca J., and Bernard M. Dickens (1986). *Issues in Reproductive Health Law in the Commonwealth.* London: The Commonwealth Secretariat.

Elkan, Walter (1980). Labour migration from Botswana, Lesotho, and Swaziland. *Economic Development and Cultural Change* (Chicago), vol. 28, No. 3 (April), pp. 583-596.

Poulter, Sebastian, and others (1981). *Law and Population Growth in Lesotho.* Roma, Lesotho: National University of Lesotho, Law and Population Project.

Ross, John A., and others (1992). *Family Planning and Child Survival Programs As Assessed in 1991*. New York: The Population Council.

United Nations Fund for Population Activities (1979). *Survey of Laws on Fertility Control*. New York.

Liberia

Nichols, Douglas, and others (1987). Sexual behaviour, contraceptive practice, and reproductive health among Liberian adolescents. *Studies in Family Planning* (New York), vol. 18, No. 3 (May-June), pp. 169-176.

Tietze, Christopher, and Stanley K. Henshaw (1986). *Induced Abortion: A World Review, 1986*. New York: The Alan Guttmacher Institute.

United Nations Population Fund, and Harvard Law School Library (1991). *Annual Review of Population Law, 1988*, vol. 15. New York: UNFPA.

World Health Organization (1979). *International Digest of Health Legislation* (Geneva), vol. 30, No. 4, p. 818.

Libyan Arab Jamahiriya

Legnain, M. M., R. Singh and A. Paruch (1984). Fertility regulation clinic in Libyan Arab Jamahiriya at Benghazi. In *Research in Family Planning*, J. Bonnar, W. Thompson and R. F. Harrison, eds. Lancaster, United Kingdom: Graham and Trotman.

Stubbs, G. M. (1980). Population policy in the Arab countries. In *Population in the Arab World: Problems and Prospects*, Abdel-Rahim Omran, ed. New York: United Nations Fund for Population Activities; and London: Croom Helm Ltd.

United Nations Fund for Population Activities (1979). *Survey of Laws on Fertility Control*. New York.

World Health Organization (1975). *International Digest of Health Legislation* (Geneva), vol. 26, No. 1, pp. 143-162.

_____, (1980). *International Digest of Health Legislation* (Geneva), vol. 31, No. 1, pp. 73-74.

Liechtenstein

United Nations (1989). *World Population Policies*, vol. II, *Gabon to Norway*, Population Studies, No. 102/Add.1. Sales No. E.89.XIII.3.

United Nations Population Fund, and Harvard Law School Library (1990). *Annual Review of Population Law, 1987*, vol. 14. New York: UNFPA.

United States of America, State Department (1989). Liechtenstein: background notes. Washington, D.C.: Bureau of Public Affairs.

Lithuania

Cook, Rebecca J. (1989). Abortion laws and policies: challenges and opportunities. In "Women's health in the third world: the impact of unwanted pregnancy", A. Rosenfield and others, eds. *International Journal of Gynecology and Obstetrics*. (Limerick, Ireland), Supplement No. 3, pp. 51-87.

_____, and Bernard M. Dickens (1988). International developments in abortion laws: 1977-88. *American Journal of Public Health* (Washington, D.C.), vol. 78, No. 10 (October), pp. 1305-1311.

Pópov, Andrej A. (1991). Family planning and induced abortion in the USSR: basic health and demographic characteristics. *Studies in Family Planning* (New York), vol. 22, No. 6 (November/December), pp. 368-377.

_____ (1992). Induced abortions in the USSR at the end of the 1980s: the basis for the national model of family planning. Paper presented at the Annual Meeting of the Population Association of America, Denver, Colorado, 30 April -2 May.

Royston, Erica, and Sue Armstrong, eds. (1989). *Preventing Maternal Deaths*. Geneva: World Health Organization.

United Nations Children's Fund (1992). Estonia, Latvia and Lithuania: overview of health, education and social safety nets and assessment of priority requirements. Report of a UNICEF Mission. 16-17 February. New York.

United Nations Fund for Population Activities (1976). *Survey of Contraceptive Laws: Country Profiles, Checklists, and Summaries.* New York.

_____ (1979). *Survey of Laws on Fertility Control.* New York.

Union of Soviet Socialist Republics, State Committee on Statistics (1988, 1989). *Naselenie SSSR, 1987 and 1988.* Moscow: Finance and Statistics.

_____ (1990). *Demografichesky Ezhegodnik SSSR, 1990* (Demographic yearbook of the USSR, 1990). Moscow: Finance and Statistics.

World Health Organization (1970). Comparative health legislation: abortion laws. *International Digest of Health Legislation* (Geneva), vol. 21, No. 3.

_____, Regional Office for Europe (1990). Family Planning in the USSR. *Entre nous: The European Family Planning Magazine* (Copenhagen, Denmark), No. 16 (September), pp. 347-512.

Zvidrinch, Peter (1992). *Trends in the Population of Estonia, Latvia and Lithuania.* Report prepared for the Population Division of the Department of Economic and Social Development of the United Nations Secretariat. Riga, Latvia: University of Latvia, Department of Statistics and Demography.

Luxembourg

Cook, Rebecca J. (1989). Abortion laws and policies: challenges and opportunities. In "Women's health in the third world: the impact of unwanted pregnancy", A. Rosenfield and others, eds. *International Journal of Gynecology and Obstetrics* (Limerick, Ireland), Supplement No. 3, pp. 61-87.

_____, and Bernard M. Dickens (1988). International developments in abortion laws: 1977-88. *American Journal of Public Health* (Washington, D.C.), vol. 78, No. 10 (October), pp. 1305-1311.

Glendon, Mary Ann (1987). *Abortion and Divorce in Western Law.* Cambridge, Massachusetts and London: Harvard University Press.

Institut national d'études Démographiques (1981). L'interruption volontaire de grossesse dans l'Europe des Neuf. *Travaux et documents,* Cahier No. 91. Paris. Presses universitaires de France.

International Planned Parenthood Federation (1989). Abortion laws in Europe. *Planned Parenthood in Europe* (London), vol. 18, No. 1 (Spring), supplement.

Knoppers, Bartha Maria, and Isabel Brault (1989). *La loi et l'avortement dans les pays francophones.* Montreal, Canada: Les Editions Thémis.

_____, Isabel Brault and Elizabeth Sloss (1990). Abortion law in francophone countires. *American Journal of Comparative Law* (Berkeley, California), vol. 38, No. 4 (Fall), pp. 889-922.

Luxembourg (1978). Law of 15 November 1978, concerning Sex Education, Prevention of Clandestine Abortion, and Regulation of the Voluntary Interruption of Pregnancy, amending art. 353 of Penal Code. *Memorial: Journal officiel du Grand-Duche de Luxembourg,* part A, 6 December 1978, No. 81, pp. 1968-1970. Translated in United Nations Fund for Population Activities (1979). *Annual Review of Population Law, 1978.* New York.

Royston, Erica, and Sue Armstrong, eds. (1989). *Preventing Maternal Deaths.* Geneva: World Health Organization.

United Nations Fund for Population Activities (1976). *Survey of Contraceptive Laws: Country Profiles, Checklists, and Summaries.* New York.

_____ (1979). *Survey of Laws on Fertility Control.* New York.

World Health Organization (1970). Comparative health legislation: abortion laws. *International Digest of Health Legislation* (Geneva), vol. 21, No. 3, pp. 347-512.

_____ (1988). *International Digest of Health Legislation* (Geneva), vol. 39, No. 2, pp. 381-382.

Madagascar

Madagascar (1962). Penal Code. *Journal officiel de la République malgache*, No. 240 (7 September).

Cook, Rebecca J. (1989). Abortion laws and policies: challenges and opportunities. In "Women's health in the third world: the impact of unwanted pregnancy", A. Rosenfield and others, eds. *International Journal of Gynecology and Obstetrics* (Limerick, Ireland), Supplement No. 3, pp. 61-87.

_____, and Bernard M. Dickens (1988). International developments in abortion laws: 1977-88. *American Journal of Public Health* (Washington, D.C.), vol. 78, No. 10 (October), pp. 1305-1311.

Henshaw, Stanley K. (1990). Induced abortion: a world review, 1990. In *Induced Abortion: A World Review, 1990 Supplement*, by Stanley K. Henshaw and Evelyn Morrow. New York: The Alan Guttmacher Institute.

Knoppers, Bartha Maria, and Isabel Brault (1989). *La loi et l'avortement dans les pays francophones*. Montreal, Canada: Les Editions Thémis.

_____, and Elizabeth Sloss (1990). Abortion law in francophone countries. *American Journal of Comparative Law* (Berkeley, California), vol. 38, No. 4 (Fall), pp. 889-922.

Royston, Erica, and Sue Armstrong, eds. (1989). *Preventing Maternal Deaths*. Geneva: World Health Organization.

Tietze, Christopher, and Stanley K. Henshaw (1986). *Induced Abortion: A World Review, 1986*. New York: The Alan Guttmacher Institute.

United Nations Fund for Population Activities (1976). *Survey of Contraceptive Laws: Country Profiles, Checklists, and Summaries*. New York.

_____ (1979). *Survey of Laws on Fertility Control*. New York.

World Health Organization (1970). Comparative health legislation: abortion laws. *International Digest of Health Legislation* (Geneva), vol. 21, No. 3, pp. 347-512.

Malawi

Cook, Rebecca J., and Bernard M. Dickens (1979). Abortion laws in Commonwealth countries. *International Digest of Health Legislation* (Geneva), vol. 30, No. 2, pp. 395-502.

_____ (1986). *Issues in Reproductive Health Law in the Commonwealth*. London: Commonwealth Secretariat.

Henshaw, Stanley K. (1990). Induced abortion: a world review, 1990. In *Induced Abortion: A World Review, 1990 Supplement*, by Stanley K. Henshaw and Evelyn Morrow. New York: The Alan Guttmacher Institute.

Malawi (1968). Penal Code 1930, Act of 1 April 1930. In *The Laws of Malawi*, rev. 1968.

Royston, Erica, and Sue Armstrong, eds. (1989). *Preventing Maternal Deaths*. Geneva: World Health Organization.

Tietze, Christopher, and Stanley K. Henshaw (1986). *Induced Abortion: A World Review, 1986*. New York: The Alan Guttmacher Institute.

United Nations Fund for Population Activities (1976). *Survey of Contraceptive Laws: Country Profiles, Checklists, and Summaries*. New York.

_____ (1979). *Survey of Laws on Fertility Control*. New York.

United Nations Population Fund, and Harvard Law School Library (1989). *Annual Review of Population Law, 1986*, vol. 13. New York: UNFPA.

World Health Organization (1970). Comparative health legislation: abortion laws. *International Digest of Health Legislation* (Geneva), vol. 21, No. 3, pp. 347-512.

Malaysia

Anonymous (1990). Malaysia: changes in abortion law. *The Lancet* (Baltimore, Maryland; and London), vol. 335, No. 8699 (19 May), p. 1209.

Aziz, Nor Laily (1978). Malaysia. In "East Asia review, 1976-77", S. M. Keeny, ed. *Studies in Family Planning* (New York), vol. 9, No. 9 (September), pp. 241-242.

Ibrahim, Ahmad (1986). Law and population. In *Population of Malaysia*. Economic and Social Commission for Asia and the Pacific Country Monograph Series, No. 13. Bangkok.

Takeshita, Y. J., Tan Boon Ann, and H. Arshat (1986). Attitude towards induced abortion in peninsular Malaysia: a Guttman scale analysis. *Malaysian Journal of Reproductive Health*. vol. 4, No. 2 (December), pp. 73-90.

Maldives

United Nations (1989). *World Population Policies*, vol. II, *Gabon to Norway*. Population Studies No. 102/Add.1. Sales No. E.89.XIII.3.

United Nations Fund for Population Activities (1982). *Maldives: Report of Mission on Needs Assessment for Population Assistance*. Report No. 49. New York.

Mali

Henshaw, Stanley K. (1990). Induced abortion: a world review, 1990. In *Induced Abortion: A World Review, 1990 Supplement*, by Stanley K. Henshaw and Evelyn Morrow. New York: The Alan Guttmacher Institute.

Knoppers, Bartha Maria, and Isabel Brault (1989). *La loi et l'avortement dans les pays francophones*. Montreal, Canada: Les Editions Thémis.

_____, and Elizabeth Sloss (1990). Abortion law in francophone countries. *American Journal of Comparative Law* (Berkeley, California), vol. 38, No. 4 (Fall), pp. 889-922.

Mali (1961). Criminal Code, Law No. 99 of 3 August 1961. *Journal officiel*, No. 98 (4 September).

_____ (1991). *Rapport sur l'état de la nation et de la République, présenté par le Gouvernement à la Conférence nationale*. Bamako.

Royston, Erica, and Sue Armstrong, eds. (1989). *Preventing Maternal Deaths*. Geneva: World Health Organization.

Tietze, Christopher, and Stanley K. Henshaw (1986). *Induced Abortion: A World Review, 1986*. New York: The Alan Guttmacher Institute.

United Nations Fund for Population Activities (1976). *Survey of Contraceptive Laws: Country Profiles, Checklists, and Summaries*. New York.

_____ (1979). *Survey of Laws on Fertility Control*. New York.

United States of America, Centers for Disease Control (1983). *Study of Abortion With Complications Requiring Hospitalization In Mali: Final Report*. Atlanta, Georgia.

World Bank (1991). Second health, population and rural water supply project. Report No. 8683-MLI. (22 February).

World Health Organization (1970). Comparative health legislation: abortion laws. *International Digest of Health Legislation* (Geneva), vol. 21, No. 3, pp. 347-512.

Malta

Shain, R.N. (1986). A cross-cultural history of abortion. *Clinics in Obstetrics and Gynaecology*, vol. 13, No. 1 (March), pp. 1-17.

Simons, J. (1982). Fertility control in Europe. In *Proceedings of the European Population Conference, Strasbourg, 21-24 September 1982*. Strasbourg, France: Council of Europe.

United Nations (1982). *World Population Trends and Policies: 1981 Monitoring Report*, vol. II, *Population Policies*. Population Studies, No. 79/Add.1. Sales No. E.82.XIII.3.

Marshall Islands

Marshall Islands (1982). Country statement. Paper prepared for the United Nations Economic and Social Commission for Asia and the Pacific, Third Asian and Pacific Conference, Colombo, Sri Lanka, 20-29 September.

Levy, Susan J., and others. (1988). Fertility and contraception in the Marshall Islands. *Studies in Family Planning* (New York), vol. 19, No. 3 (May/June). pp. 179-185.

Mauritania

Henshaw, Stanley K. (1990). Induced abortion: a world review, 1990. In *Induced Abortion: A World Review, 1990 Supplement*, by Stanley K. Henshaw and Evelyn Morrow. New York: The Alan Guttmacher Institute.

Knoppers, Bartha Maria, and Isabel Brault (1989). *La loi et l'avortement dans les pays francophones*. Montreal, Canada: Les Editions Thémis.

_____, and Elizabeth Sloss (1990). Abortion law in francophone countries. *American Journal of Comparative Law* (Berkeley, California), vol. 38, No. 4 (Fall), pp. 889-922.

Mauritania (1984). Code pénal (Ordinance No. 83-162), 9 July 1983. *Journal officiel de la République islamique de Mauritanie*, Nos. 608-609 (29 February), pp. 112.

Royston, Erica, and Sue Armstrong, eds. (1989). *Preventing Maternal Deaths*. Geneva: World Health Organization.

Tietze, Christopher, and Stanley K. Henshaw (1986). *Induced Abortion: A World Review, 1986*. New York: The Alan Guttmacher Institute.

United Nations Fund for Population Activities (1976). *Survey of Contraceptive Laws: Country Profiles, Checklists, and Summaries*. New York.

_____ (1979). *Survey of Laws on Fertility Control*. New York.

United Nations Population Fund, and Harvard Law School Library (1988). *Annual Review of Population Law, 1985*, vol. 12. New York: UNFPA.

Westinghouse Social Science International (1984). *Mauritania*. Population Policy Review: Demographic Data for Development. Columbia, Maryland.

World Health Organization (1970). Comparative health legislation: abortion laws. *International Digest of Health Legislation* (Geneva), vol. 21, No. 3, pp. 347-512.

Mauritius

Mauritius (1945). Penal Code Ordinance of 29 December 1838. *The Laws of Mauritius Review, 1945*.

Chandrasekhar, S.(1988). Growth and characteristics of population - the island of Mauritius: 1767-1987. *Population Review: Demography of Developing Countries* (La Jolla, California), vol. 32, Nos. 1-2 (January-December), pp. 11-40.

Cook, Rebecca J., and Bernard M. Dickens (1979). Abortion laws in Commonwealth countries. *International Digest of Health Legislation* (Geneva), vol. 30, No. 3, pp. 395-502.

_____ (1986). *Issues in Reproductive Health Law in the Commonwealth*. London: Commonwealth Secretariat.

Elia, D. (1980). La contraception a l'île Maurice. *Contraception, fertilité, sexualité* (France), vol. 8, No. 7 (juillet), pp. 603-605.

Henshaw, Stanley K. (1990). Induced abortion: a world review, 1990. In *Induced Abortion: A World Review, 1990 Supplement*, by Stanley K. Henshaw and Evelyn Morrow. New York: The Alan Guttmacher Institute.

Knoppers, Bartha Maria, and Isabel Brault (1989). *La loi et l'avortement dans les pays francophones*. Montreal, Canada: Les Editions Thémis.

_____, and Elizabeth Sloss (1990). Abortion law in francophone countries. *American Journal of Comparative Law* (Berkeley, California), vol. 38, No. 4 (Fall), pp. 889-922.

Mauritius, Ministry of Economic Planning and Development (1988). *National Development Plan, 1988-1989*.

Muvman Liberasyon Fem (1988). Abortion. In *The Women's Liberation Movement in Mauritius*. Rose Hill, Mauritius.

Rajcooman, Vakil, and Esther Hanoomanjee (1989). Formulation, implementation and impact of population policy in Mauritius. In *Developments in Family Planning Policies and Programmes in Africa*. Legon, Ghana: University of Ghana, Regional Institute for Population Studies.

Royston, Erica, and Sue Armstrong, eds. (1989). *Preventing Maternal Deaths*. Geneva: World Health Organization.

Tietze, Christopher, and Stanley K. Henshaw (1986). *Induced Abortion: A World Review, 1986*. New York: The Alan Guttmacher Institute.

United Nations Fund for Population Activities (1976). *Survey of Contraceptive Laws: Country Profiles, Checklists, and Summaries*. New York.

_____ (1979). *Survey of Laws on Fertility Control*. New York.

World Health Organization (1970). Comparative health legislation: abortion laws. *International Digest of Health Legislation* (Geneva), vol. 21, No. 3.

_____ (1990). Safe motherhood: abortion. A tabulation of available data on the frequency and mortality of unsafe abortion. Geneva. Unpublished report.

Mexico

Barnett, P. G. (1982). *Status Report on Population Problems and Programmes of Mexico*. Washington, D.C.: Population Crisis Committee.

Boland, Reed (1992). New abortion laws run into problems. *People* (London), vol. 19, No. 1, p. 41.

Cornejo, Gerardo, and others (1975). *Law and Population in Mexico*. Law and Population Monograph Series, No. 23. Medford, Massachusetts: Tufts University, The Fletcher School of Law and Diplomacy.

Foro Nacional por la Maternidad Voluntaria y la Despenalización del Aborto (1991). Mexico. Federal agreement for voluntary motherhood (Mexico. Pacto federal por la maternidad voluntaria). In *Conciencia Latinoamericana*, vol. 3, No. 2, pp. 13-14.

Henshaw, Stanley K. (1990). Induced abortion: a world review, 1990. In *Induced Abortion: A World Review, 1990 Supplement*, by Stanley K. Henshaw and Evelyn Morrow. New York: The Alan Guttmacher Institute.

Institute for Resource Development, Inc. (1986). *Population Policy Brief: Mexico*. Demographic Data for Development. Columbia, Maryland.

International Planned Parenthood Federation (1980). Church opposes abortion bill in Mexico. IPPF Open File: news digest of the world largest voluntary family planning organization (two weeks ending 7 March). London. Mimeographed.

Leal, Luisa M., Coordinator (1980). *El problema del aborto in México*. Mexico City: Miguel Angel Parrua.

Natali, S. E. (1980). Socio-demographic analysis of abortion (Analisis sociodemografico del aborto). In *El Problema del Aborto en México*, Luisa M. Leal, coordinator. Mexico City.

Ross, John A., and others (1992). *Family Planning and Child Survival Programs As Assessed in 1991*. New York: The Population Council.

United Nations (1989). *Case Studies in Population Policy: Mexico*. Population Policy Paper, No. 21. Sales No. E.90.XIII.27.

United Nations Fund for Population Activities (1978). *Annual Review of Population Law, 1978*. New York.

_____ (1979). *Survey of Laws on Fertility Control.* New York.

United Nations Population Fund, and Harvard Law School Library (1990). *Annual Review of Population Law, 1987*, vol. 14. New York: UNFPA.

_____ (1991). *Annual Review of Population Law, 1988*, vol. 15. New York: UNFPA.

Viel, Benjamin (1988). Latin America. In *International Handbook on Abortion*, Paul Sachdev, ed. New York; Westport, Connecticut; and London: Greenwood Press.

World Health Organization (1987). *International Digest of Health Legislation* (Geneva), vol. 38, No. 4, p. 747.

Micronesia (Federated States of)

Pulea, Mere (1986). *The Family, Law and Population in the Pacific Islands.* Suva: University of the South Pacific, Institute of Pacific Studies.

Monaco

Kuznetsov V. K., and E. V. Baranova (1980). Zaknodatel'stwa ob aborte v stranach mira: obzor literatury (Legislation on abortion in the countries of the world: a review of the literature). *Zdravookhranenie Rossiiskoi Federatsii* (Moscow), No. 5, pp. 37-40.

United Nations Fund for Population Activities (1979). *Survey of Laws on Fertility Control.* New York.

United Nations Population Fund, and Harvard Law School Library (1989). *Annual Review of Population Law, 1986*, vol. 13. New York: UNFPA.

Mongolia

Boland, Reed (1991). Abortion rights under threat in Eastern Europe. *People* (London), vol. 18, No. 1, p. 33.

Dashzeveg, G. (1992). Statement presented at the Fourth Asian and Pacific Population Conference, Bali, Indonesia, 19-27 August.

Henshaw, Stanley K. (1990). Induced abortion: a world review, 1990. In *Induced Abortion: A World Review, 1990 Supplement*, by Stanley K. Henshaw and Evelyn Morrow. New York: The Alan Guttmacher Institute.

Ross, John A., and others (1992). *Family Planning and Child Survival Programs As Assessed in 1991.* New York: The Population Council.

United Nations Fund for Population Activities (1979). *Survey of Laws on Fertility Control.* New York.

United Nations Population Fund (1991). Mongolia chooses birth spacing to save mothers, infants. *Population* (New York), vol. 17, No. 5 (May).

_____, and Harvard Law School Library (1991). *Annual Review of Population Law, 1988*, vol. 15. New York: UNFPA.

Morocco

Henshaw, Stanley K. (1990). Induced abortion: a world review, 1990. In *Induced Abortion: A World Review, 1990 Supplement*, by Stanley K. Henshaw and Evelyn Morrow. New York: The Alan Guttmacher Institute.

Houari, Amina Messaoudi (1981). *Le droit et la condition de la femme au Maroc.* Serie de recherche, 1982. ST/ECA/ATRCW/81/29. Addis Ababa: United Nations, ECA.

Knoppers, Bartha Maria, and Isabel Brault (1989). *La loi et l'avortement dans les pays francophones.* Montreal, Canada: Les Editions Thémis.

_____, and Elizabeth Sloss (1990). Abortion law in francophone countries. *American Journal of Comparative Law* (Berkeley, California), vol. 38, No. 4 (Fall), pp. 889-922.

Lapham, Robert J. (1971). Family planning in Tunisia and Morocco. *Studies in Family Planning* (New York), vol. 2, No. 5 (May), pp. 101-109.

Mauldin, W. Parker, and Sheldon J. Segal (1988). Prevalence of contraceptive use: trends and issues. *Studies in Family Planning* (New York), vol. 19, No. 6, part I (November/December), pp. 335-353.

Morocco, Ministère du plan, Direction de la statistique (1991). *Population, l'an 2062: strategies, tendances*. Rabat: Etudes démographiques, Centre d'études et de recherches demographiques.

Laraqui, A. (1972). Report on Morocco. In *Induced Abortion: A Hazard to Public Health?*, Isam R. Nazer, ed. Proceedings of the First Conference of the IPPF Middle East and North Africa Region, Beirut, Lebanon, February. Beirut: IPPF, Middle East and North Africa Region.

Royston, Erica, and Sue Armstrong, eds. (1989). *Preventing Maternal Deaths*. Geneva: World Health Organization.

Swartz, Barbara (1983). *Family Planning Legislation*. EURO Reports and Studies, No. 85. Copenhagen, Denmark: World Health Organization, Regional Office for Europe.

Tietze, Christopher, and Stanley K. Henshaw (1986). *Induced Abortion: A World Review, 1986*. New York: The Alan Guttmacher Institute.

United Nations Fund for Population Activities (1976). *Survey of Contraceptive Laws: Country Profiles, Checklists, and Summaries*. New York.

_____ (1979). *Survey of Laws on Fertility Control*. New York.

World Health Organization (1968). *International Digest of Health Legislation* (Geneva), vol. 19, No. 1, p. 217.

_____ (1970). Comparative health legislation: abortion laws. *International Digest of Health Legislation* (Geneva), vol. 21, No. 3, p. 457.

Mozambique

Anonymous (1980). Mozambique to introduce family planning services. *IPPF Law File 1980*, vol. 11 (November), pp. 12.

Da Silva, C. (1978). Why abortion? *Tempo* (Maputo, Mozambique), vol. 12, No. 388 (March), pp. 31-39.

Isaacman, B., and June Stephen (1980). Mozambique: women, the law and agrarian reform. Addis Ababa: United Nations Economic Commission for Africa.

United Nations Fund for Population Activities (1979). *Survey of Laws on Fertility Control*. New York.

Myanmar

Myanmar (1971). Penal Code of Myanmar. In *Burma: The Penal Code*. Washington, D.C.: Law Library of Congress.

Cook, Rebecca J. (1989). Abortion laws and policies: challenges and opportunities. In "Women's health in the third world: the impact of unwanted pregnancy", A. Rosenfield and others, eds. *International Journal of Gynecology and Obstetrics* (Limerick, Ireland), Supplement No. 3, pp. 61-87.

_____, and Bernard M. Dickens (1988). International developments in abortion laws: 1977-88. *American Journal of Public Health* (Washington, D.C.), vol. 78, No. 10 (October), pp. 1305-1311.

Henshaw, Stanley K. (1990). Induced abortion: a world review, 1990. In *Induced Abortion: A World Review, 1990 Supplement*, by Stanley K. Henshaw and Evelyn Morrow. New York: The Alan Guttmacher Institute.

Knoppers, Bartha Maria, and Isabel Brault (1989). *La loi et l'avortement dans les pays francophones*. Montreal, Canada: Les Editions Thémis.

_____, and Elizabeth Sloss (1990). Abortion law in francophone countries. *American Journal of Comparative Law* (Berkeley, California), vol. 38, No. 4 (Fall), pp. 889-922.

Royston, Erica, and Sue Armstrong, eds. (1989). *Preventing Maternal Deaths*. Geneva: World Health Organization.

Tietze, Christopher, and Stanley K. Henshaw (1986). *Induced Abortion: A World Review, 1986*. New York: The Alan Guttmacher Institute.

United Nations Fund for Population Activities (1976). *Survey of Contraceptive Laws: Country Profiles, Checklists, and Summaries*. New York.

_____ (1979). *Survey of Laws on Fertility Control*. New York.

World Health Organization (1970). Comparative health legislation: abortion laws. *International Digest of Health Legislation* (Geneva), vol. 21, No. 3, pp. 347-512.

Namibia

Cook, Rebecca J., and Bernard M. Dickens (1979). Abortion laws in Commonwealth countries. *International Digest of Health Legislation* (Geneva), vol. 30, No. 2, pp. 395-502.

_____ (1986). *Issues in Reproductive Health Law in the Commonwealth*. London: Commonwealth Secretariat.

Brophy, Gwenda (1990). Need for family planning in independent Namibia. *People* (London), vol. 17, No. 1, p. 46.

Henshaw, Stanley K. (1990). Induced abortion: a world review, 1990. In *Induced Abortion: A World Review, 1990 Supplement*, by Stanley K. Henshaw and Evelyn Morrow. New York: The Alan Guttmacher Institute.

Royston, Erica, and Sue Armstrong, eds. (1989). *Preventing Maternal Deaths*. Geneva: World Health Organization.

Tietze, Christopher, and Stanley K. Henshaw (1986). *Induced Abortion: A World Review, 1986*. New York: The Alan Guttmacher Institute.

United Nations Fund for Population Activities (1976). *Survey of Contraceptive Laws: Country Profiles, Checklists, and Summaries*. New York.

_____ (1979). *Survey of Laws on Fertility Control*. New York.

United Nations Population Fund and Harvard Law School Library (1989). *Annual Review of Population Law, 1986*, vol. 13. New York: UNFPA.

World Health Organization (1970). Comparative health legislation: abortion laws. *International Digest of Health Legislation* (Geneva), vol. 21, No. 3, pp. 347-512.

_____ (1975). *International Digest of Health Legislation* (Geneva), vol. 26, pp. 844.

Nauru

Cook, Rebecca J., and Bernard M. Dickens (1979). Abortion laws in Commonwealth countries. *International Digest of Health Legislation* (Geneva), vol. 30, No. 2, pp. 395-502.

Pulea, Mere (1986). *The Family, Law and Population in the Pacific Islands*. Suva: University of the South Pacific, Institute of Pacific Studies.

United Nations (1989). *World Population Policies*, vol. II, *Gabon to Norway*. Population Studies , No. 102/Add.1. Sales No. E.89.XIII.3.

Nepal

Integrated Development Systems (1986). *Abortion in Rural Nepal, A Study Report*. Kathmandu.

_____ (1982). *Women in Prison: Case Studies*. Kathmandu.

Risal, Ram P., and Ashoke Shrestha (1989). Fertility and its proximate determinants. In *South Asia Study on Population Policies and Programmes: Nepal*. New York: United Nations Population Fund.

Thapa, Prem J., Shyam Thapa and Neera Shrestha (1992). A hospital-based study of abortion in Nepal. *Studies in Family Planning* (New York), vol. 23, No. 5 (September/October), pp. 311-318.

United Nations Fund for Population Activities (1979). *Survey of Laws on Fertility Control*. New York.

_____, and Harvard Law School Library (1983). *Annual Review of Population Law, 1983*, vol. 10. New York: UNFPA.

Netherlands

Council of Europe (1991). *Recent Demographic Developments in Europe, 1991 Edition*. Strasbourg.

Henshaw, Stanley K. (1990). Induced abortion: a world review, 1990. *Family Planning Perspectives* (New York), vol. 22, No. 2 (March-April), pp. 76-89.

Ketting, Evert, and Paul Schnabel (1980). Induced abortion in the Netherlands: a decade of experience, 1970-80. *Studies in Family Planning* (New York), vol. 11, No. 12 (December), pp. 385-394.

Rademakers, Jany (1988). The Netherlands. In *International Handbook on Abortion*, Paul Sachdev, ed., pp. 333-346.

Schmitz, L. (1989). The Netherlands: silence after the storm. *Planned Parenthood in Europe* (London), vol. 1, No. 18 (Spring), pp. 13-15.

United Nations (various years). *Demographic Yearbook*.

United Nations Fund for Population Activities (1982). *Annual Review of Population Law, 1981*, vol. 8. New York.

New Zealand

Cook, Rebecca J., and Bernard M. Dickens (1979). Abortion laws in Commonwealth countries. *International Digest of Health Legislation* (Geneva), vol. 30, No. 2, pp. 395-502.

_____ (1988). International developments in abortion laws: 1977-88. *American Journal of Public Health* (Washington, D.C.), vol. 78, No. 10 (October), pp. 1305-1311.

Henshaw, Stanley K. (1990). Induced abortion: a world review, 1990. In *Induced Abortion: A World Review, 1990 Supplement*, by Stanley K. Henshaw and Evelyn Morrow. New York: The Alan Guttmacher Institute.

International Advisory Committee on Population and Law (1976). *Annual Review of Population Law, 1975*. Law and Population Monograph Series, No. 39. Administered with the cooperation of Harvard University. Medford, Massachusetts: Tufts University, The Flecher School of Law and Diplomacy.

New Zealand (1993). *Demographic Trends, 1992*. Wellington: Department of Statistics.

North, D. A., and M. J. Sparrow (1991). Trends in the contraceptive practices of women seeking abortions in the 1980s. *New Zealand Medical Journal*, vol. 104, No. 910 (24 April), pp. 156-158.

Nuthall, J. (1986). Unplanned pregnancy. *New Zealand Nursing Journal*, vol. 79, No. 7 (July), pp. 11-15.

O'Neill, J. (1982). Contraception and abortion in New Zealand: a review article. *New Zealand Population Review*, vol. 8, No. 2 (July), pp. 51-58.

Sceats, Janet (1988). New Zealand. In *International Handbook on Abortion*, Paul Sachdev, ed. New York; Westport, Connecticut; and London: Greenwood Press, pp. 347-360.

_____ (1988). Trends and differentials in abortion, 1976-1986. *New Zealand Population Review*, vol. 14, No. 2 (November), pp. 4-18.

United Nations, Economic Commission for Asia and the Pacific (1985). *Population of New Zealand*, vol. 2. Country Monograph Series, No. 12. Bangkok.

United Nations Fund for Population Activities (1978). *Annual Review of Population Law, 1977*. New York.

_____ (1979). *Survey of Laws on Fertility Control*. New York.

World Health Organization (1978). New Zealand. *International Digest of Health Legislation* (Geneva), vol. 29, No. 4, pp. 758-772.

Nicaragua

International Planned Parenthood Federation (1986). Nicaragua debate on abortion. IPPF Open File: news digest of the world's largest voluntary family planning organization (two weeks ending 28 February). London. Mimeographed.

International Women's Rights Action Watch (1988). *The Women's Watch* (Minneapolis, Minnesota), vol. 2, No. 3 (December), pp. 1-2.

Mahler, Halfdan (1989). Address to the meeting of the Regional Council in the city of Guatemala, September 1989.

Rohter, Long (1985). Nicaragua has a postwar baby boom. *The New York Times* (24 February).

United Nations. (1985). *Nicaragua*. Population Policy Compendium.

United Nations Fund for Population Activities (1979). *Survey of Laws on Fertility Control*. New York.

Viel, Benjamin (1988). Latin America. In *International Handbook on Abortion*, Paul Sachdev, ed. New York; Westport, Connecticut; and London: Greenwood Press.

Niger

Henshaw, Stanley K. (1990). Induced abortion: a world review, 1990. In *Induced Abortion: A World Review, 1990 Supplement*, by Stanley K. Henshaw and Evelyn Morrow. New York: The Alan Guttmacher Institute.

Ignegongba, Par Keumaye (1988). La politique de population au Niger. *Pop Sahel*, No. 7 (septembre), pp. 23-26.

Knoppers, Bartha Maria, and Isabel Brault (1989). *La loi et l'avortement dans les pays francophones*. Montreal, Canada: Les Editions Thémis.

_____, and Elizabeth Sloss (1990). Abortion law in francophone countries. *American Journal of Comparative Law* (Berkeley, California), vol. 38, No. 4 (Fall), pp. 889-922.

Royston, Erica, and Sue Armstrong, eds. (1989). *Preventing Maternal Deaths*. Geneva: World Health Organization.

Tietze, Christopher, and Stanley K. Henshaw (1986). *Induced Abortion: A World Review, 1986*. New York: The Alan Guttmacher Institute.

United Nations Fund for Population Activities (1976). *Survey of Contraceptive Laws: Country Profiles, Checklists, and Summaries*. New York.

_____ (1979). *Survey of Laws on Fertility Control*. New York.

World Health Organization (1970). Comparative health legislation: abortion laws. *International Digest of Health Legislation* (Geneva), vol. 21, No. 3, pp. 347-512.

_____ (1989). *International Digest of Health Legislation* (Geneva), vol. 40, No. 1, pp. 80-81.

Nigeria

Edeh, J. (1979). Abortion and the law in Nigeria: a psychiatrist's view. *Nigerian Medical Journal*, vol. 9, No. 5 (May-June), pp. 631-4.

Nigeria, (1990). *Nigeria Demographic and Health Survey, 1990: Preliminary Report*.

Nnatu, Stephen (1988). Nigeria. In *International Handbook on Abortion*, Paul Sachdev, ed. New York; Westport, Connecticut; and London: Greenwood Press.

Odejide, T. O. (1986). Offering an alternative to illegal abortion in Nigeria. *New Era Nursing Image International* (Lagos, Nigeria), vol. 2, No. 2, pp. 39-42.

Okagbue, Isabella (1990). Pregnancy termination and the law in Nigeria. *Studies in Family Planning* (New York), vol. 21, No. 4 (July/August), pp. 197-208.

United Nations Fund for Population Activities (1979). *Survey of Laws on Fertility Control.* New York.

Norway

Cook, Rebecca Y., and Bernard M. Dickens (1988). International developments in abortion laws: 1977-1988. *American Journal of Public Health* (Washington, D.C.), vol. 78, No 10 (October), pp. 1305-1311.

Council of Europe (1992). *Recent Demographic Developments in the Member States of the Council of Europe, 1991 Edition.* Strasbourg.

Glendon, Mary Ann (1987). *Abortion and Divorce in Western Law.* Massachusetts and London: Havard University Press.

Henshaw, Stanley K. (1990). Induced abortion: a world review, 1990. In *Induced Abortion: A World Review, 1990 Supplement*, by Stanley K. Henshaw and Evelyn Morrow. New York: The Alan Guttmacher Institute.

Norway (various years). *Statisk Årbok/Statistical Yearbook of Norway.* Oslo: Central Bureau of Statistics.

Østby, Turid (1981). Fertility among Norwegian women: results from the Fertility Survey, 1977. Oslo: Central Bureau of Statistics.

Skjelle, Hans (1988). Norway. In *International Handbook on Abortion*, Paul Sachdev, ed. New York; Westport, Connecticut; and London: Greenwood Press.

United Nations (various years). *Demographic Yearbook.*

Wiik, Y. (1986). The abortion issue, political cleavage and the political agenda in Norway. In *The New Politics of Abortion*, Yani Lovensduski and Joyce Autshorn, eds. Sage Studies in Modern Politics. London: Sage Publications.

United Nations (1982). *World Population Trends and Policies: 1981 Monitoring Report*, vol. II, *Population Policies*. Population Studies, No. 79/Add.1. Sales No. E.82.XIII.3.

World Health Organization (1976). *International Digest of Health Legislation* (Geneva), vol. 27, No. 3, pp. 594-604.

_____ (1980). *International Digest of Health Legislation* (Geneva), vol. 31, No. 1, pp. 115-121.

Litho in United Nations, New York
54397—November 1993—5,350
ISBN 92-1-151258-1

United Nations publication
Sales No. E.94.XIII.2
ST/ESA/SER.A/129/Add.1